Stratification and Inequality Series

The Center for the Study of Social Stratification and Inequality,
Global COE Program
Tohoku University, Japan
Volume 15

Stratification in Cultural Contexts

Stratification and Inequality Series

The Center for the Study of Social Stratification and Inequality,
Global COE Program
Tohoku University, Japan

Inequality amid Affluence: Social Stratification in Japan
Junsuke Hara and Kazuo Seiyama

Intentional Social Change: A Rational Choice Theory
Yoshimichi Sato

Constructing Civil Society in Japan: Voices of Environmental Movements
Koichi Hasegawa

Deciphering Stratification and Inequality: Japan and beyond
Yoshimichi Sato

Social Justice in Japan: Concepts, Theories and Paradigms
Ken-ichi Ohbuchi

Gender and Career in Japan
Atsuko Suzuki

Status and Stratification:
Cultural Forms in East and Southeast Asia
Mutsuhiko Shima

Globalization, Minorities and Civil Society:
Perspectives from Asian and Western Cities
Koichi Hasegawa and Naoki Yoshihara

Fluidity of Place: Globalization and the Transformation of Urban Space
Naoki Yoshihara

Japan's New Inequality: Intersection of
Employment Reforms and Welfare Arrangements
Yoshimichi Sato and Jun Imai

Minorities and Diversity
Kunihiro Kimura

Inequality, Discrimination and Conflict in Japan:
Ways to Social Justice and Cooperation
Ken-ichi Ohbuchi and Nobuko Asai

Social Exclusion: Perspectives from France and Japan
Marc Humbert and Yoshimichi Sato

Global Migration and Ethnic Communities:
Studies of Asia and South America
Naoki Yoshihara

Stratification and Inequality Series

The Center for the Study of Social Stratification and Inequality,
Global COE Program
Tohoku University, Japan
Volume 15

Stratification in Cultural Contexts

Cases from East and Southeast Asia

Edited by

Toshiaki Kimura

First published in 2013 by
Trans Pacific Press, PO Box 164, Balwyn North, Victoria 3104, Australia
Telephone: +61 (0)3 9859 1112 Fax: +61 (0)3 8611 7989
Email: tpp.mail@gmail.com
Web: http://www.transpacificpress.com
Copyright © Trans Pacific Press 2013

Designed and set by Jodie McLean Email: mail@bookprinter.com.au

Cover design by Digital Environs, Melbourne, Australia. http://www.digitalenvirons.com

Distributors

USA and Canada
International Specialized Book Services (ISBS)
920 NE 58th Avenue, Suite 300
Portland, Oregon 97213-3786
USA
Telephone: 1-800-944-6190
Fax: 1-503-280-8832
Email: orders@isbs.com
Web: http://www.isbs.com

Asia and the Pacific
Kinokuniya Company Ltd.

Head office:
3-7-10 Shimomeguro
Meguro-ku
Tokyo 153-8504
Japan
Telephone: +81-3-6910-0531
Fax: +81-3-6420-1362
Email: bkimp@kinokuniya.co.jp
Web: www.kinokuniya.co.jp

Asia-Pacific office:
Kinokuniya Book Stores of Singapore Pte., Ltd.
391B Orchard Road #13-06/07/08
Ngee Ann City Tower B
Singapore 238874
Telephone: +65-6276-5558
Fax: +65-6276-5570
Email: SSO@kinokuniya.co.jp

Cover illustration: A scenery in Medan, the largest city in Sumatra Island, Indonesia. The photo, taken by the editor, shows a stark contrast between modest houses and high-rise buildings along the river that runs through the center of the city.

All rights reserved. No production of any part of this book may take place without the written permission of Trans Pacific Press.

ISBN 978-1-920901-30-1 (Hardback)
ISBN 978-1-920901-36-3 (Paperback)

Contents

Figures vi
Tables vi
Photos viii
Contributors ix

Introduction 1
Toshiaki Kimura

1. The Pluralization and Multitiering of Society in Taiwan: Ethnicity and Social Stratification since the 1990s 7
   Ichiro Numazaki
2. The Lives of Slaves from the Perspective of Family Relations: The Case of Daegu Household Registers from the End of the Seventeenth Century to the First Half of the Eighteenth Century 31
   Mutsuhiko Shima
3. The Roles of Samurai-Class Women and the Gender System in Early Modern Japan 55
   Rumi Matsuzaki
4. Stratification and Ethnicity in An Averted Feud Incident: The Case of A Village in the Pearl River Delta, Guangdong Province 75
   Yukihiro Kawaguchi
5. Social Differences in an Emigrant Community in Modern China: A Case Study from Fuzhou City, Fujian Province 95
   Itoe Kaneshiro
6. Social Change and Transformation in Toba Batak Ethnic Associations in Medan, Sumatra 113
   Toshiaki Kimura
7. The Dynamics of Household Rituals in Mongolia: After undergoing Religious Control under the Socialist Regime 127
   Katsuhiko Takizawa

Notes 144
Bibliography 153
Index 169

Figures

Figure 1.1 Dualistic and two-tiered structure under Japanese colonial rule 9
Figure 1.2 Dualistic and two-tiered structure under Chiang Kaishek and
 Chiang Chingkuo 10
Figure 1.3 Fluidity of dualistic and two-tiered structure 12
Figure 1.4 Increase in the foreign worker population
 (number of temporary residents) 19
Figure 1.5 Change in the foreign worker population by industry
 (number of temporary residents) 20
Figure 1.6 Nationalities of foreign workers by industry
 (number of temporary residents, 2009) 21
Figure 1.7 Increase in the foreign spouse population 22
Figure 1.8 Income distribution in Taiwan (1980–2009) 26
Figure 1.9 'Pluralization' and 'multitiering' in ethnicity and social stratification
 (schematic representation) 29
Figure 2.1a Genealogy of Kimhae Kim lineage in Wŏlbae-ri, 1690 37
Figure 2.1b Marriage relations surrounding Jongho 38
Figure 2.1c Marriage relations surrounding Iwŏn 38
Figure 2.2 Genealogy of the successive heads of Danyang U Lineage 41
Figure 2.3 Households of the lineage head and his brothers, 1690 41
Figure 2.4a Long-lasting genealogy of a slave family 46
Figure 2.4b Female slave Juyang and her family, 1690 46
Figure 2.4c Information indicating Hyosŏng's wife as recorded in the register of 1720 47
Figure 2.5 Genealogy of Sŏngju Yi Kin Group in Joam-bang Il-rl, 1690 49
Figure 2.6 Slaves whose whereabouts seem to have been known long after their 'escape'
 (a case from 1738) 50
Figure 2.7 Genealogy of slaves in 1690, one of whom returns long after escaping 51
Figure 4.1 Pre-1949 villages and the formation of collectives 77
Figure 4.2 Funeral procession routes 90
Figure 5.1 Location of Fuzhou City 98
Figure 6.1 Ethnic composition of Medan City 116
Figure 6.2 Population growth in Medan 118
Figure 7.1 Spatial configuration in a yurt 140

Tables

Table 1.1 Perceptions of language use by identity and generation	14
Table 1.2 Class consciousness by ethnicity	15
Table 1.3 Generational change in class structure	25
Table 2.1 Classification of registered households	32
Table 2.2 Registered individuals and status	33
Table 2.3 Resident individuals and status	33
Table 2.4a Status relations of husband and wife in slave households, 1690	34
Table 2.4b Status relations of husband and wife in slave households, 1720	34
Table 2.4c Status relations of husband and wife in slave households, 1729–32	35
Table 2.4d Number of slave households according to statuses of head and wife	35
Table 2.5 Government appointed/ascribed position or status of the individuals in Figure 2.1a	36
Table 2.6 Ownership of household head and his wife in slave households, 1690	40
Table 2.7 Number of households of U Yŏjun's descendants and their location of residence	41
Table 2.8 Summary of slaves owned by households of U Yŏjun's descendants	42
Table 2.9 Slaves in household no.4-1, Sangin-ri, headed by U Sŏkjang, 1690	44
Table 2.10 Classification according to the slave's parents' status in Table 2.8	44
Table 3.1 Family heads and feudal lords of the Date family and their official wives	57
Table 6.1 The residents in U District according to their occupations	121
Table 6.2 The households in U District according to clan membership	121
Table 6.3 Aid by STM on the occasion of a funeral	122
Table 7.1 Overview of the survey on household rituals in Ulaanbaatar	136
Table 7.2 Overview of the survey on household rituals in Hovd	137

Photos

Photo 4.1 A reconstructed Chen lineage ancestral hall	81
Photo 4.2 Vehicle stoppers installed at the lane entrance	84
Photo 5.1 Western style houses built in the 1990s	105
Photo 5.2 Offering of a play	106
Photo 5.3 Notice of the play performance	106
Photo 5.4 Recognition of contributors through a photo display	107
Photo 5.5 Funeral procession marching through the village	108

Contributors

Itoe Kaneshiro, Ph.D. candidate in the Graduate School of Environmental Science at Tohoku University.

Yukihiro Kawaguchi (Ph.D., Tohoku University), Associate professor of cultural anthropology in the Graduate School of Arts and Letters at Tohoku University.

Toshiaki Kimura (Ph.D., Tohoku University), Associate professor of religious studies in the Graduate School of Arts and Letters at Tohoku University.

Rumi Matsuzaki (Ph.D., Tohoku University), Assistant professor in the CSSI at Tohoku University.

Ichiro Numazaki (Ph.D., Michigan State University), Professor of cultural anthropology in the Graduate School of Arts and Letters at Tohoku University.

Mutsuhiko Shima (Ph.D., University of Toronto), Professor emeritus of the Graduate School of Arts and Letters at Tohoku University.

Katsuhiko Takizawa (Ph.D., Tohoku University), Research fellow in the Graduate School of Arts and Letters at Tohoku University. Lecturer in the Center for the Advancement of Higher Education at Tohoku University.

Translators and Editor

Chapters 1–4: Minako Sato
Chapters 5 and 7: Tomoko Onuki
Chapter 6: Leonie R. Stickland
Structural Editor: Miriam Riley

Introduction

Toshiaki Kimura

This volume is a collection drawn from research results of the East Asian Division of the Center for the Study of Social Stratification and Inequality (CSSI) at Tohoku University. Cooperating with other divisions, we have tried to tackle the issue of how social stratification and inequality manifest themselves in concrete East Asian socio-cultural and historical contexts. It is in these very contexts that people recognize (or fail to recognize) and relate to (or, in many cases, just ignore) the inequality that exists in their society. We have discussed when and in what circumstances the problem of stratification has become more serious and how the tension could be eased, taking examples from East and Southeast Asian societies. We have also paid attention to the local wisdom of traditional societies to analyze inequality and stratification in cases such as ethnic associations and revolving loan systems, etc.

In this book, seven scholars who specialize in an area of East and Southeast Asia examine how the problems of stratification manifest themselves in different cultural and historical contexts. Chapter One, by Ichiro Numazaki, outlines the transformation of Taiwan society over the past twenty years, focusing on its 'pluralization' and 'multitiering'. Under the administration of Japanese colonialists and the governments of Chiang Kaishek and Chiang Chingkuo, the dualistic (outsiders versus indigenous peoples) and two-tiered (ruling versus subordinate class) structure was formed in Taiwan society. During the Japanese colonial period, the Japanese were the outsiders who constituted the ruling class, while Han-Chinese immigrants before Japanese occupation and Austronesian speaking indigenous people formed the subordinate class. This dualistic structure was maintained under the Chiang Kaishek and Chiang Chingkuo government following the Second World War, replacing Japanese with newcomer mainland Chinese military personnel and bureaucrats as the new outsiders in the ruling class. However, in the late 1970s, this structure began to destabilize as the ethnic classification around ruler and subordinate class became more complicated and 'middle class expansion' was experienced in Taiwan society. After 1990, the discourse of 'four major ethnic groups' and the perception of 'plural society' emerged. Also foreign laborers and brides began to arrive in Taiwan as the new 'outsiders'. These newcomers add novel dimensions to Taiwan's ethnicity and further complicate its ethnic composition. Concerning social stratification, Numazaki points out that 'middle class expansion' in Taiwan society continued basically through the 1990s. However, the emergence of various – economic, gender, cultural – disparities could be observed in Taiwan. Finally, Numazaki explains these changes in Taiwan society using the words 'individualization' and 'internationalization' and concludes that factors with a centrifugal potential are newly emergent while a certain level of centripetal force is working to maintain social integrity in Taiwan.

Chapter Two, by Mutsuhiko Shima, examines the form of existence of 'slaves' under the Chosŏn dynasty in Korea from the end of the seventeenth century to the first half of the eighteenth century when the slave system was altered through the adoption of the *nobi-jongmoje* system in 1729. Shima analyzes household registers of the Daegu region in Gyeongsang Province from the perspective of family relations. In conclusion, pointing out the spread of intermarriage between commoners and slaves, he finds that in terms of day-to-day social relations, only minor distinctions could be observed between commoners belonging to the lower social strata and people with slave status. Shima suspects this is why intermarriage between commoners and slaves became very prevalent before 1729 and as a result the government was compelled to institute a new measure. He also notes an apparent imbalance in the sex ratio of slaves in household registers. According to his study, however, a considerable number of male commoners actually lived as the husbands of female slaves and therefore the sex ratio of men and women living with slave-like status was far more balanced than entries in the household registers suggest. Finally, Shima refers to the existence of a slave family lineage that continued to exist alongside the households of the same owner's family line for many generations. It shows, he explains, that there was a long-term human relationship between owner and slave in these cases.

In Chapter Three, Rumi Matsuzaki focuses on the 'gender system' incorporated into the feudal administrative and family system in the early modern era in Japan (the Edo period). At that time, gender roles were divided following the conceptual distinction between *omote* and *oku*. This distinction was not only used for spatial division inside a castle or residence, but also formed the structure or system of government. The *omote* was a public sphere in which men carried out political and military functions, while the *oku* was a private sphere in which the family head and his family led their private lives. *Omote* and *oku* were clearly partitioned and women were restricted from involvement in the former. In this chapter, Matsuzaki uses the historical materials of the Date family, feudal lord of Sendai domain, in the early and middle Edo period and examines the formative process of the gender system from a diachronic viewpoint.

Matsuzaki concludes that during this period the role of the samurai-class wife changed from direct involvement in war and politics to performing a rather ritual function involving the exchanging of gifts and courtesies.

In Chapter Four, Yukihiro Kawaguchi examines the mechanism of the heightening of the ethnic boundary in modern China by focusing on a case of feud involving members of the dominant Chen lineage and boat dwellers that occurred in D village in Guandong Province in 2002. Before the founding of the People's Republic of China in 1949, the Chen lineage, claiming to have founded D village in 1131, played a major political and economic role in that village. They took advantage of its connection with the officialdom to develop one tract of land after another and owned and managed them as the common property of the lineage. Some successful members built ancestral halls to hold ancestral rituals to show off their success and prestige. Conversely, the boat dwellers were minorities who lost their competition with the dominant group and tried to establish a niche on the lowlands at the mouth of the river under ongoing development and on the water. However, after 1949 the government of the People's Republic of China began to clamp down on lineages and various religious observances, including ancestral rituals. Common property owned by lineages was distributed to the people and ancestral halls were either demolished or converted to other uses. The situation changed again due to the changing state doctrine towards modernization-oriented policy, which caused the revival of the lineage system all around China. The Chen lineage of D village also rebuilt the ancestral halls and recompiled their genealogy at that time. Kawaguchi argues this re-recognition of the historical value of the lineage was one of the background factors of the feud between Chen lineage members and boat dwellers. He concludes that this kind of reconnection between present and past through 'history' or 'culture' strongly appeals to the interested parties in contemporary China and serves to highlight the historically constructed ethnic boundaries and hierarchical relationships.

In Chapter Five, Itoe Kaneshiro deals with an immigrants' native village in southeastern China, Village X, and shows how the villagers attempt to transform economic capital (income acquired overseas) into various forms of symbolic capital to differentiate themselves from others. Village X has dispatched many overseas immigrants since the 1980s. Years later, the funds acquired by migrants were gradually remitted home and the village was said to be a 'wealthy village' by outsiders. However, not all immigrants are thought to be successful by other villagers. Kaneshiro points out the importance of the 'Green Card' and 'American citizenship' for immigrants who went to the US in terms of the recognition of successfulness among the villagers. In addition, she notices that certain actions are expected from a successful immigrant: the luxurious feast held on the opportunity of their first homecoming; the renovation of houses of wood or brick to four or five story concrete houses; and donations or contributions to the ancestral shrines or public works projects. According to Kaneshiro, nowadays the most prominent way for immigrants to show their successfulness in their hometown is via lavish rites of passage, especially funeral ceremonies. Two to three hundred people are invited to the ceremony and treated with sumptuous food and gifts there. Interestingly, referring to Bourdieu's concept of 'symbolic battle at the "sites"', she argues that these 'weapons' for battle are based on the cultural code shared within the village. In a sense, Kaneshiro's study clearly shows how economic differences caused by immigration work manifests itself in a concrete cultural context.

In Chapter Six, Toshiaki Kimura examines the functional change of the ethnic association founded by a minority group, Toba Batak migrants, living in a multi-ethnic urban city, Medan, on Sumatra Island, Indonesia. In his famous work, E. Bruner mentioned this association in his early studies based on research conducted in the 1950s and called attention to their wisdom to invent the mutual aid association based on the traditional worldview and value system. After his study, during the second half of the twentieth century, Indonesian society achieved rapid economic growth under the Suharto regime, leading to further migration to the cities including Medan. The social conditions around migrants have changed drastically during the period. A half-century has passed since the migration boom and the second and third generation has grown. Kimura endeavors to tackle the issue as to what the ethnic association means for those involved by comparing the constitutions of three associations. According to his research, some functions of the association such as ritual participation have been maintained, but its elaborate lists of the various contributions both material and in terms of manpower changed to prioritize financial support. The revolving loan and scholarship function reported by Bruner has gone. In contrast, ethnic associations established in the 1980s performed new functions: providing aid in times of natural disaster or hospitalization due to illness. Kimura concludes that the ethnic associations in the late twentieth century are more focused on the function of insurance against risks to life and health rather than on aid to establish a base for their livelihood.

Chapter Seven, by Katsuhiko Takizawa, focuses on the phenomenon of 'religious revival' after democratization in Mongolian society. Mongolia was governed by a socialist regime from 1924 to 1990. During the socialist era, all religious activities were banned and more than 17,000 monks were executed by the purge that took place mainly around 1937. The temples that amounted to 800 before the purge were all destroyed or closed by 1940, except Gandan Temple that was restored in 1944 under the strict control of the government. After 1990, as the Mongolian government changed their policy to capitalism and liberalized religion, and religious activities were revived both by native religions and new entrants such as Christianity and Bahaism. Takizawa analyzes the conditions underpinning this revival and points out the role of household that maintained and reproduced religious practices against their elimination from the public sphere during the socialist period in Mongolia.

Topics dealt with in this volume are diversified, from religious to economic concerns. It is our purposes in the CSSI that scholars in different fields are gathered together to exchange ideas with each other. I hope our discussion and especially, this book will provide a strong step on the way to further study on the field of stratification and inequality in cultural contexts.

The publication of this volume was made possible by a grant offered by the Center for the Study of Social Stratification and Inequality (CSSI) in the GCOE Program at Tohoku University, whose financial support is greatly acknowledged. I appreciate Airin Izumi and Fukuo Ootomo for their excellent administrative work and kind help. I also thank Professor Yoshio Sugimoto, Director of Trans Pacific Press, for his patient support of this book project and Ms Miriam Riley for her thorough and meticulous editorial work.

1 The Pluralization and Multitiering of Society in Taiwan: Ethnicity and Social Stratification since the 1990s[1]

Ichiro Numazaki

Introduction

This chapter presents an overview of the 'pluralization' and 'multitiering' of 'Taiwan society'[2] over the past twenty years, and outlines my hypothesis as to how the changes of the past two decades should be interpreted. In this chapter, the term 'pluralization' is used to mean not only an increase in social divisions but also a rise in the complexity of social differentiation. It can be rephrased as the 'accelerated multiplication of social dimensionalities'. Conversely, 'multitiering' refers to the increase in the fractionation and multilayeredness of the hierarchical composition of socio-economic strata.

Taiwan society has been undergoing a transformation along with major political and economic changes since the 1990s. This chapter focuses particularly on the transformation of *zuqun*,[3] or ethnicity, and social stratification in the 1990s and 2000s. I shall argue that ethnicity and social stratification in Taiwan society were 'dualistic' and 'two-tiered' until the end of the 1980s, but that they have been undergoing rapid pluralization and multitiering since then. As a result, the increasing complexity of Taiwan society may have intensified the problems of social integration. This chapter also proposes the hypothesis that the changes to ethnicity and social stratification in contemporary Taiwan can be characterized as processes of 'individualization' and 'internationalization'.

I used to expect that further democratization and economic development in Taiwan society would lead to further '*Taiwanhua*' (Taiwanization) and 'middle class expansion' (Numazaki 1998, 1999, 2002). My projection was that the *shengji maodun* (literally 'contradiction between provincial identities'),[4] which characterized Taiwan society under the rule of Chiang Kaishek and Chiang Chingkuo, would gradually be resolved through the growing bilingualism among both Waishengren (literally 'people who originated outside the province', meaning those who came to Taiwan from the Chinese mainland after the end of Japanese colonial rule) and

Benshengren (literally 'people who originated inside the province', indicating those who had lived in Taiwan under Japanese colonial rule) and increasing intermarriage between the two groups, while discrimination and disparity between Han and non-Han residents would diminish through the political recognition of 'Aborigines' and improvements in their economic status; these changes would engender a common 'new Taiwan consciousness' that could result in the formation of an 'integrated Taiwan society', in spite of various social and cultural differences. I also expected that the economic disparity would continue to shrink on the back of stable economic growth.

Against my projection, however, there emerged the possibility that political and economic upheaval since the late 1980s and especially during the 2000s is gradually fractionating Taiwan society. Accordingly, in this chapter I would like to draw attention to 'new diversities' with a centrifugal potential that have emerged from the transformation of Taiwan society in the last two decades and examine whether such a potential is actually threatening social integration.

This chapter is comprised of four sections. I first provide an overview of the dualistic and two-tiered structure of Taiwan society prior to the 1990s in order to set the benchmark for social changes thereafter. The following two sections describe the pluralization and multitiering of ethnicity and social stratification. The closing section considers whether the pluralization and multitiering of society will act as a centrifugal or centripetal force and explores the question 'are the various components of Taiwan society being glued together or torn apart?'

The dualistic and two-tiered structure prior to 1990

The formation of a dualistic and two-tiered structure

In Taiwan, a society that was characterized by a dualistic conflict between 'outsiders' and 'indigenous peoples' and a two-tiered structure consisting of the 'ruling class' and the 'subordinate class' was formed under the administration of Japanese colonialists and under the governments of Chiang Kaishek and Chiang Chingkuo (Ahern and Gates 1981; Copper 1996; Numazaki 1998).

The Japanese colonial period
During the Japanese colonial period, the Japanese were the outsiders who constituted the ruling class, while Han-Chinese migrants who had been in Taiwan prior to the Japanese occupation, their descendants and the Austronesian-speaking peoples, who were the indigenous population of Taiwan, formed the subordinate class.

A dualistic conflict between the Han-Chinese population as the outsiders and the Austronesian-speaking population as the indigenous peoples had existed prior to Japanese occupation. Many plain-dwelling indigenous peoples, however, had been incorporated into the Han-Chinese migrant society through sinicization and intermarriage by the time the Japanese arrived and thus the main players in the dualistic conflict against the Han-Chinese were high mountain tribes who rejected assimilation and maintained their own cultures. The sinicized tribes were called Pingpufan (plains savages) or Shufan (tamed savages), whereas non-sinicized tribes were called Shengfan (wild savages) inhabiting *fanjie* (savages' territories). The *fanjie* was a *huawaizhidi* (uncivilized land) to the Han-Chinese and the habitation areas of the outsiders and the unsinicized indigenous peoples were clearly separated, even though they had contact through trade and some intermarriage.

The Japanese colonial government maintained the horizontal structure of division between the Han and the Shengfan, and built a system of government upon it. As a result, a vertically divided dual structure consisting of the ruling class and the subordinate class was formed, and the horizontally divided dual structure within the subordinate class was preserved (Figure 1.1).

Figure 1.1 Dualistic and two-tiered structure under Japanese colonial rule

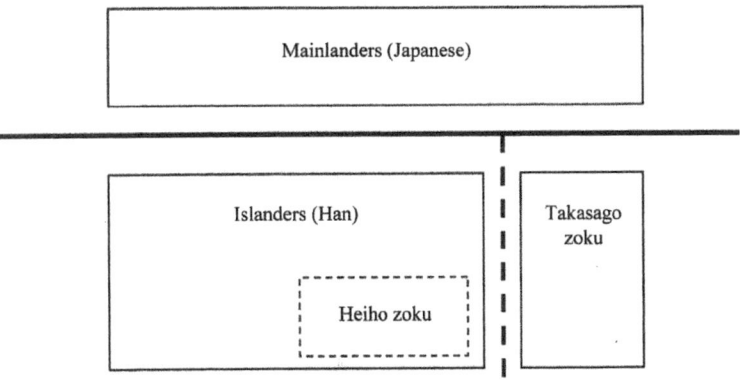

Source: Prepared by the author.

The colonial government called the Japanese, the ruling outsiders, Naichijin (Mainlanders) and the indigenous Han of the subordinate class

Hontōjin (Islanders), and categorized the Pingpufan (Shufan) aborigines as Heiho zoku (Plains tribes) and the Shengfan aborigines as Takasago zoku (Formosan tribes). Islanders were divided further on the basis of the place of origin or the language/dialect between the Hoklo and the Hakka, and between immigrants of Changzhou and Chuanzhou backgrounds among the Hoklo population. While there were ethnic clashes[5] between these groups during the Qing dynasty period, the disparity and conflict between subgroups within the Islanders group became relatively inconspicuous during the Japanese colonial period, as the disparity and conflict between the Islanders and Mainlanders became prominent. Towards the end of the Japanese colonial period, urban elites with secondary and tertiary education among the Islanders came to possess a common 'Islander consciousness' and mounted campaigns to demand the rights of self-government and cultural expression. This was the beginning of the primordial form of 'Taiwan consciousness'. The 'Plains tribes' underwent further sinicization during the Japanese colonial period, but they did not completely lose their own manners, customs or languages. This would have important implications from the 1990s. Although the unsinicized 'Formosan tribes' were forced to assimilate with the Japanese under the military authorities of the colonial government, they generally preserved their own ethnic cultures. Still, the Japanese language that was forced upon them under the assimilation policy gave them a 'common language' beyond ethnic boundaries. Together with the designation of the Takasago zoku (Formosan tribes), the Japanese language appears to have served as the catalyst behind the budding 'collective consciousness' against the Han and the Japanese.

Figure 1.2 Dualistic and two-tiered structure under Chiang Kaishek and Chiang Chingkuo

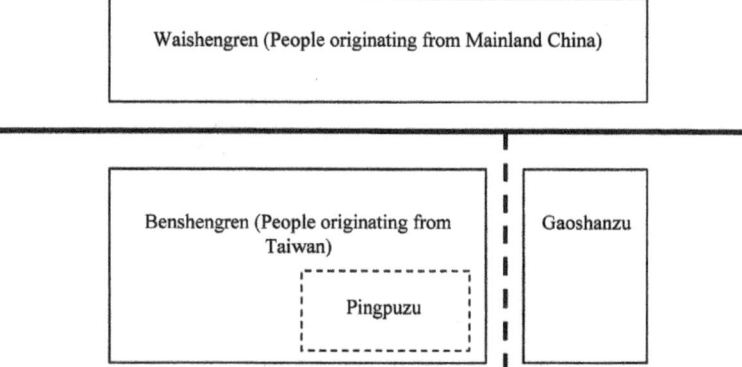

Source: Prepared by the author.

A characteristic of the period of Japanese rule was that the dualistic structure consisting of outsiders and indigenous peoples was incorporated into a larger two-tiered structure comprising the ruling class and the subordinate class, as shown in Figure 1.1. This dualistic structure was passed on to the government of Chiang Kaishek (of the Kuomintang = KMT (Chinese Nationalist Party)), who came to power after the Second World War. The KMT, military and bureaucrats of mainland Chinese origin replaced the Japanese as the new outsiders in the ruling class. The earlier Han-Chinese settlers and the Austronesian-speaking peoples remained in the subordinate class (Figure 1.2).

The KMT government period

After Chiang Kaishek took over the reins, new immigrants from Mainland China were called Waishengren and the Han people who had been in Taiwan since the Japanese colonial period were called Benshengren.[6] This classification corresponded to the division between Naichijin and Hontojin during the Japanese period.

The KMT government also essentially kept the division structure of the Austronesian-speaking peoples from the Japanese colonial period. The designation of Heiho zoku (Pingpuzu) was retained, while that of Takasago zoku was replaced with Gaoshanzu (high mountain tribes), Shandi tongbao (mountain compatriots) or Shanbao, and their 'assimilation' into Han culture was enforced. The designation of mountain compatriots was adopted to emphasize that they were part of the 'Chinese' population.

In contrast to Chiang Kaishek's administration, Benshengren in the subordinate class called themselves Tai-oan-lang (Taiwan people) and referred to Waishengren as Tiong-kok-lang (Chinese people). This suggests that they did not recognize new outsiders as those belonging to Taiwan, nor themselves as part of the Chinese.

A definitive event for the division between Waishengren and Benshengren was the 2.28 Incident in 1947 (Lai et al. 1991; Ka Girin (He Yi-Lin) 2003). The oppression and massacre by the KMT security forces, which caused 20,000 deaths according to one estimate, opened a deep rift in Taiwan society. While people were not even allowed to openly talk about the incident for a long period of time, a deep distrust of the opposite party grew not only in the minds of Benshengren on the victim's side but also in the minds of Waishengren on the oppressor's side. Thus the seeds of the so-called 'contradiction between provincial identities' were cast.

According to Wang Fuchang (2003: 79–82), however, the awakening and dissemination of such 'Benshengren consciousness' did not emerge during the 1950s and 1960s. Despite a sense of political oppression, Benshengren and Waishengren began to have closer social contact and relations that were leading to higher levels of social integration. The Benshengren consciousness began to manifest along with a movement for political democratization that gathered pace in the 1970s (Wang 2003: 82–88). Wang argues that this resulted in the creation of the 'modern ethnic imagination', where Taiwan had multiple cultural groups of different origins and waves of migration, which were neither superior nor inferior to one another and which were politically equal. The state thus had an obligation to guarantee equal political, economic, social and cultural opportunities to all of them. In these circumstances, ethnic conflicts were becoming more visible.

Yet, it is safe to say that the basic dualistic and two-tiered structure shown in Figure 1.2 above was more or less unchanged until around the mid-1970s. Diversities within the provincial population were yet to manifest, and activism among the Austronesian-speaking peoples was still weak. While Taiwan was undergoing industrialization and economic growth and concomitant social mobility from rural villages to cities and from agricultural to various other occupations, Chiang Chingkuo inherited political power after the death of his father, Chiang Kaishek, and maintained government by Waishengren. At this time there was a general overlapping of ethnic classification and social stratification.

Fluidity in the dualistic and two-tiered structure

This structure began to destabilize in the latter half of the 1970s and 1980s. Society was unsettled by two kinds of movements: ethnic demerging and merging and a rise and fall in terms of social stratification. These are schematized in Figure 1.3 below.

Figure 1.3 Fluidity of dualistic and two-tiered structure

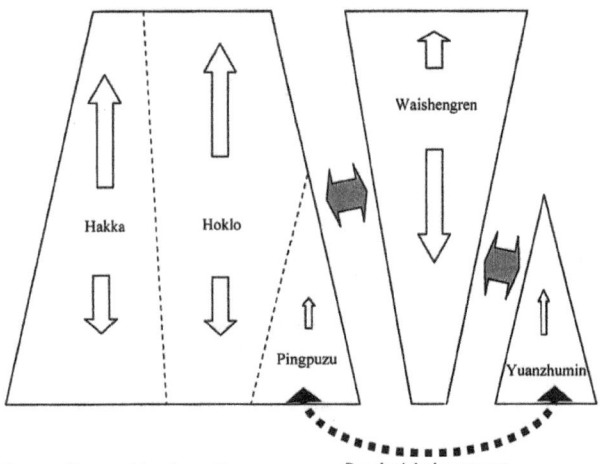

Source: Prepared by the author.   Pan-aboriginal movement

Ethnicity

According to Wang (2003: 133–145), a distinction between the Hoklo and Hakka within the Benshengren population came to the surface in terms of language during the 1980s and led to the rise of movements to preserve the language and revive the culture of the Hakka people. This was triggered by a sense of threat felt by the Hakka-speaking population when the increasingly heated anti-government campaign led by the Democratic Progressive Party (DPP) touted 'Taiwanese nationalism' and asserted their own identity by using the 'Taiwanese language' at their gatherings. The 'Taiwanese language' usually refers to Taiwanese Hokkien or Hoklo (Minnan dialect), and does not include Hakka. This is why movements demanding that Hakka and Hoklo be recognized as equal languages and Hakka- and Hoklo-speakers as equal ethnic groups have emerged.

The Hakka people formed a minority among Taiwan's Han society, and many of them had become the so-called 'Hoklo-Hakka' who were heavily influenced by Hoklo linguistically and culturally. The differences between the Hakka and Hoklo people had been tending to diminish for a long time from the Japanese colonial period to the KMT period (Wang 2003: 129–132).

Because the heightening of 'Benshengren consciousness' often presented 'Hoklo centrism', however, the Hakka people were moved to perceive themselves as a distinct ethnic group to counteract it. The result of this was a disaggregation of ethnic identities among Benshengren, or a double-tracking of their ethnic movement, although it stopped short of complete separation.

Conversely, social barriers between Benshengren and Waishengren were diminishing. Intermarriage between the two groups increased, albeit gradually. According to a 1991 survey, the rate of intermarriage was 12.2% in the twenty to thirty-nine age group while it was only 7.1% in the forty to sixty age group at the time of the survey (Wang 1993: 83–84). The enforcement of *guoyu* (national language) (Mandarin-based standard Chinese) education by the KMT led to increased fluency in and reduced resistance to the national language among the younger generations of Benshengren. Conversely, the younger generations of Waishengren were also learning and becoming fluent in Taiwan Hokkien. As shown in Table 1.1 below, the increasing bilingualism in both groups was making communication easier beyond the ethnicity barrier. Based on these, Wang Fuchang (1993) admits that the merging of Benshengren and Waishengren was progressing as far as ethnic relations during the 1980s were concerned.

Thus it is clear that Taiwan's Han society was undergoing the fluidization of the ethnicity structure, characterized at once by the differentiation of ethnic groups/subgroups and the melting down of ethnic barriers.

Table 1.1 Perceptions of language use by identity and generation

%

	National language (Mandarin)					
	Benshengren		Waishengren		Total	
Generation	Fluent	Wish to use actively	Fluent	Wish to use actively	Fluent	Wish to use actively
20–29	77.4	35.0	92.7	75.6	79.4	40.3
30–39	53.9	37.1	88.3	83.3	57.4	41.8
40–49	42.7	26.3	83.9	83.9	46.1	31.1
50–59	21.5	10.5	81.8	72.7	25.1	14.2
60–64	13.1	7.1	68.2	59.1	24.5	17.9
Total	49.3	20.9	85.5	77.6	53.1	34.1
	Hoklo (Taiwanese Hokkien)					
	Benshengren		Waishengren		Total	
Generation	Fluent	Wish to use actively	Fluent	Wish to use actively	Fluent	Wish to use actively
20—29	82.5	88.7	39.0	39.0	76.8	82.2
30—39	91.5	95.8	71.7	41.7	89.5	90.3
40—49	89.2	97.7	51.6	25.8	86.1	91.7
50—59	83.7	97.7	63.6	27.3	82.5	93.4
60—64	83.2	100.0	18.2	27.3	69.8	84.9
Total	87.7	95.5	52.1	35.2	84.0	89.0

Source: Wang Fuchang (1993: 89, 92). Original source: Academia Sinica (1991) *Taiwan diqu shehui yixiang diaocha* (Taiwan social opinion survey), periodical survey no. 2.

The 1980s also saw the beginning of new movements among Austronesian-speaking peoples. In 1983, students at the National Taiwan University began to publish the *Gaoshanqing* (Mountains are green) magazine on an irregular basis. The Taiwan Yuanzhumin quanli cujinhui (Alliance for the promotion of aboriginal rights in Taiwan) was organized in December 1984, which redefined them as 'Yuanzhumin' (Aborigines), who were the original rulers of Taiwan and not *fan*/Banjin (barbarians), Takasago zoku, 'High mountain tribes' nor 'Mountain compatriots'. Further, they proposed a 'pan-Aboriginal identity' beyond internal linguistic and cultural differences, and released 'Yuanzhumin quanli xuanyan' (The declaration of the rights of the aboriginal peoples) in 1988 to embark on campaigns to restore their rights, including land rights (Xie Chengzhong 1987; Wang Fuchang 2003: 112–119). The new ethnic group category of Yuanzhumin was thus born. These movements spread to the highly sinicized 'Plains tribes' as well, and some of them began to seek their own aboriginal identity based on non-Han languages, manners, customs and religion.

A major transformation in the dualistic ethnicity structure therefore began to take place in the 1980s.

Social stratification

Taiwan's industrialization and economic growth prompted many Benshengren to move out of farming villages into cities and diversify into various occupations. A majority of them became factory laborers, but a considerable number started their own businesses and became the owner-operators of small and medium-sized companies. Some managed to found large-scale corporate groups and join the ranks of the capitalist class (Numazaki 1989, 2004; Lin Zhongzheng and Lin Heling 1993).

Many Waishengren worked as soldiers, policemen, public servants and school-teachers. As the private-sector economy developed and the income of the Benshengren increased, disparities between Waishengren and Benshengren decreased. Conversely, retired low-ranking soldiers who were called *laobing* (war veterans) or *rongmin* (honorable citizens) saw their already low standard of living deteriorate further (Hu 1989; Hu Taili 1993).

In general, though, Taiwan experienced a 'middle class expansion'. The Gini coefficient continued to fall up to the end of the 1970s and remained at 0.28–0.30, despite a slight increase during the 1980s (Xingzhengyuan Zhijichu 2010: 21). As Table 1.2 shows, the majority of residents came to perceive themselves as middle-class, regardless of their ethnicity.

Table 1.2 Class consciousness by ethnicity

				(%)
	Hoklo	Hakka	Waishengren	Total
Upper class	0.7	1.9	1.6	0.8
Upper middle class	9.0	11.1	18.5	9.6
Middle class	51.1	46.3	53.2	48.8
Lower middle class	12.2	15.7	8.9	11.6
Working class	19.7	16.7	8.9	17.7
Lower class	7.4	8.3	8.9	7.3
Total	100.0	100.0	100.0	100.0

Source: Lin Zhongzheng/Lin Heling (1993: 119). The original source: Academia Sinica (1991) *Taiwan diqu shehui yixiang diaocha* (Taiwan social opinion survey), periodical survey no. 2.

Aborigines were the only exception. Increasing numbers of Aboriginal peoples moved out of the mountains into cities, but they were still placed at the bottom of the social hierarchy. Their income as at 1985 was fifty-seven to sixty percent of the national average in Aboriginal communities on the highlands and plains and sixty-seven percent for Aborigines living in urban areas (Wang 2003: 109). In 1991 it was still fifty-nine to sixty-two percent in Aboriginal communities on the highlands and plains and seventy-two percent for urban Aborigines.

Thus the previous two-tiered hierarchy began to undergo a major change. The structure consisting of the upper and lower layers was transformed into an assemblage of trapezoids (see Figure 1.3). Ethnicity and social stratification started to show completely different dimensionalities.

Pluralization and multitiering in ethnicity

What are the changes to Taiwan's ethnic composition since the 1990s? In essence, the process of internal demerging and merging within Taiwan that began in the 1980s progressed and produced the theory of 'four main ethnic groups' (Wang 2003; G. Li 2008).[7] In addition, new elements arrived from the outside of Taiwan in the form of an influx of 'new immigrants' consisting of foreign workers and foreign spouses.

Four major ethnic groups

Wang Fuchang (2003: 151–157) argues that following the flourishing of 'Benshengren consciousness' during the 1970s and 'Aboriginal consciousness' and 'Hakka consciousness' during the 1980s, 'Waishengren consciousness' manifested during the 1990s. It was the result of an increasing sense of crisis felt by Waishengren in response to the growing Taiwanization of politics under Lee Teng-Hui, and the intensifying confrontation with Mainland China under Chen Shui-Bian. Apart from a few groups that had developed their own identity, such as *rongmin* ('honorable citizens' or retired soldiers) (Hu 1989, 1993), Waishengren never formed a common 'Waishengren consciousness' because of their diverse origins, languages and dialects. This was the first time that they recognized themselves and were recognized by others as an ethnic group.

This gave rise to the discourse that Taiwan had 'four major ethnic groups' comprising Hoklo (Minnan), Hakka, Yuanzhumin and Waishengren, each of whom had their own history, culture and language. This discourse spread widely throughout society. It led to the perception that their cultures and languages were equal and that Taiwan society was a 'plural society' with multiple cultures and languages. This was the emergence of 'cultural pluralism' (T. Wu 2008; K. Li 2008).[8]

The principal characteristic of the four major ethnic groups discourse is the juxtaposition of Hoklo, Hakka, Yuanzhumin and Waishengren as equal ethnic groups. Members of each group may have a perception of being a minority in various senses or being discriminated against or oppressed. Because of that, they strongly assert equality between their own ethnic group and others. In reality, no single ethnic group controls real political and economic power over the other groups anymore.

All four ethnic groups have already 'taken root' in Taiwan society. Although Waishengren alone still retain some flavor of 'outsider', it has been sixty years since their arrival and even the first generation have spent a major part of their lives in Taiwan. The second and third generations who now account for a majority of Waishengren were born and raised in Taiwan. Consequently, it has become difficult to understand ethnicity in Taiwan society from the conventional dualistic and two-tiered perspective based on ruler/ruled and outsider/indigenous, and internal diversity is increasing within each ethnic group.

In the case of Yuanzhumin, for example, the fostering of pan-Aboriginal consciousness beyond cultural and language boundaries is taking place simultaneously with differentiation based on individual subgroups' unique cultures and languages. The government rapidly issued new policies on Yuanzhumin from the 1990s and the special status of Yuanzhumin in particular was established under the DPP administration (Huang 2010). At the 1994 National Assembly, the term 'Shandi tongbao' (Mountain compatriots) was officially replaced by 'Yuanzhumin'. The Council of Aboriginal Affairs (renamed the Council of Indigenous Peoples in 2002 by the Executive Yuan) was set up as one of the central ministry-level agencies in 1996. The fourth constitutional amendment in 1997 included additional articles concerning the Aboriginal peoples[9] and now the Constitution clearly declares that '[t]he State affirms cultural pluralism and shall actively preserve and foster the development of aboriginal languages and cultures' and '[...] safeguard the status and political participation of the aborigines. The State shall also guarantee and provide assistance and encouragement for aboriginal education, culture, transportation, water conservation, health and medical care, economic activity, land, and social welfare' (Article 10).[10] The draft Indigenous Peoples Basic Act (Aboriginal Basic Law) that was first tabled in 1999 was finally passed in 2005. A state-run television station for Aborigines was launched in 2004.

In addition to Ami, Paiwan, Atayal, Bunun, Puyuma, Rukai, Tsou, Saisiyat and Tao (Yami), who were previously recognized as 'Mountain compatriots', more Aboriginal peoples were given official recognition. Thao and Kavalan, who were recognized in 2001 and 2002 respectively, were 'Plains tribes'. A section of the Atayal people were given recognition as a separate ethnic group as Truku in 2004, and Sakizaya was separated from Ami and given recognition. Sediq was recognized as the fourteenth Aboriginal group in 2008. Other 'Plains tribes' are now seeking separate Aboriginal status.

What does the recognition of additional Aboriginal peoples mean? It signifies the official 'endorsement' of ethnic identity at a sublevel below the four major ethnic groups. Their legal status and rights are guaranteed as a group. They have collective identity as Yuanzhumin in contrast with the other three major ethnic groups. Yet, they are Truku, not Atayal, Sakizaya or Ami, in terms of more specific and local ethnic identity. Unlike Thao and Kavalan who were newly recognized as Aboriginal groups, Truku and Sakizaya already had Aboriginal status. Nevertheless, they demanded their own group names. Such an identity politics is qualitatively different from the so-called *zuqun zhengzhi* (ethnic politics). One aspect of the pluralization and multitiering of ethnic structure is revealed here.

The case of Waishengren is also complex. They are not only Waishengren but also the Shandong or Zhejiang people. They can also be 'Taiwan people' and/or 'Chinese people'. Corcuff (2008) argues that Waishengren are becoming progressively 'Taiwanized', as an increasing number of them perceive themselves as part of the Taiwan people. Corcuff makes a bold prediction that they will eventually have 'Taiwan' identity. However, some sections of the Waishengren community retain a strong orientation toward the 'Republic of China' (Kamizuru 2012). Although their political identity lies in the Republic of China, Kamizuru's informants speak of their affection for Taiwan and regard themselves as 'legitimate residents' of the island. The ethnic identity of these people, who claim they are part of Taiwan society notwithstanding the different circumstances of their immigration to Taiwan, cannot be grasped one-dimensionally.

The complexity of the situation also applies to the Hoklo and Hakka peoples. The four-group ethnic classification is only one view, and it cannot capture the full picture of ethnicity in contemporary Taiwan. Identity is diverse within each ethnic group, and plural and multilayered even within each individual person.

New immigrants

In the 1990s, new 'outsiders' began to arrive in Taiwan in increasing numbers. They included foreign laborers from Southeast Asian countries and *waiji xinniang*, or 'foreign brides'[11], from Mainland China and Southeast Asian countries who married into Taiwan. These two groups add new dimensions to Taiwan's ethnicity and further complicate its ethnic composition.

Foreign workers
As Figure 1.4 shows, workers from Southeast Asian countries such as Indonesia, Malaysia, the Philippines and Thailand began to arrive in large numbers from the 2000s. The total number of foreign workers exceeded 300,000 people in 2000 and steadily rose to 350,000 in 2007, albeit with some regional fluctuations.

The Pluralization and Multitiering of Society in Taiwan 19

Figure 1.4 Increase in the foreign worker population (number of temporary residents)

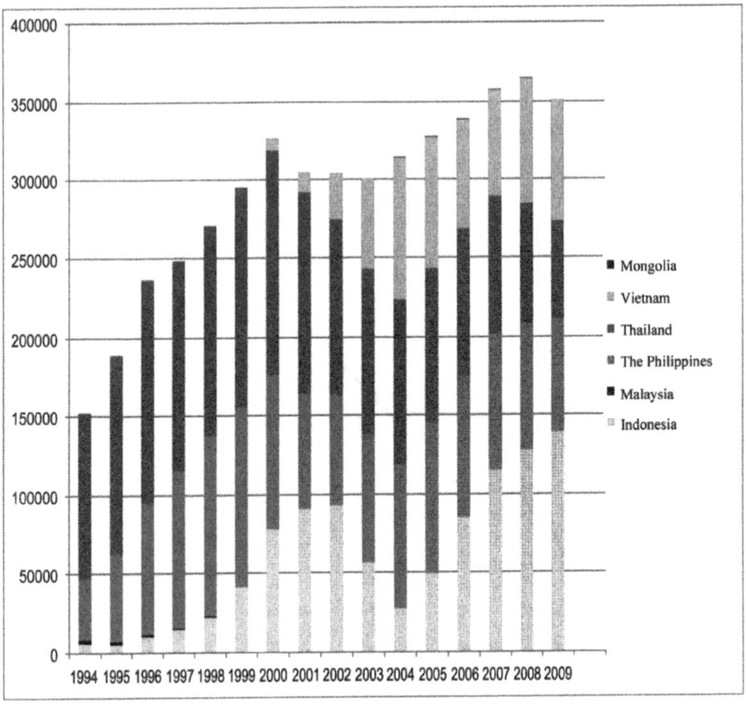

[Bar chart showing foreign worker population from 1994 to 2009, broken down by country of origin: Mongolia, Vietnam, Thailand, The Philippines, Malaysia, Indonesia]

Source: Prepared by the author, based on data from Xingsheng Yuan Laogong Weiyuanhui (Council of Labor Affairs), *99 nian banlaodong tongji nianbao* (Annual labor statistics report for 1999: 316).

Figure 1.5 shows changes in the number of foreign workers by industry. There are three interesting points to note here. Firstly, the number of foreign workers in manufacturing and construction increased rapidly during the 1990s, but the increase flattened out in manufacturing and the numbers fell in construction during the 2000s. Secondly, the number of foreign nurses and care workers surged from the mid-1990s throughout the 2000s. Thirdly, the number of foreign domestic workers has been gradually falling in the 2000s after exceeding 10,000 people by the end of the 1990s.

Foreign workers in manufacturing and construction are mostly men, and nurses, care workers and domestic workers are mostly women. Foreign male workers were imported to replace Taiwan men and covered a shortage of low-wage non-skilled laborers at factories and construction sites. They have multinationalized the base-level blue-collar labor market. Conversely, the influx of foreign female workers occurred in response to an increase in demand for nursing and aged care and a change in the home environment due to a falling birth rate and aging population. They have not only multinationalized the medical and welfare ancillary labor market but also tapped into Taiwan homes as ancillary workers in aged care, domestic work and childcare.

Figure 1.5 Change in the foreign worker population by industry (number of temporary residents)

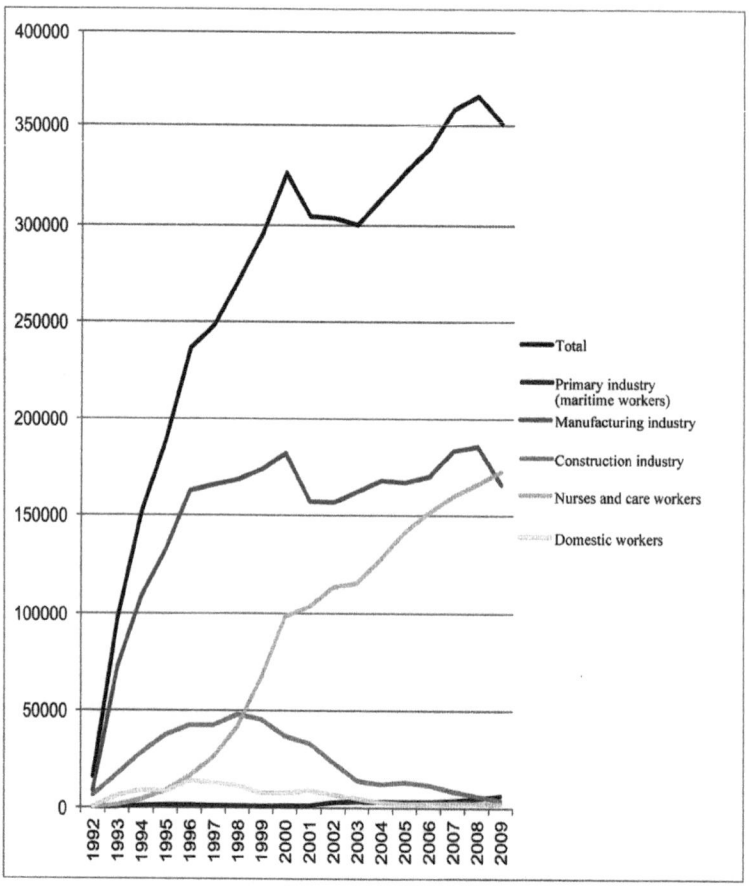

Source: Prepared by the author based on data from Xingsheng Yuan Laogong Weiyuanhui (Council of Labor Affairs), *99 nian banlaodong tongji nianbao* (Annual labor statistics report for 1999: 312–313).

Figure 1.6 shows the composition of foreign workers by industry and nationality as at 2009. The diagram clearly demonstrates national characteristics. Since industry type and gender are closely related, these characteristics can be summarized as follows. A majority of Indonesian workers are female ancillary workers on the frontline of medicine and welfare such as nurses and care workers. In the case of Philippine and Vietnamese workers, many men work in manufacturing and considerable numbers of women work as nurses, care workers and domestic workers. A majority of Thai workers are male and are employed in manufacturing and construction.

Figure 1.6 Nationalities of foreign workers by industry (number of temporary residents, 2009)

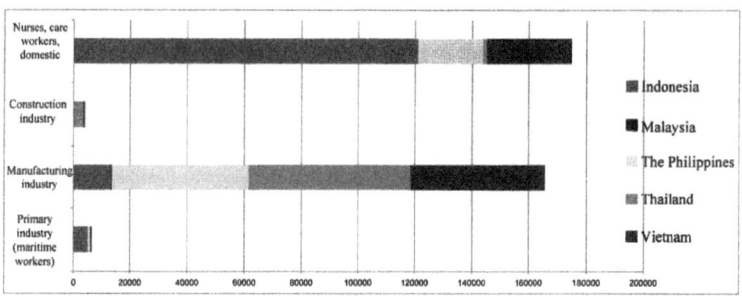

Source: Prepared by the author based on data from Xingsheng Yuan Laogong Weiyuanhui (Council of Labor Affairs), *99 nian banlaodong tongji nianbao* (Annual labor statistics report for 1999: 314).

Note: Only ten Malaysians are included in the manufacturing industry.

Although their numbers are still relatively small, these linguistically and culturally diverse people are present not only at various workplaces but also inside family homes in contemporary Taiwan society. They are not always fluent in the 'national language'. This may not be a problem at worksites involving simple physical labor, but it poses a serious problem for nursing and care-giving in clinical and domestic settings. Nevertheless, in recent years foreign workers have supplied a large part of the ancillary workforce in medical care and welfare. New ethnic relations are being formed in these non-conventional fields.

Waiji xinniang (foreign brides)
The influx of 'brides' from foreign countries is increasing even more rapidly than foreign workers (Figure 1.7). As more Taiwan youth are marrying later or not marrying at all, many Taiwan men are opting to find spouses outside of Taiwan. The main sources of foreign brides are Mainland China (including Hong Kong and Macau) and Southeast Asian countries such as Indonesia and Vietnam. Marriage to Mainland Chinese rose to sixteen percent of Taiwan's total marriages in 1997 and reached twenty-one percent in 2003 (Wan Hongzen 2008: 114). On the other hand, the ratio of marriage to Southeast Asian people hovered at around eleven percent for the same period. For over a decade, one-fourth to one-third of the total number of nuptials in Taiwan have been 'international marriages'.

Figure 1.7 shows that the number of international marriages to foreigners other than Mainland Chinese and Southeast Asians is also increasing, although the overall number is still small. It includes many Taiwan women marrying foreign men as well as the reverse.

Figure 1.7 Increase in the foreign spouse population

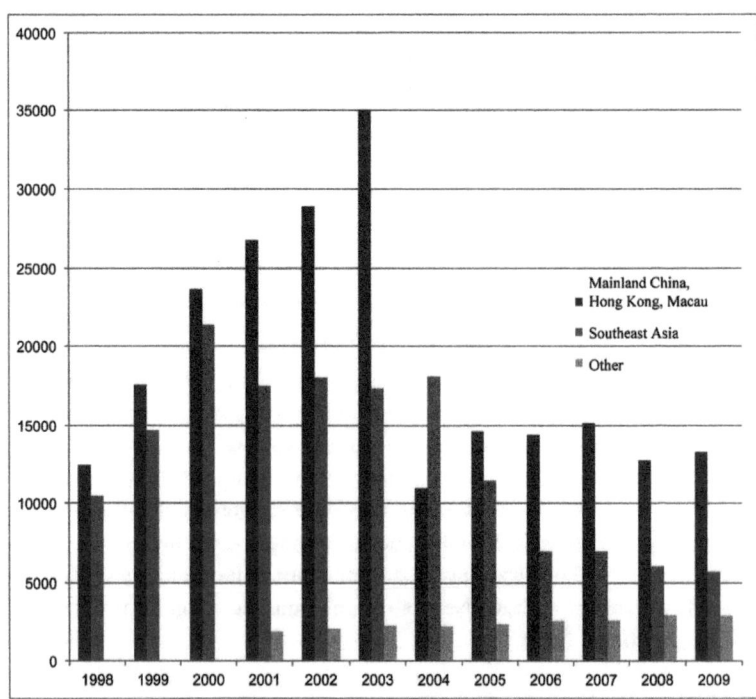

Source: Prepared by the author based on data from Xingzhengyuan Zhijichu (2009: 24–25) *Shehui zhibiao tongji* (Social indicators statistics).

It appears that Taiwan men typically take wives from 'developing countries', while Taiwan women take husbands from 'developed countries'. In other words, this involves the phenomenon of international hypergamy (marrying up). This phenomenon has been observed in the past but its expansion is a recent development. The surge in the number of matrimonial immigrants from Mainland China and Southeast Asia in particular is a social trend that is likely to have a signicicant impact on Taiwan society for a long period through child rearing and education.

The most marked influence at present arises in relation to Taiwan's ethnic composition. An extensive 'cultural pluralization' that is beyond comparison with intermarriage between Taiwan's ethnic groups in the past has begun in the homes of many newly married couples. And this cultural pluralization is a process in which various dimensions such as gender dynamics, food culture and language use are intricately intertwined.

For example, studies by Wang Hongren et al. (Tian and Wang 2006; Wang and Tien 2009) report that Taiwan men who marry Vietnamese women tend to think that men should play the breadwinner role in the family and seek 'traditional' virtues in women. Conversely, it has been pointed out that Vietnamese women who marry Taiwan men have a relatively conservative idea about gender roles in comparison to today's Taiwan women (M. Li 2003). One study reports that there are no major differences in terms of values about marriage and family life between Taiwan husbands and Vietnamese wives (H. Zhang 2007: 69–94). Wang Hongzen (2008: 115) argues that in addition to economic reasons that are usually emphasized, the 'masculinity' culture of Taiwan men is contributing to the rise in matrimonial immigrants from Southeast Asia. The gender cultures of Taiwan and Vietnam jointly affect these international marriages.

While Vietnamese brides endeavor to fit into Taiwan homes as 'good wives' according to their conservative idea of gender roles, they maintain their Vietnamese ethnicity by forming Vietnamese cooking groups with other Vietnamese women and gradually incorporating Vietnamese food in their home cooking (K. Lin 2006). Slowly but surely, they are changing Taiwan's food culture.

According to Zhang Hanbi (2007: 112–119), Vietnamese wives use the national language (Mandarin Chinese), Taiwan Hokkien, Hakka and Vietnamese at home, depending on whom they are speaking to. The Vietnamese language has contributed to Taiwan's multilingual situation.

Brides from Mainland China and Hong Kong share Han culture and the 'Chinese language', but they often encounter a 'foreign culture' in their lives in Taiwan, since the island society followed a separate path from Mainland China and Hong Kong for about 100 years. If the husband's parents are Benshengren, the wife may have to learn to speak Taiwan Hokkien. Even the marriage between Taiwan men and Mainland Chinese women more or less adds to the country's multicultural situation.

The 'individualization' and 'internationalization' of ethnicity

The above overview of the pluralization and multitiering of ethnicity in Taiwan society since the 1990s suggests that the changes are not merely an increase in the ethnic categories or the diversification of classification criteria. They entail the 'individualization' and 'internationalization' of ethnicity.

Foreign brides are a typical example of 'individualization'. They do not exist in groups. The Vietnamese nationality is an attribute of one woman within one family. People around her experience Vietnamese ethnicity through their individual contact and relationships with her.

This is also the case with foreign domestic workers in homes and foreign laborers at factories and construction sites. Above all, Taiwan residents belonging to the so-called four major ethnic groups are perhaps coming in contact with people of other ethnicities as individuals rather than competing with them as groups.

New immigrants such as foreign workers and foreign brides are also typical examples of 'internationalization'. The Vietnamese wife does not sever her relationship with her 'birth family' back home after marriage. The ethnic relations of her Taiwan husband will extend beyond national boundaries through her. Similarly, foreign workers are creating new networks of ethnic relations between their home countries and Taiwan, and Taiwan's four major ethnic groups are also forming ethnic relations beyond national boundaries as Taiwan strengthens its ties with Mainland China and its economy undergoes globalization.

Consequently, ethnicity is individualized at the micro level, and simultaneously internationalized at the macro level. 'Ethnic groups' are less and less groupish than they used to be. Ethnicity in Taiwan is being transformed from a collective entity into an individual characteristic or personal 'ethnic-ness', which is developing globally at the same time.

Pluralization and multitiering in social stratification

'Middle class expansion' in Taiwan society continued basically from the 1990s to the 2000s (Su 2008, 2009). Despite occasional crises, Taiwan's economy continued to grow and the national income continued to rise. The GDP per capita rose to be on par with Japan on a purchasing power parity basis. Conversely, new disparities are starting to emerge. As a result, pluralization and multitiering are progressing in Taiwan's social stratification.

The ongoing middle class expansion

Table 1.3 shows Taiwan's class composition by generation in recent years. A common feature in both the survey respondent's class and their father's class is a steady decrease in farming and an increase in other occupations among the younger generations. The professional and clerical worker classes expanded markedly, suggesting a white-collar expansion.

Table 1.3 Generational change in class structure

	Male				Female			
Generation (birth year)	1928–45	1946–55	1956–65	1966–75	1928–45	1946–55	1956–65	1966–75
Respondent's class	%	%	%	%	%	%	%	%
Professional	18.7	26.9	29.5	26.7	9.6	19.0	24.0	29.3
Clerk/administrator	4.3	6.7	7.7	7.6	10.9	18.3	27.8	42.2
Self-employed	20.9	27.8	24.1	23.2	16.2	19.5	17.1	10.3
Farmer	29.4	10.0	6.1	11.6	35.8	9.4	3.8	0.7
Skilled worker	12.2	16.1	20.4	17.9	11.8	15.5	15.8	9.7
Semi-skilled worker	14.6	12.6	12.2	13.1	15.7	18.3	11.6	7.9
Father's class	%	%	%	%	%	%	%	%
Professional	9.6	13.9	13.0	17.0	8.6	12.9	16.0	19.2
Clerk/administrator	4.0	5.5	6.1	5.4	3.4	7.0	5.6	7.3
Self-employed	14.3	16.8	20.4	27.2	12.6	17.3	22.9	25.2
Farmer	60.9	47.0	37.3	23.0	65.9	47.0	33.4	19.1
Skilled worker	4.6	8.2	12.5	15.0	4.3	7.1	10.7	15.0
Semi-skilled worker	6.6	8.7	10.8	12.4	5.2	8.7	11.4	14.3

Source: Prepared by the author based on data from Su Guoxian (2009: 111). Original source: *Taiwan shehui bianjian jiben diaocha1992–2005* (Social change in Taiwan basic survey, 1992–2005).

What is interesting about Table 1.3 is that the self-employed class in the respondent's class alone is shrinking in the generations born after the 1956–65 period among both men and women. This suggests a trend toward salaried employment in the younger generations and in turn a decrease in the so-called *laoban* (literally 'Boss' or an independent owner-manager of a large or small enterprise).[12] It is said that the younger generations show a strong preference for public-sector employment, perhaps because it is becoming increasingly difficult to start up independent enterprises as the economy matures.

In terms of subjective class consciousness, the percentage of people who considered themselves as belonging to the 'middle class' was around fifty percent among men and about sixty percent among women in the 1990–2006 period, and the numbers showed an upward trend from 2002 to 2006 (Su 2008: 196).

The emergence of new disparities

A more detailed examination also reveals the emergence of various disparities. Figure 1.8 shows changes in income distribution inequality based on the ratio of the top and bottom income quintiles and the Gini coefficient. Both indices demonstrate that the income gap has been widening, albeit slightly and slowly.

Figure 1.8 Income distribution in Taiwan (1980–2009)

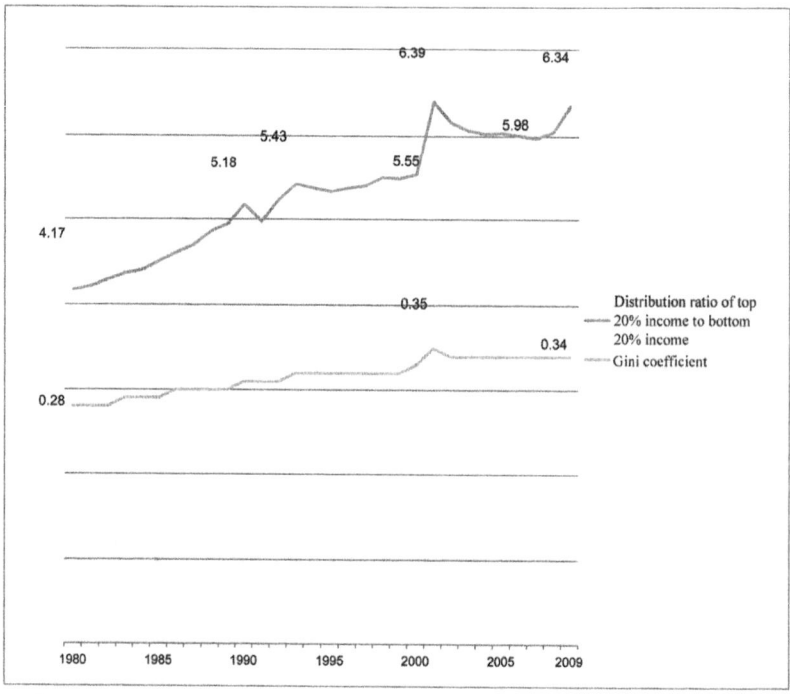

Source: Prepared by the author based on data from Xingzhengyuan Zhijichu (1998: 21) *Jiushiba nian jiating shouzhi diaocha baogao* (Household economy survey report for 1998).

Economic disparity

For instance, the income gap is widening even more between Aborigines and the non-Aboriginal Taiwan people. According to a survey, in 1985 the average income of Aboriginal families was 210,000 yuan, while Taiwan's overall average income was 460,000 yuan; a differential of about 2.3 times. The differential increased to over three times in 2006 as the average Aboriginal family income was 320,000 yuan, while the average Taiwan family income was over one million yuan (Y. Zhang et al. 2010: 90).

With regard to disparity between Benshengren and Waishengren, one analysis reports that a higher proportion of Waishengren belonged to the middle and upper classes in 1994 (N. Wu 1997), but a later study found that the gap has been decreasing because Waishengren have not been able to maintain their class status (Su and Yu 2007).

While gaps between ethnic groups other than Aborigines are diminishing, those between classes appear to be increasing. In comparing household finances between 1992 and 2007, Lin Zonghong (2009: 128–130) reports that the income of the capitalist class rose the most and the wages of professionals and skilled workers also increased, while the income of clerical workers and the self-employed decreased. The wages of non-skilled workers rose but they remained at the lowest of all classes. Lin concludes that disparities between classes are widening.

There is another curious change afoot. Gaps between the top and bottom income quintiles are widening in terms of household size and number of persons working. The average household size in 2006 was 4.37 persons in the top quintile class as against 1.82 persons in the bottom quintile class. The average number of persons working was 2.32 persons in the top quintile class as against 0.59 persons in the bottom quintile class. The top quintile had 3.93 times more working persons than the bottom quintile in 2006, which is a twofold increase from 1.82 times in 1980 (Su 2008: 195). This appears to point to the impoverishment of single households, such as solitary elderly people and single-mother households.

Gender gaps
Gaps between women and men appear to have decreased in the last two to three decades. Between 1981 and 2006, the employment rate among women increased from thirty-nine to forty-nine percent, the percentage of women with university or higher education in the workforce rose from twenty-six to forty-five percent and the ratio of the female to the male wage also increased from sixty-four to over seventy-nine percent (Z. Lin 2009: 123). Between 1992 and 2007, the numbers of women in the professional, managerial and capitalist classes increased (Z. Lin 2009: 124–125).

On the other hand, a comparison of the generations who were born before and after 1970 shows that the percentages of women entering the upper managerial and capitalist classes are smaller in the latter group (Z. Lin 2009: 125). According to survey reports (Xue 2004, 2008), the number of single-woman households is increasing as more women divorce or stay unmarried, and the ratios of single-woman households and single-mother households are high in the low-income class and households with children are more impoverished than those without. Another possible reason for the increase in the number of single women in the lowest class is the presence of foreign women who work as nurses, care workers and domestic workers.

Thus it appears that 'gaps between women' are widening while 'gaps between men and women' are narrowing. The disparity between 'wealthy Taiwan housewives' and 'foreign maids' frankly portrayed by Lan Pei-Chia (2006) and Lan Peijia (2008) is a prime example of this trend.

'Cultural' gaps

The increasing population of foreign workers and foreign brides is creating new cultural inequalities. Foreign workers are positioned at the bottom of society not just in terms of income. They have no choice but to endure cultural hardships due to their language difficulties and unfamiliarity with Taiwan's Han culture. Moreover, many feel that they are exposed to prejudice and discrimination in Taiwan. Just like foreign workers, many foreign wives have limited language skills and are unfamiliar with Taiwan's Han culture (Se et al. 2007b).

Having a foreign mother may have an adverse impact on a child's education (Se et al. 2007a). Mothers who are not fluent in the national language may be unable to read notices and instructions from schools or help with their children's homework. Children from multinational families are more likely to be disadvantaged in this respect.

A new kind of 'racial discrimination' is also emerging. According to Lan Peijia (2005), an employment agency for foreign domestic workers carried out an advertising campaign promoting 'obedient Indonesians' as opposed to 'unmanageable Filipinas'. This led to a decrease in the employment of Philippine domestic workers and an increase in the demand for their Indonesian counterparts.

Thus the increased complexity in ethnicity due to the increasing numbers of new immigrants is contributing to the pluralization and multitiering of Taiwan's social hierarchy by way of a rise in cultural inequalities.

The 'individualization' and 'internationalization' of social stratification

The above overview of the transformation of Taiwan's social stratification in the last two decades reveals widening disparities in various dimensions, contrary to the entrenchment of middle-class consciousness. The hierarchical structure is complicated not only by ethnic classification, education and occupation but also a combination of factors such as gender, age, marital status, a spouse's nationality, whether or not one has children, and so on.

Consequently, as in the case of ethnicity, social stratification shows new tendencies of 'individualization' and 'internationalization'. Social stratification can no longer be discussed on the basis of family units or within Taiwan's national boundaries. This is not limited to foreign workers and foreign brides. As the activities of corporate owners and managers in the middle and upper classes extend overseas, an increasing number of families experience living in foreign countries. Their children grow up to become bilingual and bicultural. An increasing number of middle- and upper-class parents send their children to English-speaking kindergartens to prepare for their future life in overseas countries. Individual factors such as experience living abroad or English language skills can exert a great influence over one's future position in the social stratification and the relative importance of these individual factors are strongly influenced by international ones.

Conclusion

Figure 1.9 is a schematic representation of pluralization and multitiering in ethnicity and social hierarchy. Large frameworks no longer exist and small boxes are arranged one above the other and side-by-side in a multidimensional space. Figure 1.9 is represented three-dimensionally, but the number of dimensions is of course not limited to three. Each box contains a diverse array of individuals who more or less share similar characteristics but do not constitute a coherent group at all.

Figure 1.9 'Pluralization' and 'multitiering' in ethnicity and social stratification (schematic representation)

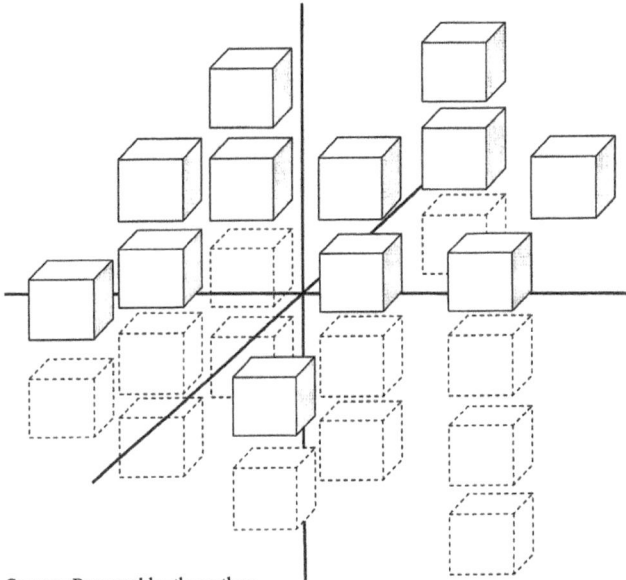

Source: Prepared by the author.

The diagram in Figure 1.9 indicates that the existing ethnic groups and social strata are fractionized and diversity is increasing. The dimensions of this diversity are also multiplying. This is the contemporary manifestation of pluralization and multitiering in Taiwan society. This seems to suggest that the constituent members of Taiwan society are becoming more diverse and distinct. Will the increasing diversity act as a centrifugal force and make the integration of Taiwan society more difficult? Or will it not act as an impediment, and will some centripetal force overcome such diversity to maintain the integrity of Taiwan society? In closing, I would like to consider this point.

If the ethnic consciousnesses of Hoklo and Hakka strengthen and lead to a clear division of support for political parties, ethnic grouping may act as a centrifugal force in the sense that their preexisting unity as Benshengren will weaken. Language and cultural barriers may also act as a centrifugal force between the Han and the new non-Han immigrants.

However, there is the possibility that centripetal forces may act beyond the boundaries between ethnic groups. As mentioned above, not only Benshengren, who were forced to use the 'national language', but also Waishengren are becoming bilingual and intermarriage between ethnic groups is increasing. These are perhaps acting as a centripetal force by strengthening their relationships beyond differences. Between the Han and Yuanzhumin, the continuation of support for the KMT by the latter group may prompt the KMT to act as a centripetal force to bring the two groups closer together (Ishigaki 2012). Even those with the strongest Waishengren consciousness remain in Taiwan and assert that they are legitimate members of Taiwan society (Kamizuru 2012). This is perhaps one example of the centripetal force at work in Taiwan.

Some scholars and the government seem to promote 'cultural pluralism' as a centripetal force to maintain social integration, while retaining linguistic and cultural diversity among ethnic groups and new immigrants (Tanoue 2012). It remains to be seen as to whether this attempt will succeed.

Contrary to the discourse of 'Taiwanization', the complexities in Taiwan society continue to grow. Further, 'individualization' and 'internationalization' in ethnicity and social stratification may make integration difficult even within a single family, and the increase of new immigrants may call for social integration at a level beyond the confines of Taiwan. What is certain is that factors affecting the integration of Taiwan society are multiplying and becoming ever more complex. Nevertheless, there are no serious conflicts between ethnic groups or social strata, and new immigrants have not caused any major social problems thus far.

It appears that factors with a centrifugal potential are newly emerging, while a certain level of centripetal force is working to maintain social integrity in contemporary Taiwan society. As a Taiwan specialist, I would like to continue to watch as to whether the centrifugal force will strengthen or a centripetal force will be sustained in the future.

2 The Lives of Slaves from the Perspective of Family Relations: The Case of Daegu Household Registers from the End of the Seventeenth Century to the First Half of the Eighteenth Century

Mutsuhiko Shima

This chapter presents a tentative study on the forms of existence of people recorded as slaves in household registers in Korea from the end of the seventeenth to the mid-eighteenth century, from the perspective of their family relations. The household registers used here are of the Daegu region in Gyōngsang Province. The analysis first focuses on the overall conditions of local society at the time and then attempts to paint a distinct picture based on individual cases. Material on the slaves under detailed analysis is derived from the records on the household of the head of the Danyang U lineage and those of his nearest relatives from 1690 to 1753. This lineage held the highest social status in the area at the time.

Legal and institutional conditions concerning the determination of slave status

According to historian Hiraki Makoto (1971), various arguments were put forward concerning the legal framework of the system of hereditary slave status, which had been in place since the middle of the Koryŏ dynasty period (1039). The system was repeatedly revised until a final decision was made regarding its structure in January 1729. While the term *nobi-jongmoje* (a system in which children inherit the slave status of their mother) had been in use since the beginning of the slave system, in reality all children whose father or mother was a slave inherited the slave status. This resulted in a decreased population of commoners by the middle of the Chosŏn dynasty period. In order to secure a sufficient population of commoners to perform *yangyŏk* (government duties assigned to commoners), a change to the system of *nobi-jongmoje* was proposed in 1669, and the system was subsequently revised multiple times until it was finalized in 1729 (Hiraki 1971).

The household registers that feature in this study cover the period of these frequent legal changes as well as over twenty years post establishment of the final form of the system. As a result, we must be mindful of the circumstances surrounding the slave system when considering the form of social existence of slaves through our analysis of household registers. In particular, one of the social conditions that necessitated the legal change was intermarriage between commoners and slaves, which must have been widespread in those days. It is important that we pay attention to the way this situation was reflected in the household registers.

Yi Yŏnghun (2001: 264) argues that the slave system collapsed following the adoption of *nobi-jongmoje* in 1729. It is undeniable that this posed a major change to the hereditary slave system, leading to a decrease in the overall size of the slave population. However, it is doubtful as to whether it is appropriate to call it a 'collapse', as such. Although the class system falls outside of my expertise, this issue relates to the fact that there remained a large population of *hain* (persons of subordinate status) who were stuck with their former slave status after the class system was officially abolished as part of the Kabo reform in 1894, and the structure of society was maintained on that basis.[1]

Yi also states in the same paper that *sinobi* (government-owned slaves) possessed almost the same level of personal liberty as did commoners (2001: 253), and this forms another point of interest for the present study.

An overview of slavery in Joam-bang and Wŏlbae-bang

Records of slaves in Daegu household registers

Table 2.1 Classification of registered households

Year	Total	Commoner households	Slave households	Proportion of slave households
1690	463	349	114	24.6%
1720	283	234	49	17.3%
1729/32	366	316	50	13.6%

Note: 'Slave households' refers to those in which either or both household heads and their spouses are of slave status.

Table 2.1 shows a breakdown of all registered households into commoner and slave households, based on the status of the household head. Slave households refer to those of *oegŏ-nobi* (slaves who live away from their owners), with the husband or wife or both holding slave status. Households of 'emancipated former slave' status are also included in this category for the purpose of this study, on the basis that the individuals 'were slaves until recently'. While we have all household registers for 1690 for both

Joam-bang and Wŏlbae-bang, we have 1720 records for Wŏlbae-bang only, and we are missing half of the Wŏlbae-bang records for 1729/32; therefore a full comparison could not be made. However, it is generally found that it was quite common for people of slave status to establish their own households (approx. fifteen to twenty-five percent) during this period.

Table 2.2 Registered individuals and status

Year	Total registered individuals	Registered individuals of slave status	Proportion of slaves
1690	2768	1200	43.4%
1720	2217	1012	45.6%
1729/32	2699	1096	40.6%

Note: Household registers include individuals not currently resident in the area due to either being dead, or, in the case of slaves, living elsewhere or having escaped.

Table 2.2 is a list of registered individuals classified by status for this period and shows us that forty to forty-five percent of the total population belonged to the slave class. However, the figures include considerable numbers of slaves owned by the household head who were not living in the area at the time because they resided elsewhere or had escaped. In consideration of this, Table 2.3 shows the percentages of people of slave status in the total resident population of the area. According to this, from the end of the seventeenth to the first half of the eighteenth century the proportion of people of slave status in the local community was quite high (around thirty percent). I shall carry out the following analysis with this in mind.

Table 2.3 Resident individuals and status

Year	Total population	Slave status population	Proportion of slaves in the total population
1690	2094	743	35.5%
1720	1586	520	32.8%
1729/32	1943	545	28.0%

Marital relations of slave household couples: Commoner/ slave intermarriage

Tables 2.4a, 2.4b and 2.4c show status relations of husband and wife in slave households for each year. Where widower/widow households are excluded and emancipated former slaves are counted as slaves, status relations of the household head and his wife in slave households for the period are summed up in Table 2.4d. This shows that more than thirty percent of marriages in slave households were between commoners and slaves. It is found that the

Table 2.4a Status relations of husband and wife in slave households, 1690

Status of husband	Status of wife: slave	widowed or unmarried slave	emancipated former slave	daughter of lower officer of local government	commoner	status unidentifiable	total number of wives or widows
slave	69	59		1	1	7	1
widowed or unmarried slave	5		1				
emancipated former slave	8	6			2		
lower officer of local government	1	1					
commoners, including one emancipated due to old age	27	25			2		
status unidentifiable	6	6					
total number of husbands or widowers	116						112

Table 2.4b Status relations of husband and wife in slave households, 1720

Status of husband	Status of wife: slave	slave (widowed or unmarried)	emancipated former slave	commoner	status unidentifiable	total number of wives or widows
slave	34	18		8	8	
emancipated former slave	2	1	1			
emancipated former slave, widower	7	7				
commoner	6	6				
total	49					50

Note: In one case, a male slave first married a slave, then a commoner.

status of a commoner spouse (the status of a male household head and, in the case of a commoner wife, the status of her father) tends to be of lower stratum among commoners, including *ŏyŏng-gun*, *jŏngbyŏng*, *boin* and *jangin*. It appears that there was no rupture to social relations between the commoners of lower strata and those of slave status.

As an example suggesting this possibility, I shall describe the following case of the coexistence of commoner and slave households within a patrilineal kinship group.

Table 2.4c Status relations of husband and wife in slave households, 1729–32

		Status of wife				
		slave	slave (widowed or unmarried)	emancipated former slave	commoner	total number of wives or widows
Status of husband	slave	24	18		6	
			12			
	emancipated former slave	1	1		1	
	emancipated former slave, widowered	9				
	commoner	4	4			
	total	38				41

Table 2.4d Number of slave households according to statuses of head and wife

				Number of households in which slaves and commoners are married	
Year	Total number of slave households	Number of slave households excluding those headed by widowers or widows	Numbers of households in which husband and wife are both slaves	Number of households excluding those in which the status of either of the partners is unidentified	Number of household including those in which the status of either of the partners is unidentified
1690	114	108	65 (57.0%)	36 (31.6%)	43 (39.8%)
1720	49	48	19 (39.6%)	15 (31.3%)	29 (60.4%)
1729/32	50	29	19 (65.5%)	10 (34.5%)	10 (34.5%)

Case 1: Kimhae Kim lineage, Wŏlbae-ri hamlet in Wŏlbae-bang administrative village

This lineage is a patrilineal kinship group of twenty-three households, which was the second largest group in Joam-bang and Wŏlbae-bang after the Danyang U lineage of Sangin-ri.

Table 2.5 presents a list of the *jikyŏk* (officially assigned positions or statuses) of all men who appear on the genealogy in Figure 2.1a. All men in the first five generations were of commoner status in various positions. Overall, the status of the lineage was not very high as we can see from examples such as Ik in the first generation whose position was *jŏngbyŏng* and Chŏnŭl in the fourth generation whose position was *napsok bongsa*, *napsok* meaning 'purchased with rice'. It is highly likely that positions such as *gyomsabok* of Guise in the third generation and *busagwa* of Saryong in the fourth generation were also bought with rice.[2] Even though the lineage might not belong to the upper social strata, it formed a large-scale kinship

Table 2.5 Government appointed/ascribed position or status of the individuals in Figure 2.1a

Generation 1	Generation 2	Generation 3	Generation 4	Generation 5	Generation 6	Generation 7
Ik:	Gunbok:	Guise:	Saryong:	Yŏkwan:	Siŏn:	Ilbang:
Jŏngbyŏng	Jŏlchung-Janggun,	Jŏnryŏk-Buui,	Ŏmochanggun, Haeng	Jŏngbyŏng	Ŏpmu	Muhak, Sundaejol
	Chŏmji-Junchubusa	Gyŏmsabok	Yongyangui Busagwa		Sŏkmin: Muhak, Sunjaega	
					Üichŏl: Ŏbo	
					Sŏkchŏl: Gŭmuigun	
			Chŏnŭl: Napsok Bongsa	Kŭkkwang: Jŏngbyŏng	Jongho: Gŭmuibo	Iwŏn: Sano Sunabyŏng
				Hojip: Ŏyŏnggun		Guibang: Suboyŏng Janggunkwaan Sosgang Byŏngin
				Surip: Chungikui	Hogŏl: Ŏyŏnggun Hogang: Chungchanul	Yŏŏp: Subo Sunmagun
				Surin: Chungikui, Ŏmochanggun	Hosŏn: Gŭmuibo	Chŏlju: (adopted by Suyang below)
						Chŏljun: Giboyŏng Janggungwan
						Chŏlhŭng: Gŭmuibo
					Hosang: Chungikui	
				Kiyŏng: Muhak	Homyŏng: Ŏyŏnggun	
					Hosŏng: Ŏbo	
					Bowŏn: Sano	
					Mallyong: Sano Sokogun	
				Suyang: Chungikui	Chŏlju: Chungikui, Sŏnryak Janggun	
			Samyŏng: Pobo	Jŏngmin: Muhak, Sundaejŏl		

group that had economic status high enough to purchase government posts with rice. Chŏnŭl (fourth generation) is the only person with *napsok*

Figure 2.1a Genealogy of Kimhae Kim lineage in Wŏlbae-ri, 1690

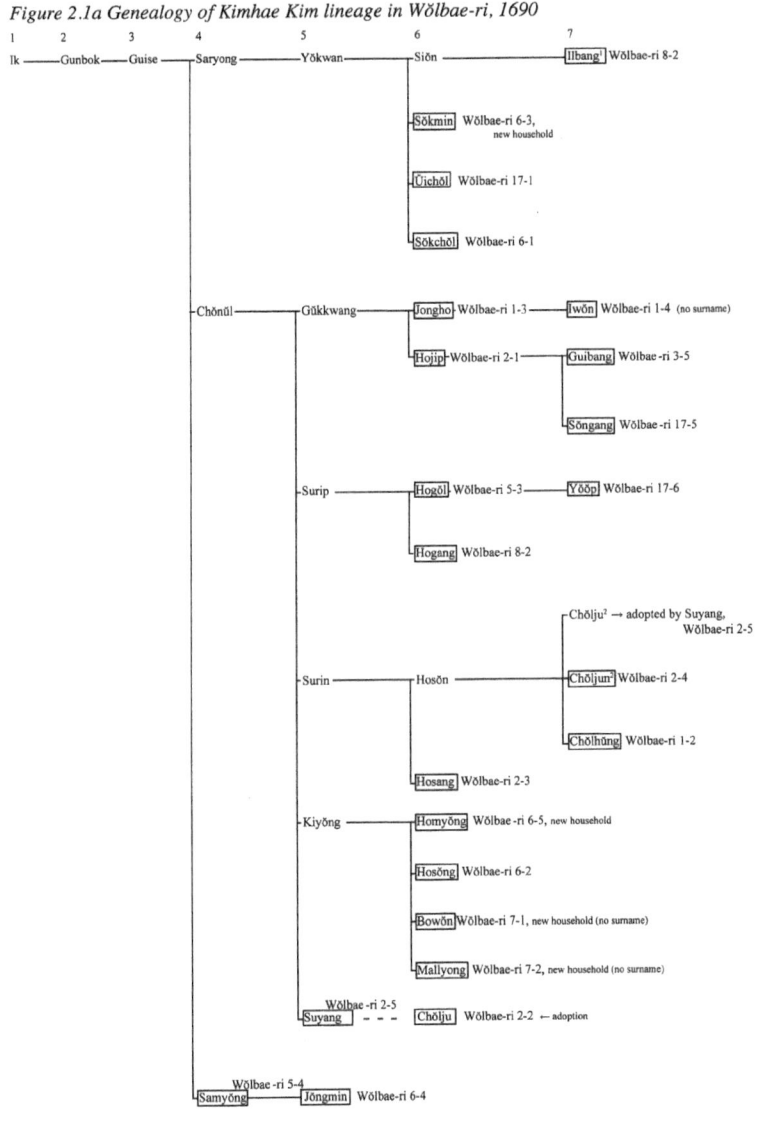

Notes:
1. ☐ denotes the household head.
2. Chŏlju and Chŏljun are of the same age but born of different mothers. It is not known which of the mothers was the lawful wife of their father.

mentioned in the position title. Of his seventeen descendant households, eight fall into the category of slave households for the purpose of the present study. In other words, commoner and slave households coexisted within this lineage.

Figure 2.1b Marriage relations surrounding Jongho

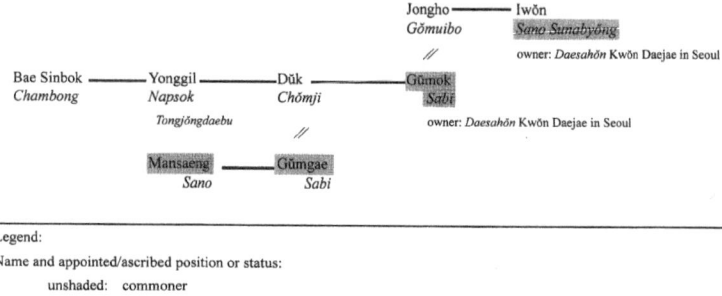

Legend:
Name and appointed/ascribed position or status:
   unshaded: commoner
   shaded: slave
Appointed/ascribed positions and statuses are shown in italics.
   Marriage sign || partners are both commoners or slaves;
                  //   marriage between a commoner and a slave;
                  // ?   child of slave status but born of a commoner father, suggesting that the mother is a slave.

Figure 2.1c Marriage relations surrounding Iwŏn

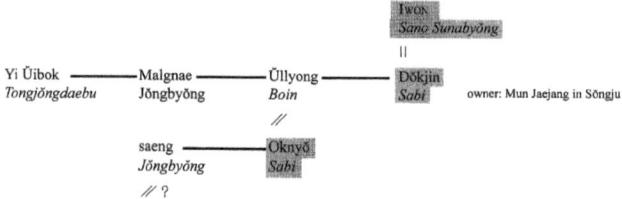

The sole reason for these eight households to become slave households was intermarriage between commoners and slaves. Let us look at the circumstances in more detail based on the case of Jongho and his son Iwŏn whose names appear at the top of the family tree.

Jongho, who was a commoner (*gŭmwuibo*), married Gŭmok, who was a *sabi* (female slave owned by an individual). All of her paternal ancestors were commoners but it is highly likely that their positions were purchased with rice. Gŭmok's slave status resulted from the marriage between her father Dŭk (one character undecipherable) (*chŏmji*) and her mother Gŭmgae, who was a *sabi*.

Son Iwŏn from this marriage became a *sano* (male slave owned by an individual) because of his mother's slave status. As Iwŏn himself married a *sabi*, theirs was a marriage between slaves. However, it is likely that the *sabi* status of his wife Dŏkjin resulted from her father's (*boin*) marriage to a *sabi*, and the *sabi* status of her mother Oknyŏ also resulted from her father's (*jŏngbyŏng* (one character undecipherable) *jŏng*) marriage to a *sabi*. In view of these circumstances, it is highly probable that the *tongjŏng daebu* position, ranking very high, of the wife's paternal great grandfather was purchased with rice.

The examination of genealogical records of the ancestors of slave status spouses in intermarriages between commoners and slaves has revealed the existence of a history of multiple intermarriages. This is true for the remaining six cases of slave households who descended from Chŏnŭl.

- Hojip (*ŏyŏng-gun*): Both parents of his wife (*sabi*, whose owner was Bang Yŏngil of Sŏngju) were slaves but their fathers were commoners (*jŏngbyŏng*), and therefore it is surmised that marriage to slaves occurred in their generation.
- Hogŏl (*ŏyŏng-gun*): The father of his wife (*sabi*, whose owner was *yuhak* Yu Jŏk of Kongju) was a commoner (*jŏngbyŏng*) and her mother was a *sabi*. As her mother's father was also a *jŏngbyŏng*, it is surmised that her mother became a slave because her father married a female slave.
- Hogang (*chungchanui*): The father of his wife (*sabi*, whose owner was Bae Sinmin of Daegu) and her maternal grandfather (*jŏngbyŏng*) both married *sabis*. Intermarriage between commoners and slaves continued for three generations, including that of Hogang's wife.
- Homyŏng (*ŏyŏng-gun*): The status of his wife (*sabi*, whose owner was *yuhak* Yun Gye who lives in (undecipherable)) resulted from her father's (*tongjŏng daebu*) wife (*sabi*) whose father (*boin*) presumably married a *sabi*.
- Bowŏn: Bowŏn's *sino* (government-owned male slave) status resulted from his mother's *sibi* (government-owned female slave) status, which resulted from her maternal grandfather's (*tongjŏng daebu*) marriage to a slave. The status of Bowŏn's wife (*sabi*, whose owner was Bae Gihan of Daegu) resulted from the slave-status wives of both her father (*jŏngbyŏng*) and maternal grandfather (*jŏngbyŏng*). Homyŏng and Bowŏn above were half-brothers and their statuses were different because their father (*muhak*) married a slave as his second wife or concubine.
- Mallyong (Bowŏn's brother, *sano*): The genealogy of his wife (*sabi*, whose owner was Yi Aegwang of Daegu) shows that her father (*jŏngbyŏng*) and paternal grandfather (*jŏngbyŏng*) married slaves.

In each of the above cases, the ancestral record of the slave-status wife shows a history of intermarriages between commoners and slaves. These examples suggest that commoners and slaves associated with one another with hardly any distinction in their day-to-day social lives, including marriage that formed the core of family life, despite a clear legal distinction between them (from the government's point of view). Cases of intermarriage in this lineage are only found among the descendants of Chŏnŭl. I suspect that this was because his sons (in positions such as *jŏngbyŏng, chungchanui* and *muhak*) just happened to marry women of slave status or were receptive to such marriages, rather than because Chŏnŭl himself had some kind of problem.

It is also worth noting that many of the *sangjŏn* (owners) of the slave-status spouses in these examples lived away from the area (they might have lived in Daegu but not in the Joam-bang and Wŏlbae-bang areas). This points to the possibility that owners had little involvement in the marriage of the slaves living away from them. Let us now look at the relationship between the residential locations of slave household couples and the owners of all slave households (living away from their owners).

Table 2.6 Ownership of the household head and his wife in slave households, 1690

Type 1	both are government slaves	1
Type 2	both have same owner	6
Type 3	either one of the couple is owned by a Danyang U lineage member	8
Type 4	other than Types 1–3	83
	total	98

Note: None of the owners of the slaves in Type 4 reside in Joam-bang or Wŏlbae-bang.

Table 2.6 shows the results of an ownership analysis for ninety-eight of 114 slave household couples for 1690, excluding cases of unknown ownership where both the household head and his wife were emancipated former slaves. It is impossible to rule out the possibility of owner involvement in slaves' marriages in the case of Types 1–3, but perhaps there is no need to pay special attention to it as there were cases of elopement by slaves owned by the same owner, as mentioned below. Among the eighty-three cases where the husband and the wife had different owners in Type 4, a majority of owners lived in faraway places such as Seoul and other provinces. Judging from this condition, it is unlikely that owners were involved in the marriages of slaves who lived away from them; it is more likely that slaves were at liberty to choose their own spouses. This is not to say that no constraints were placed on the lives of live-away slaves by their owners, but their daily existence appears to have been autonomous to a large extent.

The existence of slaves owned by the descendant of the Danyang U lineage

A summary of Danyang U Yŏjun's descendants and their slaves

Figure 2.2 Genealogy of the successive heads of Danyang U Lineage

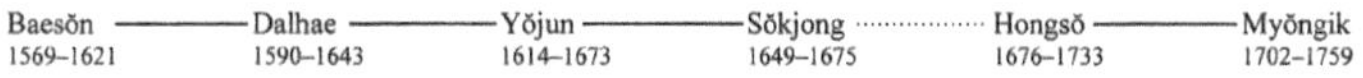

Baesŏn 1569–1621
Dalhae 1590–1643
Yŏjun 1614–1673
Sŏkjong 1649–1675
Hongsŏ 1676–1733
Myŏngik 1702–1759

Figure 2.3 Households of the lineage head and his brothers, 1690

Yŏjun
Sŏkjon
Mrs. Jo, widow
Sangin-ri 3-4
Sŏkhyŏn
Sangin-ri 3-2
Sŏksŏ
Sangin-ri 2-1
Sŏkjang
Sangin-ri 1-4

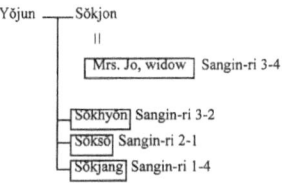

The Danyang U lineage in the Wŏlbae area increased in number and came to form a distinctive patrilineal group sometime after the mid-seventeenth century. Based on some notable cases, this section will focus on the households of the descendants of Yŏjun (Figure 2.2), a grandson of U Baesŏn, who later became *jongga* (the household of the lineage head) of this lineage, to examine the family situation of the slaves they owned. In 1690, Yŏjun's descendants included four households headed by four brothers (Figure 2.3) and increased thereafter as shown in Table 2.7.

Table 2.7 Number of households of U Yŏjun's descendants and their location of residence

Year	Wŏlbae-bang Sangin-ri	Joam-bang Il-ri	Total
1690	4	0	4
1720	4	(at least 1)	(5)
1729/32	5	3	8
1738	5	3	8
1744	10	4	14
1753	11	4	15

According to Table 2.8, the total number of slaves owned by the households of U Yŏjun's descendants increased gradually from 1690. However, *solgŏ nobi* (male and female slaves who live within the household of their owners) comprised less than thirty percent of the total. Based on sex, the total number of male slaves was about one half of that of female slaves, and the number of male slaves living within the owner household was extremely small.

Table 2.8 Summary of slaves owned by households of U Yŏjun's descendants

1690	Total number of registered slaves				Number of slaves whose marriage partners are recorded			
	male	female	sex unidentified	total	male slaves whose wives are recorded	status of wives	female slaves whose husbands are recorded	status of husbands
Sŏlgŏ	6	27		33	1	slave	1	commoner
Oegŏ	15	14		29	5	commoners (4), slave (1)	4	commoners
escaped	24	29		53	2	commoners		
deceased	2	3		5	2	commoners, both escaped		
total	47	73	0	120	10		5	

Sŏlgŏ: living in the household of the owner

Oegŏ: living away from the owner

1720	Total number of registered slaves				Number of slaves whose marriage partners are recorded			
	male	female	sex unidentified	total	male slaves whose wives are recorded	status of wives	female slaves whose husbands are recorded	status of husbands
Sŏlgŏ	7	30	1	38			4	commoners
Oegŏ	7	11		18	1	commoner	4	slaves
escaped	29	34		63	3	commoners (2), slave (1)		
deceased	1	7		8	1	commoner, escaped	1	slave
total	44	82	1	127	5		9	

1729/32	Total number of registered slaves				Number of slaves whose marriage partners are recorded			
	male	female	sex unidentified	total	male slaves whose wives are recorded	status of wives	female slaves whose husbands are recorded	status of husbands
Sŏlgŏ	3	44		47	1	commoner	2	commoners
Oegŏ	13	21	1	35	5	commoners (4), slave (1)	1	slave
escaped	37	36		73	3	commoners	3	slaves
deceased	1	3		4				
emancipated		2		2				
total	54	106	1	161	9		6	

The *solgŏ nobi* lived in their owner's households and carried out agricultural and miscellaneous domestic duties. The *oegŏ nobi* cultivated farmland away from the owner's residence, which was either the property of their owner or belonged to someone else. In the latter case, the *oegŏ nobi* cultivated farmland as tenant farmers. In both cases, they were liable for the payment of certain taxes called *singong* (tribute) to the owner (Kim

Yongman 1997, Ch 2). In terms of the relationship with their owners, for the time being let us define 'escape' as temporary desertion from this specific master-servant relationship. In some cases the household head would capture escapees and bring them back or return them to his control as live-away slaves, but the majority of escaped slaves remained on the loose for decades while still being recorded as slaves on the household register. This perhaps served as a claim of ownership on the part of the household head. The fact that nearly one half of the slaves owned by the households under examination escaped suggests that the level of control over slaves was such that slaves could abscond easily if they wished.

Marital status of slaves owned by the U lineage head and his close relatives

According to the marriage records of slaves (Table 2.8, right), only slightly over ten percent of the slaves had spouses. However, this does not seem to indicate that the rest of the slaves were unmarried. The reason for this is information on the mothers of the slaves. Each slave's parents were recorded, perhaps because they related to the derivation of slave status and therefore the location of ownership, and thus it is possible to extract marital information about individual slaves indirectly from this source.

Let us take the records of thirteen slaves (two escaped, one transferred and ten lived within the household) owned by Sŏkjang (1690, Sangin-ri household no. 4-1), Yŏjun's fourth son, as an example (Table 2.9). None of the thirteen slaves have their spouses recorded in the register, but ten have information about their father and mother, two have information about their mother only and one has no parentage record (a male slave named Hansari). There is no parentage record for Hansari here because his record was transferred to another household register.[3] The remaining twelve slaves can be grouped according to the status of their parents as shown in Table 2.10. The prefix '*ban*' in the slave status terms *banno* and *banbi* signifies 'of the same owner' (Wagner 1974).

It is possible to point out two things from the information in Table 2.10. Firstly, the two cases where the father was a *banno* and the mother was a commoner confirms that a child of a commoner mother became a slave if their father was a slave, contrary to the system of *nobi-jongmoje* (maternal inheritance of slave status) as pointed out in the legal debate at the time. Secondly, and this probably has more important implications, all cases except one in which parents were slaves of the same owner were marriages between slaves and outsiders who had no direct relationship with the slaves' owners, and seven of the twelve cases were intermarriages between commoners and slaves.

Table 2.9 Slaves in household no.4-1, Sangin-ri, headed by U Sŏkjang, 1690

Name	Sex	Age	Father	Status	Mother	Status	Notes
Dŏksang	male	23	Myŏnggŭm	Sano	Juyang	Banbi	escaped in 1687
Hanok	female	31	Sŭngryong	Sano	Yongdŏk	Banbi	
Aejŏng	female	39			Sadae	Banbi	
Iljin	female	39	Ŭngryong	Banno	Sajin	commoner	
Sook	female	17	Kim Sŏkmun	commoner	Okmae	Banbi	
Hansari	male						Left for the household of Yuhak Na (unreadable) in Sŏngju
Jagŭn	female	29	Kim Nanbok	commoner	Guichun	Banbi	
Illyong	male	36	Ŭngryong	Banno	Sajin	commoner	escaped in 1686
Dolyŏ	female	11	Kim Aesŏn	commoner	Iljin	Banbi	second child of Iljin
Jachun	female	9	Kim Aesŏn	commoner	Iljin	Banbi	third child of Iljin
Janyŏ	female	7	Kim Aesŏn	commoner	Iljin	Banbi	fourth child of Iljin
Hanjin	female	7			Hanok	Banbi	first child of Hanok
Saryong	male	46	Ŭngryong	Banno	Mujin	Banbi	newly registered

Note: Sano: male slave of another owner

Table 2.10 Classification according to the slave's parents' status in Table 2.8

Mother	Father	Number	Names of slaves concerned
Banbi	Banno	1	Saryong (M)
Banbi	slave of other owner	2	Dŏksang (M), Hanok (F)
Banbi	unknown	2	Aejŏng (F), Hanjin (F)
Banbi	commoner	5	Sook (F), Jagŭm (F), Dolyŏ (F), Jachun (F), Janyŏ (F)
commoner	Banno	2	Iljin (F), Illyong (M)

Note: Ban in Banbi and Banno mean '(slave) of the same owner'.

There are two more points of note regarding the latter. Firstly, where the slave's father was recorded as a *sano* (individual-owned male slave), the female slave owned by the U lineage living within the household took a male slave owned by another party as her husband. The slave husband's owner was not recorded. It was obviously not a matter of concern to the administrator of the household register.

Another important point is as follows; regarding the sex ratio of slaves living within the owner's household, I mentioned earlier that the ratio of males to females was extremely small. When we look at their marital relations, however, we find that commoner males or male slaves owned by someone else married live-in female slaves in the majority of cases. It is reasonable to assume that they resided in the household of their spouse's owner. In that case, the actual living conditions of the legally commoner-status husband or wife of a slave would be no different from the living conditions of live-in slaves. In other words, the effective sex ratio in the population belonging to the slave equivalent category, including the husbands and wives of slaves, would be considerably closer to parity than the estimate obtained from the household registration records. From the slave owner's point of view, if there were many male slaves who escaped, men who married their live-in female slaves filled these vacancies, as they could be put to work for him.

It is also notable that many of the spouses of live-in slaves were of commoner status, although the number in this category may not be certified. This situation corresponds to the prevalence of intermarriages between live-away slaves and commoners and confirms my earlier observation that there was no rupture in social relations among them.

Long-lasting genealogy of a slave family

Case 2 (Figure 2.4) reconstructs the genealogy of a slave family based on information in the household registers. It is considered to be a very unique case in that, although the number of individuals involved is small, at least some of them continued to live within the household of the U lineage head for a long period of time. I shall trace how the form of residence of this slave family changed over time.

In 1690, Juyang (age fifty-three, born in 1638) was a live-in female slave owned by Mrs. Jo, the widow of lineage head Sŏkjang, whose father Hŭinam was a *banno* (i.e., a male slave owned by the U family as was Juyang). As Juyang's mother was a commoner, she inherited slave status from her father. Her mother probably married live-in slave Hŭinam and spent her life within the household of her husband's master. Judging from Juyang's age, Hŭinam was likely born in the early 1600s. By comparing this genealogy with that of the U lineage head's household in Figure 2.2, it is found that this slave family served the household of the U lineage head for four successive generations of masters from the time of Baesŏn.

While Juyang, her eldest son Hyosŏng (age thirty-two) and fourth son Dŏkman (age eleven) lived within the household of Mrs. Jo (age forty-three), the widow of Yŏjun's eldest son Sŏkjong, Juyang's eldest daughter Sodŏk (age twenty-four), third son Dŏksang (age twenty-three) and second daughter Dŏkkŭm (age fourteen) were registered in the households of Sŏkjong's three younger brothers respectively (Dŏksang escaped). Conversely, Juyang's second son Hyohŭi (age twenty-nine) and her younger brother Gŭmmu and his wife escaped from Mrs. Jo's household.

Figure 2.4a Long-lasting genealogy of a slave family

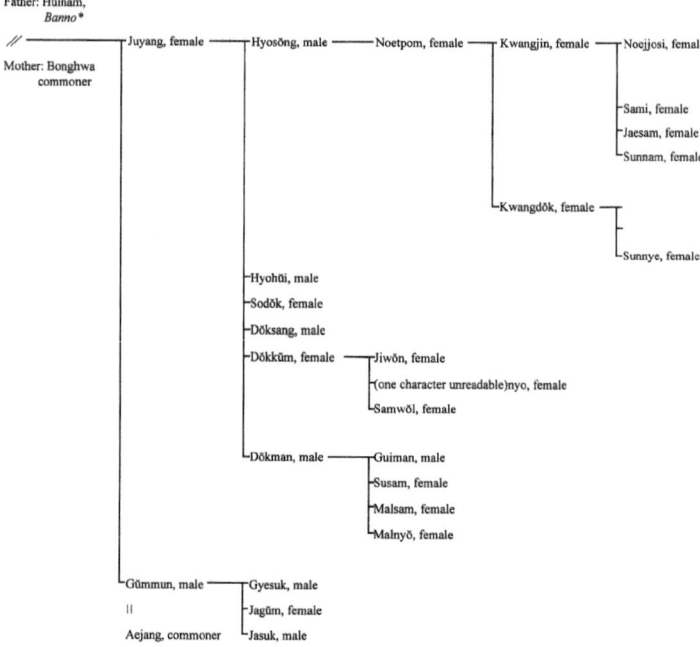

Note: *Ban* in *banno* means 'owned by the same master'.

Figure 2.4b Female slave Juyang and her family, 1690

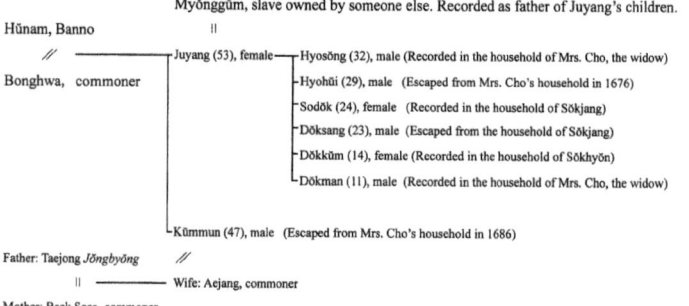

Figure 2.4c Information indicating Hyosŏng's wife as recorded in the register of 1720

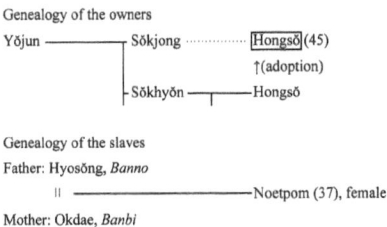

Note: The household register of 1690 does not record Hyosŏng's wife.

There is no record of Juyang's husband, but as the father of all her children is recorded as slave (or individual-owned slave) Myŏnggŭm, Juyang probably maintained a marital relationship with a male slave named Myŏnggŭm owned by someone else for a long period within the household of her owner.[4]

There is no record of the wife or children of Juyan's eldest son Hyosŏng, who was aged thirty-two in 1690. However, while the 1720 household register shows Hyosŏng as already deceased, the household register of Hongsŏ, Sokjong's adopted son who succeeded Mrs. Jo's household, shows Hyosŏng's daughter Noetpom (age thirty-seven, born in 1684) as a live-in slave and her mother as the 'slave Okdae owned by the same owner'. This indicates that Hyosŏng was already in a marital relationship with Okdae in 1690 and their daughter was seven years old by that time.

That Okdae was a *banbi* means that she was a female slave owned by a Danyang U lineage member, but her name is not found in the 1690 register. However, the 1720 register shows that there was a female slave (escaped) named Sŏlyang within Noetpom's master's household, whose mother was *banbi* Okdae. This confirms that there was a female slave named Okdae within the household when Hyosŏng belonged to the same household. As Sŏlyang, aged thirty-nine in 1720, was two years older than Noetpom, her mother was likely to have been of similar age to Hyosŏng.[5]

Noetpom, aged forty-six in 1729, was living within the household of the owner together with her daughter Gwangjin (age fourteen), whose father is recorded as 'father Gaedol, a male slave owned by an individual', suggesting that Gaedol was the husband of Noetpom. The 1738 register shows that Noetpom's second child Gwangdŏk (age twenty-one) was also a slave living within the household whose father was also recorded as Gaedol. This suggests that the marital relationship between Noetpom and Gaedol began before 1715. As for Gaedol's affiliation, the 1720 register contains male slave Gaedol (age thirty-eight) within the household of Mrs. Sŏ, who was the wife of U Sŏkpyŏng, the *dangsuk* (father's cousin) of

Noetpom's owner Hongsŏ. He is recorded to have 'escaped in 1715'. I suspect that Mrs. Sŏ gave tacit approval to the marriage between her slave and Noetpom, who was owned by the lineage head's household within the same hamlet, by treating Gaedol's status as escaped on Mrs. Sŏ's side of the record. Gaedol was aged forty-seven in 1729, the same age as Noetpom. There are other similar cases we can discuss (see Supplementary Case 3 below). In these cases, 'escaped' does not signify 'emancipated' status, but it can be interpreted here that the owner effectively removed the slave's obligation to pay a tribute and released the slave from the master-servant relationship by treating him as 'escaped' on the household register. It appears to be a compassionate act on the part of the owner.

This slave family continued to live within the household of U Myŏngik until 1753. There is no record of the parents of the two daughters (Gwangjin and Gwangdŏk) in the 1744 register, but their mother Noetpom is still listed as living within the same household. Their father Gaedol might have passed away by then. Children of Gwangjin (Noetjosi age sixteen; Sami age eleven; Jaesam age nine; Sunnam age five) and Gwangdŏk (third child Sunnye age three) appear in the 1753 household register for the first time. Although no record of the husbands of Gwangjin and Gwangdŏk is found anywhere, it is reasonable to think that their husbands lived with them as in the cases of their grandfather Hyosŏng and mother Noetpom.

In summary, six generations of male and female slaves descending from male slave Hŭinam, his eldest daughter Juyang and her eldest son Hyosŏng consistently lived within the household of six generations of U lineage heads from Baesŏn to Dalhae, Yŏjun, Sŏkjong, Hongsŏ and Myŏngik, as if leading parallel lives. However, these two lines of descent clearly differed in that the master's line was strictly patrilineal while the slave family line was carried on through both male and female descendants, depending on the generation.

Supplementary Case 3
The 1690 register of Sangin-ri, household no. 3-2 (headed by Yŏjun's second son Sŏkhyŏn) includes an entry to the effect that 'male slave Hangŭm, status *sunabyŏng*, departed to set up a new household in Joambang', and there is a corresponding household in Joam-bang Il-ri headed by 'male slave Hankui, status *sunabyŏng*, thirty-six years old, owned by U Sŏkhyŏn who lives in Daegu'. A reconstructed genealogy of this family in Figure 2.5 shows a patrilineal kinship group consisting of four households. They were emancipated in Baekji and Munui's generation but Hankui (Hangŭm), who for some reason was the only son who had remained an individual-owned slave, appeared to have been allowed to establish a new household in Joam-bang Il-ri where his relatives lived.

Figure 2.5 Genealogy of Sŏngju Yi Kin Group in Joam-bang Il-rl, 1690

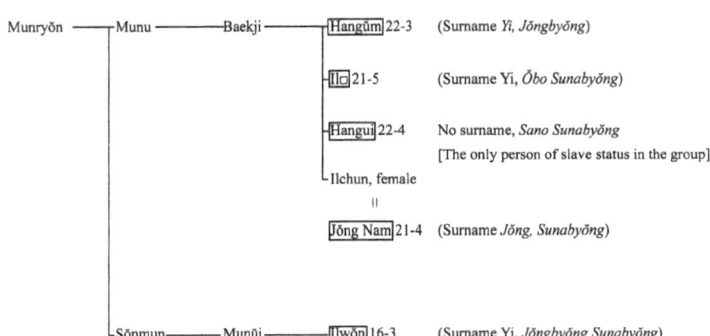

As an aside, the register of Sangin-ri, household no. 3-1 (headed by Yŏkyŏn, U Sŏkhyŏn's uncle) for the same year contains an entry to the following effect: 'female slave Ilchun, forty-six years old, whose father is Baekji, a slave of the same master, mother is a commoner Ingae, and husband is Jŏngnam, a slave by another owner, escaped in 1689'. The female slave Ilchun and her husband Jŏngnam were actually the couple who headed the household of Joam-bang Il-ri, household no. 21-4 who were 'Jŏngnam, status being *sunabyŏng* of Daegu government, whose wife is Yi Ilchun, forty-six years old, father is an emancipated former slave Baekji, grandfather is slave Mungil, and great-grandfather is slave Munryŏn' (Figure 2.5). This appears to be another case in which the owners released their slaves by treating them as 'escaped' on the household register. All the people named in Figure 2.5 had left the area by 1720.

Returning to Case 2, let us take a quick look at the lives of Juyang's younger brother and children other than Hyosŏng.

Her brother Gŭmmun, second son Hyohŭi and third son Dŏksang, escaped before 1690 and there is no sign of them returning. While her eldest daughter Sodŏk was living within the household of Yŏjun's third son Sŏksŏ in 1690, her whereabouts after that time are unknown. Her second daughter Dŏkkŭm, who lived within the household of Yŏjun's second son Sŏkhyŏn in 1690, was living within the household of Sŏkhyŏn's third son Honggui in 1720. She was forty-four years old at the time and there is no record of her husband or child. In 1729, however, Dŏkkŭm (age fifty-four) was recorded as living away from of the owner Honggui's household and having household no. 6-5 newly established in the same hamlet of Sanging-ri, along with her two daughters (age nineteen and fifteen). This means that she had been in a marital relationship with someone since at least 1710 or earlier. The whereabouts of Dŏkkŭm and her daughters after 1729 are unknown. The household register has no record of *hŏryang* (emancipation) or escape. Did she immigrate to another place with her husband and did her owner give tacit approval?

Case 2.2: Juyang's fourth son Dŏkman (age eleven), who lived within the owner's household with his mother in 1690, presents a curious case. While the 1720 and 1729 registers of U Hongsŏ's household describe him as 'escaped in 1696', it appears that Dŏkman entered a marital relationship during that period with female slave Sŏllyang (a daughter of Okdae, who is suspected to have been the wife of Hyosŏng, Juyang's son mentioned earlier), who 'escaped' from the same Hongsŏ's household in 1709. The 1738 register reports that some of their children returned, or were brought back, to live within the household of Myŏngik, Hongsŏ's eldest son (Figure 2.6). This example demonstrates that not only the owner but also fellow slaves knew the whereabouts of 'escaped' slaves.

Figure 2.6 Slaves whose whereabouts seem to have been known long after their 'escape' (a case from 1738)

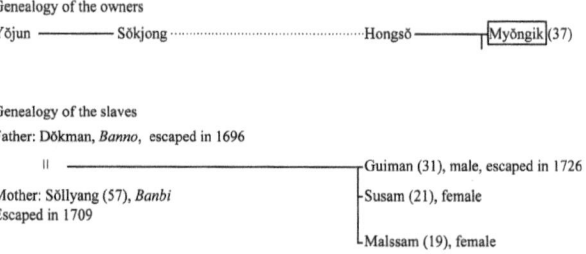

Genealogy of the owners
Yŏjun ———— Sŏkjong ·····························Hongsŏ ————┬─Myŏngik (37)

Genealogy of the slaves
Father: Dŏkman, *Banno*, escaped in 1696
 ‖ ──────────────────────────┬─Guiman (31), male, escaped in 1726
Mother: Sŏllyang (57), *Banbi* ├─Susam (21), female
Escaped in 1709 └─Malssam (19), female

Returned slaves

Case 4: Figure 2.7 outlines a genealogy chart of female slave Oknang and her family who belonged to the household of the U lineage head (widow Mrs. Jo) in 1690. In this family, her first son Ŭisang (age seventeen) escaped in 1683, her second son Ŭimyŏng (age eleven) escaped in 1684, and Oknang herself aged forty-three escaped in 1685. Ŭisang 'returned and reregistered' in the household of Sangin-ri, household no. 3-1 (headed by Hongsŏ, Mrs. Jo's adopted child) in 1720, more than thirty-five years after his escape. He then established a new household at Sangin-ri, household no. 4-2. He was a sixty-five year old widower at the time.[6] In other words, he returned to the master's household as an old widower after many years on the run and was allowed to set up a separate household.

Figure 2.7 Genealogy of slaves in 1690, one of whom returns long after escaping

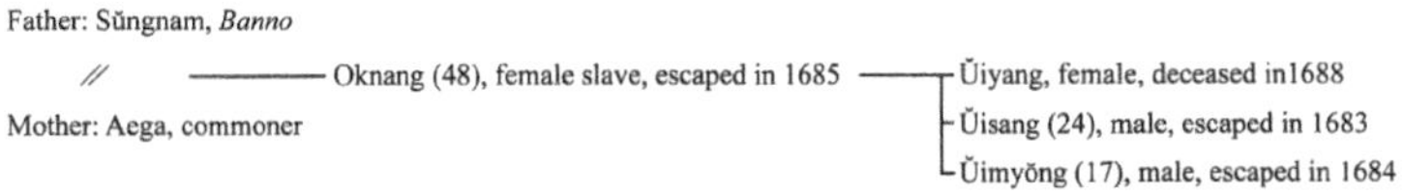

Father: Sŭngnam, *Banno*
// ———————— Oknang (48), female slave, escaped in 1685 ——— Ŭiyang, female, deceased in 1688
Mother: Aega, commoner   ├ Ŭisang (24), male, escaped in 1683
                          └ Ŭimyŏng (17), male, escaped in 1684

Note: The household head in 1690 was Mrs. Jo, widow of Sŏkjang, the lineage head.

Case 5: The 1690 household register of Sangin-ri, household no. 3-2 (headed by Sŏkhyŏn) has entries pertaining to a slave family who escaped in 1659 (male slave Sarip age forty-six, his wife, a commoner named Jang Ŭnggŭm age forty-five, their first son male slave Wangrip age twenty-one, and second son Oksaeng age eighteen). Apparently, the sons were born after Sarip escaped. He most probably also married his commoner wife after escaping. The 1690 record shows that the owner knew all the developments in the family of the 'escaped' slave. In 1720, female slave Gyehwa (born in 1673), the daughter of Sarip and Ŭnggŭm, was 'newly registered' with the household of Hongchŏl, owner Sŏkhyŏn's second son. A daughter who was born after the family escaped returned to the household of a son of the original master at the age of forty-eight, some sixty years after the family escaped. The 1729 record also shows that her two daughters – female slaves Sahwa (age seventeen) and Gyewŏl (age thirteen) – as well as Gyehwa lived within the household of the owner. Although there is no way of confirming Gyehwa's husband or the father of Sahwa and Gyewŏl for lack of record, it is conceivable that Gyehwa turned to her parents' owner for help when she lost her husband and had trouble making a living. The mother and her two daughters are reported as living within the household of their owner Honghyŏp until 1744, but Sahwa (age forty-one) and Gyewŏl (age thirty-seven) escaped again in 1748 according to the 1753 register. The same register describes their mother Gyehwa as 'deceased', suggesting her passing sometime between 1750 and 1753. In other words, Sahwa and Gyewŏl ran away, leaving behind their elderly mother in her seventies.

Conclusion

The results of my observations on the above cases can be summarized as follows in the form of a tentative conclusion.

1. I have pointed out that there was little distinction between commoners belonging to the lower social strata and people with slave status in day-to-day social relations, based on the prevalence of intermarriage between commoners and slaves among slave household couples living away from their owners. However, the commoner class men who married female slaves also included some who had enough financial resources to purchase government posts with rice.

2. The quantitative analysis of slaves owned by the descendants of Yŏjun of the Danyang U lineage has found that escaped slaves accounted for nearly one half of all slaves. Conversely, regarding marital relations that formed an important part of the family relation aspect of the slave population, the parental records of slaves have shown the existence of long-term stable marital relationships among slaves living within the owner's household as well. Intermarriages between commoners and slaves were also prevalent here.

   According to Yi Yŏnghun's interpretation, the husband of a female slave typified a commoner fallen on hard times at the peak of slavery (before the introduction of *nobi-jongmoje* in 1729), but it did not necessarily indicate social or economic ruin in the following period (Yi 2001: 260–266). It seems, however, that conditions even before and after 1729 were such that it is difficult to draw a clear line discriminating between those of commoner status and slave status at the level of daily life, including intermarriage relations, and it is perhaps unnecessary for us to regard intermarriages between commoners and slaves as reduced circumstances for the former. It may make more sense to think that this is why intermarriage between commoners and slaves became very prevalent and as a result the government was compelled to institute a new measure. In this regard, the almost equal status relationship between government-owned slaves and commoners identified by Yi was probably applicable to individual-owned slaves to a large extent in terms of the actual conditions of life.

3. Another point as noteworthy as the previous is the sex ratio between male and female slaves. As there is a clear imbalance in the sex ratio of male and female slaves recorded in household registers, there is obviously a large number of *nugu* (illegally unregistered individuals), particularly on the male side. Contrary to this apparent imbalance, however, marital relationship records of the parents of slaves clearly shows that a considerable number of men actually lived as the husbands of female slaves and therefore it would be more reasonable to think that the sex ratio of men and women living with slave-like status was far more balanced than entries in the household registers suggest. While owners were unlikely to have been concerned with the marriages of their live-away slaves, I wonder what kind of involvement owners had in the marriages of their live-in slaves as they received their husbands or wives into their households.

4. Finally, the case analysis of the family relations of live-in slaves and their continuity has revealed the existence of a slave family line which continued to exist alongside the households of the same owner's family line for many generations. There are examples of escaped slaves or their descendants returning to the household of the original owner after more than fifty years. In particular, there are more than a few cases that suggest a certain kind of moral economy (Scott 1976) in the relationship between the owner and the slave beyond the dimension of their master-servant relationship: the case of an elderly slave returning to the former master from whom he had escaped as a young man; the case of an elderly widower being taken back into the household of the owner of his already deceased slave wife; the case of daughters escaping and leaving their elderly mother behind; the case of slave parents escaping and leaving their young children behind, and so on. Kim Yongman (1997) devotes one section to explaining the *bangyŏk* (release from obligation) of individual-owned slaves by drawing on various documentary records. Circumstances suggestive of such a state of affairs also emerge from the analysis of household registers themselves.

Among the cases of 'escaped' slaves recorded in household registers, many of them would have gone missing after escaping. However, it appears that in quite a few cases owners and fellow slaves knew the whereabouts of the escaped slaves. Treatment of some of the cases has to be construed as tacit but overt approval by the owner. Herein is the problematic area that requires further study. Considering the fact that nearly one half of slaves escaped, we may need to adopt the perspective that the slaves living within the household of the owner were 'slaves who chose not to escape'. It would be reasonable to think that there was a long-term human relationship, including a mutual emotional bond, between the owner and the slave in these cases.

3 The Roles of Samurai-Class Women and the Gender System in Early Modern Japan

Rumi Matsuzaki

Introduction

Why are gender inequalities still apparent in contemporary Japan, despite significant economic development and extensive sociological studies? I believe elucidating how the realities of gender have changed and examining their background from a historical point of view are effective approaches in exploring and resolving factors underpinning the problem of gender inequalities in contemporary society. This study aims to shed light on the actual state and transformation of the roles of women and the gender system in early-modern Japan from a historical perspective and explore their background factors.

To begin with, I briefly explain Japan's early-modern history. Japan was in the midst of the Warring States period from the latter half of the fifteenth century to the latter half of the sixteenth century, during which rival warlords called *sengoku daimyos* battled for dominance. One of them, Oda Nobunaga, embarked on the unification of the whole country only to fall short of his goal. His vassal, Toyotomi Hideyoshi, took over Nobunaga's endeavor and successfully unified Japan in 1590. After Hideyoshi's death, Tokugawa Ieyasu established the shogunate government (*bakufu*) in Edo (present-day Tokyo) in 1603.

Japan's early-modern society was founded on the feudal system ruled by the samurai (warrior class) government. It consisted of the Tokugawa shogunate as the central government, headed by the Tokugawa shogun and 260–270 feudal lords (*daimyos*) administering their domains (*han*) and functioning as regional governments across the country. The seat of the shogunate government and the shogun's residence were both located in Edo Castle. Each regional feudal lord had a residence in Edo and had to spend alternate years in his territory and Edo. The samurai class was the ruling class at the top of Japan's social hierarchy, and the rest of the population was divided into various classes and vocations such as farmer, townsman, artisan and merchant.

The families of shogun and feudal lords that possessed governmental authority in the samurai society of early-modern Japan were founded on the system of gender role division between the *omote* and the *oku*, both spatially and institutionally. The conceptual distinction between *omote* and *oku* was used for spatial division inside a castle or a residence as well as forming the structure or system of the shogunate or the domain. The *omote* was a public sphere in which men carried out political and military functions, while the *oku* was a private sphere in which the family head and his family led their private lives. *Omote* and *oku* were clearly partitioned and women were restricted from involvement in the former. Let us call this structure of *omote* and *oku* distinction the 'gender system'.

As early-modern Japan was a society that did not allow samurai-class women to inherit family estates or be involved in politics, women have rarely been the subjects of study in the field of political and social history. Most studies have only analyzed historical documents exchanged between men and ignored those between women. However, some advancement in the study of women's history during the 1980s offered us a clearer view of matters concerning samurai-class women in early modern times such as status, property, inheritance and marriage. Since the 1990s, there have been several studies incorporating the concept of gender (e.g., Nagano 1990; Walthall 2001). In recent years, an increasing number of studies analyzing women of the families of shogun, feudal lords and their vassals and the *oku* have been published (e.g., Matsuo 2008; Fukuda 2005; Sugano 2008).

There are, however, some problems with these preceding publications. While the majority focus on the analysis of women in the context of laws and institutions such as regulations and office organization, studies on the realities of women's roles or the gender system remain rare. I argue that the way laws/institutions and the realities interact, or the gap between them, is the very location in which the characteristics of a particular period or society manifest themselves. Time periods and historical resources available for analysis are limited, and there are currently separate studies that are looking at distinct eras and localities. There is a need for reinterpretation of the results of individual studies by properly positioning them within the framework of early-modern society.

Accordingly, this study makes good use of documents exchanged between women as part of historical resources for analysis and examines the specific roles played by samurai-class women and the realities of the gender system from a diachronic point of view. It then considers the process of their formation and transformation and the political, social and economic factors behind them.

Methodology

The region and family chosen for this analysis are the Sendai domain and the Date family. During the Edo period, the Sendai domain was located in the north of Japan covering present-day Miyagi prefecture and part of Iwate and Fukushima prefectures. The head of the Date family was a ruler in Japan's Tohoku (northeastern) region from the end of the twelfth century to the nineteenth century and reigned as the feudal lord of the Sendai domain during the Edo period. I chose them because it was easy to follow changes, as the territory and lordship went almost unchanged throughout the Edo period, and because there were numerous extant historical materials.

Preceding studies on women of the Date family in the Sendai domain include an analysis of the Warring States period (Endō 2003) and an investigation of the latter part of early modern times (Yanagiya 2001a, 2001b, 2003a, 2003b), but every preceding study is confined to a narrow time period and none have examined the early and middle Edo period. There is a need to shed light on how the realities of the women and the *oku* of the Date family analyzed in preceding studies changed over time as well as to explore the background factors behind the shift and the characteristics of each time period.

For that purpose, this study covers an extended period of time, from the Warring States period to the middle of the Edo period. It corresponds to the time from the lordship of Date Terumune, the father of Sendai domain founder Masamune, to Date's fifth feudal lord Yoshimura. By analyzing the roles of the official wife of the feudal lord (family head), the characteristics of marriage and the formative process of the gender system from a diachronic viewpoint, the fragmented pieces of information presented in preceding studies can be considered in light of the politics and economy of the shogunate government and the domain and social transitions.

Table 3.1 Family heads and feudal lords of the Date family and their official wives

Family head/feudal lord	Official wife	Official wife's origin
Terumune	Hoshunin	Daughter of Mogami Yoshiaki, the lord of Yamagata Castle
Domain founder, Masamune	Princess Mego	Daughter of Tamura Kiyoaki, the lord of Miharu Castle
Second lord, Tadamune	Princess Furi	Adopted daughter of the second shogun Tokugawa Hidetada
Third lord, Tsunamune		
Fourth lord, Tsunamura	Princess Sen	Daughter of Inaba Masanori, the lord of the Odawara domain
Fifth lord, Yoshimura	Princess Fuyu	Adopted daughter of Koga Michitomo, a court noble
Sixth lord, Munemura	Princess Tone	Adopted daughter of the eighth shogun Tokugawa Yoshimune

Historical materials used for analysis include *Date jike kiroku* (Documents of the Date family),[1] which is the official history of the Sendai domain, *Date ke monjo* (Date family archives),[2] the family's collection of historical documents, as well as *Masamune ki* (Records of Date Masamune),[3] *Date Masamune genkō roku – Kimura Uemon oboegaki* (The words and actions of Date Masamune – Kimura Uemon memoranda)[4] and *Date Masamune kyō denki shiryō* (Resources for the biography of Lord Date Masamune),[5] which are historical materials about Date Masamune.[6]

Samurai-class women in the period of the unification of Japan

Pre-Toyotomi government era

Firstly, let us look at the actions and the marriages of samurai-class wives based on the cases of the Date family and other northeastern families prior to the establishment of the Toyotomi government. This period corresponds to the lordship of Date Terumune and the early part of Date Masamune's reign over the Sendai domain. In the Tohoku region, warlords were fighting for territorial domination until 1590.

1. The wife of Ashina Morioki, a warlord based in Aizu, was an adopted daughter of Date Terumune (she was actually his biological sister). After marrying into the Ashina family, she wrote a letter to Terumune to report on the Ashina family's defeat in a battle with the Tamura family and the details of the damage sustained.

2. The wife of Nikaidō Moriyoshi, a warlord based in Sukagawa, was a daughter of Date Harumune, Terumune's father. Since Moriyoshi's eldest son had been adopted by the Ashina family and his second son had died young, the Nikaidō family did not have an heir when Moriyoshi died. Consequently, she took charge of household administration as the family representative. The Ashina family and the Date family appeared to be supportive of her at the time. Later on, Date Masamune, her nephew, made a peace proposal to her but she refused. A battle between her family and the Date family ensued and her family was defeated.

3. The wife of Tamura Kiyoaki, a warlord based in Miharu, was a daughter of Sōma Akitane, a warlord based in Sōma, and mother of Princess Mego, the official wife of Date Masamune. After the death of her husband, she consulted her vassals and decided to administer

the affairs of her family territory according to Date Masamune's instructions. This was because her late husband had intended to adopt Masamune's son as the heir to the Tamura family if he had a son, and she decided to rely on the Date family until the birth of her grandson. She administered her territory with the cooperation of Masamune. When the relationship between Masamune and Mego worsened, the Tamura family was divided into the Date faction and the Sōma (her birth family) faction. In one incident, the Sōma family attempted to take over the Tamura family. Although the family takeover was prevented by Tamura's vassals, it became obvious that she had been in secret communication with the Sōma family. After receiving advice from her husband's mother and vassals, Masamune forced her into retirement and put Kiyoaki's nephew in the position of family representative.

4. Hoshunin, the wife of Date Terumune, was a younger sister of Mogami Yoshiaki and the mother of Date Masamune. She presented guns for Masamune and his army, who had inherited the family estate upon her husband's death, when he went off to war. When the Date family went into battle with the Mogami family and other warlords, she acted as a mediator for peace at the request of Yoshiaki (Endō 2003).

The above examples show that the warlord's wife in Case (1) maintained her connection with her birth family, the wife in Case (2) depended on her matrimonial family, the wife in Case (3) was reliant on her birth family and the wife in Case (4) was an intermediary between her birth and matrimonial families. Warlords arranged marriages with nearby warlords in those days, as they could not do so with those distant. Engagements were made according to the varying interests of individual families of the time and women who were given and taken in marriage were treated as reciprocal hostages. Women did not always become real members of the matrimonial family for this reason. They maintained their connection with both the birth family and the matrimonial family, and it was uncertain as to whether they would take the side of the former or the latter in a dispute. Some of the warlord's wives took control of the family territory as the family representative after the husband's death. Samurai-class women in the Warring States period assumed roles that directly engaged in politics or war, and greatly influenced the rise and decline of their families.

The transition period from Toyotomi government to Tokugawa shogunate

Let us look at the roles of the wife and the *omote* and *oku* in the Date family during the transition period from 1590, when Masamune submitted to Toyotomi Hideyoshi to the establishment of the Tokugawa shogunate.

Princess Mego, the official wife of Masamune
Princess Mego, the official wife of Sendai domain founder Date Masamune, moved from the castle in Yonezawa to the family residence in Kyoto in 1590 in response to Toyotomi Hideyoshi's request to Masamune to send his wife and children to Kyoto. She fulfilled the role of political hostage to the Toyotomi regime while receiving stipends. She subsequently moved to other residences in Fushimi and Osaka and lived in Edo from 1603.

Mego was not just an idle hostage while away from her homeland. She sent a messenger to Tokugawa Ieyasu's close aide in 1600 and received advice that she should present a gift when Ieyasu made an entry into Osaka Castle. In other words, she played an important role in demonstrating Masamune's intention to serve Ieyasu in a manner that was practicable as his official wife, amid the rising tension between Ieyasu and Toyotomi Hideyori.

Hoshunin, Masamune's mother
During this period, Hoshunin, the widow of Date Terumune mentioned above, acted on her own initiative as a female member of the Date family as well as a female member of the Mogami family.

While Masamune participated in Toyotomi's Korean invasion, she sent letters and money to the battlefront. It is clear that she supported her son at the front indirectly through financial assistance. At the time of a battle between Tokugawa Ieyasu and Uesugi Kagekatsu of Aizu in 1600, she asked the Date family to send troops to the relief of the Mogami family. She was likely to have obtained information from the Mogami family, as she knew the progress of the battle, including information about the enemy side, and advised Masamune through letters addressed to his vassals.

While she acted as a member of the Mogami family as she made her own judgments about situations in order to avert a family crisis, she also acted as a member of the Date family by giving advice to Masamune based on military information obtained from the Mogami family.

Non-segregation of the omote *and* oku
In 1589, Masamune decided to increase a certain vassal's fief, and the details of this policy were communicated to a female vassal, who was a Hoshunin's lady's maid and Masamune's nursemaid. When Masamune

departed his homeland in 1590, he entrusted dealings with Toyotomi government officials to his male vassal and told him to consult the aforementioned female vassal during his absence.

These examples suggest that male and female vassals were in contact on a daily basis and in the absence of their master, female vassals were involved in territorial administration together with their male counterparts. This means that during this period the *omote* and *oku* were not yet clearly segregated.

The establishment period of the Tokugawa shogunate

We now look at the wife's roles, marriage and the *omote* and *oku* in the Date family up to the time of Masamune's death in 1636. This period corresponds to the reigns of the second shogun Hidetada and the third shogun Iemitsu of the Tokugawa shogunate.

Princess Mego, the official wife of Masamune

Domestic roles: Let us look at the roles of the official wife within the household based on the case of Princess Mego, who was Masamune's official wife. She sent for Masamune's vassals from time to time to lecture them to serve well, and gave them clothes and other gifts. In other words, she bestowed advice and gifts to vassals in the service of Masamune. Garments for presentation to the shogun were made under her instruction. At the time of a fire, she ordered vassals in the *oku* and controlled them. Before his death, Masamune left word to Mego to periodically give their son Tadamune advice about maintaining their family's prosperity and not offending the shogun and to ensure that their eldest daughter didn't behave in an officious manner. Mego was in charge of the disciplining of the feudal lord's children.

As the *oku* system was not yet completely established at that time, the official wife played diverse roles in terms of the feudal lord's children, vassals and the whole *oku*.

External roles: Next are the roles of the official wife outside of the household. My analysis of historical documents has found a record of gifts exchanged between Masamune and members of the Tokugawa shogun's family from 1611 onward. It is likely that Mego, as the official wife of a feudal lord, began the practice of exchanging gifts with the shogun's family. She sent her female vassal as a messenger to Edo Castle to present gifts to the second shogun Hidetada and the third shogun Iemitsu. In return, from time to time the shoguns sent their male messengers to present gifts. The Date family's relationship with the shogun's family was closest while Masamune was still alive, and the retired shogun Hidetada and the incumbent shogun Iemitsu often visited the Date's family residence.

On these visits, Mego exchanged gifts with the shoguns together with Masamune and their son Tadamune.

The exchanging of gifts between Mego and members of the shogun's family was very important in maintaining the close relationship between the Date family and the shogun's family as the Tokugawa shogunate achieved stability after the demise of the Toyotomi family.

Thus Mego, as the official wife of the domain founder, built the foundation of the official wife's roles inside and outside of the household while performing diverse functions at a time when the Tokugawa shogunate was consolidating its power and regulations and institutions were being established in both the government and the domains.

The characteristics of marriage

What were the characteristics of marriage during this period? Masamune married off his eldest daughter to Tokugawa Ieyasu's eighth son. This marriage was decided on the basis of the close relationship between Masamune and Ieyasu. Masamune's son Tadamune married the second shogun Hidetada's adopted daughter Princess Furi. These two cases were designed to reinforce the connection between the Date and Tokugawa families through marriage, and the significance of marriage as a means to secure peace had diminished.

The marriage between Masamune's fourth daughter and a feudal lord's son was arranged by the good offices of the third shogun Iemitsu, as Masamune wished to find a suitable husband for her because she was his youngest child and her birth mother was the daughter of masterless samurai in Osaka. All other illegitimate daughters of his were married off to his vassals.

While all daughters, whether legitimate or illegitimate, were married off to forge alliances with other warlords during the pre-Toyotomi government era, the basic trend after that period was to marry off legitimate daughters to feudal lord families and illegitimate daughters to vassals. The married daughters were expected to serve the matrimonial family as the official wife of the family head. This shows that marriage no longer provided surety for peace in this period.

Separation of the omote *and* oku

At the time of the general year-end cleaning in this period,[7] all male vassals left the *omote* before Mego and the female vassals entered into it. The women were assigned to different rooms to partake in festivities. This indicates that the *omote* was usually occupied by men and the *oku* by the official wife and female vassals, and that the residence was partitioned so that there was no contact between male vassals and the official wife and female vassals. Gender-based spatial separation was instituted during this period.

Samurai-class women at the beginning of early modern times

What were the roles of samurai-class women and the gender system in the Edo period?

Firstly, let us look at the wife's roles and the *omote* and *oku* of the Date family when the shogunate-domain system was firmly established. This period corresponds to the reigns of the third shogun Iemitsu and the fourth shogun Ietsuna.

The second feudal lord Tadamune (1636–1658)

Princess Furi, the official wife of Tadamune
Domestic roles: Princess Furi, the official wife of the second feudal lord Tadamune, was permitted to adopt her husband's illegitimate son Tsunamune as a brother for her own son after the death of his birth mother. Later on, she chose Misawa Hatsuko, one of her female vassals, to be Tsunamune's concubine upon consultation with her husband.

External roles: As Furi was an adopted daughter of the second shogun Hidetada, her dealings with the shogun's family were somewhat different to those of Mego. Following the example set by Mego, Furi usually sent her female vassal as a messenger to Edo Castle to present gifts to the shogun's family, but she sometimes visited Edo Castle personally as well. Although the official wife of a feudal lord was not allowed to visit Edo Castle, Furi was able to do so as an adopted daughter of the shogun, even after she was married off to a feudal lord family.

Thus, Furi performed her in-house role as the official wife of the Date family by raising the feudal lord's sons and choosing their concubines while maintaining her connection with the shogun's family through her position as the shogun's adopted daughter.

The oku *regulations*
One feature of this period was the establishment of the *oku* within the secondary enclosure of Sendai Castle, which was built in 1638. Also, regulations governing the affairs of the *oku* at the family's Edo residence were set out in a document called *Okugata hatto sadamegaki* (Regulations of the *oku*) in 1643. The regulations were issued to male vassals who were involved in *oku* matters, and can be summarized as follows.

- Male vassals involved in the affairs of the *oku* may usually have free passage to the rooms of *tsubones* (female senior vassals) to attend to their business and are permitted to go wherever necessary

in emergencies, including a fire, to direct female vassals in order to prevent injuries.
- To revise any regulations concerning the *oku*, they must consult the male chief official and communicate with *tsubones*. If they are unable to make a decision on any matter, they must consult immediately.
- They are required to decide whether to admit visitors such as relatives of the vassals to the *oku* on a case-by-case basis.
- They must treat vassals of Mitsumune, Tadamune's second son, in the same way they treat other vassals employed in the *oku*.
- If they are uncertain about any matters concerning the *oku*, they must discuss with fellow vassals and ask or report to *tsubones*.
- When they are unable to come to work due to illness or other reasons, they must consult *tsubones* and find a replacement.
- If they find anyone disobeying orders at the time of emergencies, they must report them.

These regulations are the first set of rules concerning the *oku* of the Date family, and it is likely that the family began to institute clear rules for the *oku* around this time. The shogunate set regulations concerning the *ō-oku* (the *oku* in Edo Castle) in 1659 and 1670. The 1659 version established rules about access to the *oku* and designated the female senior vassal of the *ō-oku* as the central figure for its administration (Nagano 1990). These rules are similar to those for the *oku* of the Date family, and they were both set out in the middle of the seventeenth century. In other words, this period during which the governmental structures and systems progressed in both the shogunate and the domains was also a watershed for the establishment of rules concerning the *oku*.

The third feudal lord Tsunamune (1658–1660)

Tsunamune, the third feudal lord of the Sendai domain, inherited the family estate in 1658 but was ordered by the shogunate to withdraw from public life due to impropriety and forced into retirement. Tsunamune therefore had no official wife. Misawa Hatsuko, his concubine, became the birthmother of the fourth feudal lord Tsunamura and represented the women of the Date family during this period. I would like to examine her status based on her roles, actions and treatment.

Misawa Hatsuko, Tsunamune's concubine
Hatsuko participated in memorial services for the previous family heads of the Date family together with her husband Tsunamune, son Tsunamura

and other children of the Date family. She exchanged letters and gifts with the family's children and relatives. She acted as *ohaguro-oya* (the organizer of the coming-of-age ceremony of painting woman's teeth black) for other concubines' daughters. She often gave gifts to the vassals of her son Tsunamura. In other words, Hatsuko took on roles that were similar to the basic roles of the official wife in any other period, and carried out such duties as participating in the Date family's memorials, maintaining relations with consanguineous and affinal relatives, getting involved in the rites of passage for the family's daughters, and presenting gifts to vassals. However, she did not perform the official wife's external role of exchanging gifts with the shogun's family.

As Hatsuko gave advice about the hiring of female vassals when consulted by her son, it is clear that she had a good grasp of female vassals. She was also involved in decision-making in terms of her children's spouse selection, as she privately advised her son Tsunamura regarding the marriage of her husband Tsunamune's fifth daughter that she would be better to marry into a feudal lord family with a residence in Edo because Tsunamune wished to keep at least one of his daughters in Edo.

Upon Hatsuko's passing, her funeral was attended by the feudal lord Tsunamura, his official wife Princess Sen, Tsunamune's daughters and the family's vassals. The family conducted her memorials after this time, and musical performances at their Edo residence were suspended for such occasions.

Based on the above, it is conceivable that although Hatsuko was not recognized as an official figure of the Sendai domain by the shogunate, she was acknowledged as such and treated as the de-facto official wife within the domain.

Samurai-class women in the middle of early modern times

Let us next examine the roles of the wife of the Date family, marriage and the *omote* and *oku* in the middle of the Edo period. This period covers to the reigns of the fourth shogun Ietsuna to the eighth shogun Yoshimune.

The fourth feudal lord Tsunamura (1660–1703)

Princess Sen, the official wife of Tsunamura
Domestic roles: Historical documents from this period give us glimpses of stipends issued to the official wife. The official wife received stipends and used them to manage the finances of the *oku*. Wages to the employees of the

oku were handed out by the official wife in the case of female vassals and by the feudal lord in the case of male vassals.

Sen was the daughter of a chief official of the shogunate and was married off to the Date family as the official wife of its fourth feudal lord Tsunamura. When the financial trouble of the *omote* became worse due to a series of expenditures, she proposed to her husband that spending should be cut in all areas and she was prepared to receive a reduced stipend and would ask for extra allowances only when she ran short due to additional expenses. Tsunamura replied that her proposal was a sensible one, but since tight domain finances affected loans to vassals of the domain, it would be better to use the proposed savings as loans to the vassals since the interest would help Sen's finances and the *omote* finance could borrow money from the interest or use it when Sen ran short due to additional expenses. After her retirement, the new feudal lord Yoshimura intended to continue giving her an equivalent stipend. However, as she was now retired she requested that he reduce the amount.

These examples clearly show that Sen played an economic role in improving the overall finances of the Sendai domain by understanding the financial situation of the *omote* and managing the finances of the *oku* by, for example, suggesting a reduction of her own allowances. Even though the *omote* and *oku* were spatially divided, the official wife acted with the interests of the *omote* as well as the *oku* in mind. She was in a position of responsibility for the survival of the family ('*ie*') together with her husband, the feudal lord.

External roles: Immediately after marrying Tsunamura in 1677, Sen asked to send a female messenger (a female vassal) to Edo Castle and began the ritual of exchanging gifts and courtesies with the shogun's family. From then on, she presented the shogun, his wife and his daughters with gifts and good-luck charms at the new year, midsummer, midwinter, year-end, five festival days as well as on other occasions. She received year-end gifts from the shogun through his male messenger every year, and occasional gifts from the shogun's wife and daughters as well.

The exchanging of gifts with the shogun's family by Sen was designed to contribute to the stability of the family ('*ie*') by resuming the official wife's important external ritual role with the shogun's family, which had stopped in the previous generation when the third feudal lord Tsunamune did not have an official wife, by reinforcing the family's closeness to the shogun's family based on her special lineage as a daughter of a chief official of the shogunate and by restoring the relationship of trust between the two families. This trust had been shaken due to Tsunamune's forced retirement and the internal squabbles of the Date family in Tsunamura's childhood.

Thus Sen assumed the external role of rituals involving the shogun's family as the official wife of the Date family (after a period of suspension of the practice after Furi) while she had a good grasp of the family's financial situation, which was dire enough to frequently issue austerity measures, and managed the finances of the *oku*.

The characteristics of marriage
What were the characteristics of marriage during this period? Let us consider this based on the matrimonial decision-making process in the Date family.

Sen was chosen for the feudal lord Tsunamura's marriage because she was a daughter of the shogun's chief official and able to assist Tsunamura, who had inherited the lordship when he was very young due to Tsunamune's forced retirement (Yanagiya 2003b). For Tsunamune's fourth son, the daughter of a court noble was chosen as his wife because no suitable candidate was found among the daughters of the family's vassals. The two families had had social relations since the times of Masamune, and the court noble was a good friend of Tsunamura. The feudal lord's sons other than the heir were usually adopted by his vassals as husbands of their daughters, but if no suitable candidate was found among vassals' daughters their spouses were chosen from among the daughters of court nobles instead.

Many of the retired Tsunamune's daughters married his vassals in Sendai. This was because although Sendai was distant from Edo, he would be able to summon them from Edo at any time if they were married to his vassals. In fact, his daughters often traveled to Edo to see their father. His fifth daughter was married off to the son of a feudal lord because Tsunamune wished to keep at least one daughter near him in Edo. Thus the marriages of the retired Tsunamune's daughters reflected his wishes as their father rather than as feudal lord.

For marriage between the future fifth feudal lord Yoshimura and Princess Fuyu, the spouse selection was influenced by the fact that Yoshimura was adopted by Tsunamura from a branch family of the Date clan. Just in case Tsunamura had his own male child in future, the family was hesitant to choose a feudal lord's daughter. Quasi-feudal lord families called *kouke* were also ruled out, as their presence in Edo might cause complications. They searched for and decided on a court noble's daughter. As they had done for Tsunamune's fourth son mentioned earlier, the Date family had maintained good relations with and had respect for court noble families since Masamune's times, and therefore they considered marriage arrangements with court noble families whenever they encountered difficulties in the spouse selection process.

When we look into the association with the feudal lord families of matrimonial relatives during this period, it is clear that from the establishment period of the Tokugawa shogunate onward those who became related through marriage continued such relationships for generations and cooperated with one another to support their families.

The control of the oku

Segregation of the *oku* was enforced more thoroughly during this period. A written oath submitted by male vassals stationed at the boundary between the *omote* and *oku* promises not to flirt with female vassals as well as not to disobey the master's orders. When female vassals entered and exited the residence's gate, they had to carry a pass.

An order issued to female vassals in 1694 concerning access by shamans stated that they should be checked every time they were admitted to the residence, and permission should be sought from a male chief official before they were allowed entry to the *oku* because there were many followers of heretical beliefs around town. This example shows that female vassals routinely met religious figures at the *oku* who had had relatively free access to the area until this time, but that the practice came under strict control in the latter half of the seventeenth century. During this period, many samurai's widows, wives and children visited Buddhist temples and some widows claimed to be disciples, wore robes and visited temples without any male chaperons. Since such practice was thought to corrupt public morals even though religious devotion was commendable, an order was issued that from then on female visitors to temples should accompany attendants. In other words, not only women at the *oku* of the Date family but also samurai-class women in general had contact with religious figures, and these regulations were issued for the purpose of preventing a harmful impact on public morals. The order to restrict access of religious figures in 1694 can be regarded as one of the measures to control public morals as well as a measure to control access to the *oku*.

Conversely, control over public morals was used as leverage to reinforce restriction on contact between the Date family's female vassals and the members of the *omote*, in addition to the coming and going of samurai-class women in general. Yamakawa (1983) reports on the everyday life of samurai-class women in the Mito domain at the end of the Edo period, based on the interviews of her mother and local elders as well as historical documents. One interesting article states that allowing a samurai-class woman to go out unaccompanied was considered to be a vulgar action that reflected badly on the reputation of the family head. It appears that unaccompanied outings by women were generally considered a taboo in the samurai society of early modern times. This was perhaps because of the fear of corrupting the bloodline of the family through its women's contact with men other than the family head.

The fifth feudal lord Yoshimura (1703–1743)

Princess Fuyu, the official wife of Yoshimura
Domestic roles: Princess Fuyu, the official wife of the fifth feudal lord Yoshimura, wrote a letter to her husband as summarized below.

> Although I gave birth to five daughters, only two of them have survived and the rest died young and I have no male child. As I am becoming infirm year by year, I may not be able to have any more children. You have been telling me that you would not marry off my daughters to your vassals. In that case, if I do not have a son, my bloodline will disappear from the Date family. I have always wished that my bloodline would live on within the Date family for generations and failing this, I could waste the kind intentions for my adopted father and birth father and my marrying into the major family of Date would be meaningless. I therefore wish to marry off my young sister in Kyoto to a vassal's son or a branch family of the Date clan, so that my bloodline will continue as part of the Date family into the future. If my wish is granted, I will have my sister near me just like a servant and train her to be a good wife of a vassal.

Fuyu's wish was granted and she brought her very young sister to Edo to train and eventually married her off to the son of a vassal as her adopted daughter. Her letter demonstrates that as a court noble's daughter she fully understood the meaning of her marriage into a major domain like the Date family, and that she was endeavoring to perform her duties faithfully. At the same time, it is notable as an example that points to the official wife's involvement in spouse selection. By the way, Fuyu did later give birth to her husband's heir, Munemura.

Another notable role she played was for the selection of female pages for Princess Tone, who was to become her son Munemura's official wife. Tone was an adopted daughter of the eighth shogun Yoshimune, and when she moved from Edo Castle she came with her own female vassals appointed by the shogunate. As Tone became bored for lack of entertainment after her marriage and suffered from chronic illness, feudal lord Yoshimura thought of getting female pages for her. Instead of following the prescribed selection process, Yoshimura asked the shogunate to put Fuyu in charge of page selection for Tone, and shogun Yoshimune gave approval. Fuyu vetted candidates, sometimes together with Munemura or Tone, and even after a selection was made, Munemura consulted her about where to farm out female pages. When they were ready to be sent to Tone's residence, Fuyu interviewed them and assigned her female senior vassals to escort them from her main residence to that of Tone.

Fuyu issued orders to raise some of the vassals' babies in the *oku* of the Date family and changed the names or job titles of female vassals. Thus she was entrusted by the feudal lord and even the shogun with matters concerning the management of the *oku* of the Date family.

Further, Fuyu demonstrated her respect for the ancestors of the Date family by conducting memorials for the previous feudal lord Tsunamura and his wife Sen and donating lanterns and bells to their mausoleums. When her daughter had a refractory illness, she ordered the selection of physicians. She wrote a letter to her son Munemura about moral lesson on how to be a good heir and endeavored to care for all children. She tried to live frugally to save money and had her savings distributed to vassals. When the domain finances were so strained that her stipends sometimes fell into arrears and the weddings of the feudal lord's daughters had to be kept modest, Fuyu supported the Date family's finances from the *oku* just as her predecessor Sen had done.

External roles: Fuyu also sent her female messenger (a female vassal) to Edo Castle to present gifts to the shogun's family. She sent her representatives to present funeral offerings at the Buddhist memorial service for the shogun's family. Just as Sen did, she conducted the ritual with the shogun's family. A record of gifts exchanged between her and the shogun's family indicates that she presented gifts to the fifth shogun Tsunayoshi, the sixth shogun Ietsugu, the seventh shogun Ienobu, the eighth shogun Yoshimune and their official wives and birth mothers, and she sometimes received gifts from the shogun at occasions that Sen had not during the reign of Tsunamura. Thus Fuyu kept a closer relationship with the shogun's family compared with her predecessors. This is likely because she was a relative of the official wife of shogun Ienobu (Teneiin). After Ienobu's death, Ietsugu succeeded his father at a very young age, and Teneiin as Ietsugu's legal mother continued to wield strong influence within the shogun's family. Fuyu naturally came to have close relations with Ietsugu and Yoshimune through Teneiin.

Thus Fuyu frequently exchanged courtesies with the shogun's family by making use of her noble birth and contributed to the maintenance of the good relationship between the Date family and the shogun's family.

The above examples show that although Fuyu was from a court noble family, she did her utmost to play the roles of the official wife of a samurai-class family both internally and externally after marrying into the Date family. She did much more than the official wives of previous periods had done, and even shogun Yoshimune praised her wisdom. This is perhaps one of the reasons why the way the *oku* operated in Fuyu's times was stated as ideal in a regulation called *Onokugata kakushiki* (The codes of the *oku*), which was issued years later (Yanagiya 2001b).

Dress regulations for female vassals and the function of the oku
Dress regulation for female vassals: A sumptuary decree concerning the dress standards for samurai-class men and women was issued in 1718, and a separate one was issued concerning female vassals of the *oku* at Sendai Castle. The latter decreed that the female pages and some senior vassals should usually wear a silk dress, but anything more luxurious than *habutae* silk which they had brought with them and which they had been permitted to wear until the previous year was prohibited, and that lower female vassals should wear a cotton dress. The *oku* female vassals at the family's Edo residence were also ordered to typically wear a silk dress. In 1721, it was communicated to feudal lord families that the shogun felt that their female vassals were wearing extravagant dresses and they should wear more modest clothes, and that feudal lords should tell their female vassals to dress modestly even when they were sent to Edo Castle as messengers. In 1724, a sumptuary decree was issued this time by the shogunate that frugality should be practiced in terms of correspondence, gifts, weddings, entertaining, tools and meals and that even a feudal lord's wife should dress modestly.

As various aspects of life were getting rather extravagant and the cost of living was rising during this period, the Sendai domain's financial difficulties were deepening. More and more female vassals wore luxurious clothing that was disproportionate to their status. This is why a number of sumptuary decrees were issued by not only the Date family but also the shogunate.

The function of the *oku*: While it is possible to confirm the existence of a female vassal whom the official wife dispatched to Edo Castle as her messenger in performing her external role of exchanging gifts and courtesies with the shogun's family from the times of Mego, the official wife of the first feudal lord Masamune, one can glean information about their specific roles and arrangements from documents from the middle of the early modern times.

The female messenger was always a senior female vassal who visited Edo Castle on behalf of the official wife when she wanted to present gifts or express her gratitude to the shogun's family. She was sometimes received in audience by the shogun or his official wife, and received gifts from the shogun or a message from his official wife. She was summoned at times by female vassals at the *ō-oku* in Edo Castle to pass on instructions to her mistress. In other words, the female messenger acted as intermediary between the feudal lord's official wife and the shogun's family.

This mediating role was utilized to the fullest in relation to the engagement of Munemura, the fifth feudal lord Yoshimura's son. Munemura was engaged to marry Tone, the fifth shogun Yoshimune's adopted daughter, in accordance with Yoshimune's wishes. Until their engagement was officially announced, Yoshimune's personal wishes and instructions were communicated to the Date family from female vassals of the *ō-oku* in Edo Castle to Fuyu's female vassals who were dispatched to the Castle as her messengers. Female vassals of both the shogun's family and the Date family played the role of mediating private communications between shogun Yoshimune and feudal lord Yoshimura.

Conversely, a male vassal was sent to Edo Castle when the feudal lord presented gifts to the shogun's family. This messenger was a mid-level male vassal who was dispatched by his feudal lord to Edo Castle to present gifts, for courtesy visits and to express gratitude to the shogun's family. They were sometimes summoned to the chief official's official residence to receive the orders of the shogunate or they visited this residence to seek advice on gifts for the shogun.

Based on the above, male and female messengers each played the role of intermediary in the domain of *omote* and that of *oku* through separate channels: the feudal lord–male messenger–shogun's family (chief official) channel and the official wife–female messenger–shogun's family (*ō-oku* female vassal) channel. The gender-based communication channels were used between the shogun's family and the feudal lord's family, corresponding to the early modern gender system of *omote* and *oku*; and the *oku* channel functioned not only as a channel for exchanging gifts and courtesies between the official wife and the shogun's family, but also as a channel for private or secret communication and negotiation.

Conclusion

Japan's unification period, which corresponds to the transition period from medieval times to early modern times, was an era when the external roles of the wife of the samurai-class family shifted from direct involvement in war and politics that influenced the survival of the family to the exchanging of gifts and courtesies. The roles of the official wife were formulated during the establishment period of the Tokugawa shogunate government. The transformation of the samurai-class wife's roles was closely intertwined with the formation of the early modern gender system under which the *omote* and *oku* were increasingly segregated spatially as well as the stabilization of centralized political power. The nature of marriage also changed from a Warring-States union to an early modern union, as its significance as a politically expedient means to guarantee peace decreased while its importance as a means to form ties between the Date family and the shogun's family, other feudal lord families and vassals increased.

In the early part of early modern times, the government structure and various systems were consolidated both in the shogunate and the domains and the formulation of rules concerning the *oku* was also initiated. The segregation and control of the *oku* came to be more thoroughly enforced by the middle part of early modern times. This happened for the purpose of controlling the deterioration of public morals that was becoming a social problem at the time and preventing the bloodline of the family ('*ie*') from being tainted by men other than the feudal lord.

Thus the *oku* was spatially severed from the *omote* and the public domain, and this is the very reason that the *oku* was able to function as a channel for private and secret communication and negotiation for political purposes and the official wife and her female vassals living in that space were able to play active roles. The official wife was not only entrusted by the feudal lord with the affairs of the *oku*, but also assumed an economic role in improving the finances of the *omote* by controlling those of the *oku* within the household. Externally, on the other hand, she contributed to the building and maintenance of a good relationship with the shogun's family through exchanging gifts and courtesies. In other words, although the *omote* and the *oku* were spatially and institutionally separated, the official wife was concerned with matters not only of the *oku* but also of the *omote* in her conduct, as she was responsible for the preservation of the family ('*ie*') together with her husband who was the feudal lord.

Pre-modern China and Korea, i.e., the Ming and Qing dynasties and the Chosen dynasty and its ruling class called *yangban*, were similar to Japan's early modern samurai society in that they were founded on Confucian culture, the palace was spatially divided between the *omote* (a public space) and the *koukyū* (a private space), and women were ostensibly unable to participate in politics. However, Japan's early modern society was ruled by military men called samurais and family units ('*ie*') formed the foundation of society and held political power. Conversely, pre-modern China and Korea were ruled by civilians, and it was patrilineal kinship groups that formed the foundation of society and performed a political function. In future I plan to elucidate the characteristics of each country in East Asia, including Japan, and the principles common to all East Asian countries through a comparative-historical study of how these differences in social structure defined the state of women, families and gender in each.

4 Stratification and Ethnicity in An Averted Feud Incident: The Case of A Village in the Pearl River Delta, Guangdong Province

Yukihiro Kawaguchi

Introduction

Xiedou (feuds) refers to violent conflicts in rural areas in China that often flare up between villages, lineages or different ethnic groups.[1] On 8 July 2002, a feud between resident groups was averted in D village, Guangzhou City, Guangdong Province. Although the police managed to control the situation before it could develop into a brawl, a heated quarrel broke out between two groups, a dozen or so people on each side carrying metal pipes and other weapons, which was tense enough to make the village head who was present at the scene comment later that 'there would have been fatalities if they actually came to blows'.

Parties to the incident included people who belonged to a large kinship group that used to form the majority group in the village and people who belonged to a former minority group of boat dwellers. The direct cause of this conflict can be traced back to claims in relation to the village made by the majority side for certain rights which were considered unreasonable by current standards from an official standpoint. Background factors to their arguments and actions include the ethnic boundary and hierarchical relationship that have developed between the majority and the minority over a long period of time and the heightened majority consciousness caused in recent years by a marked resurgence of their patrilineal descent group, or lineage organization.

I now examine how the historically constructed ethnic boundary and hierarchical relationship are able to manifest today and what they mean to people living in the rural communities of contemporary China, based on the case of this averted feud incident.

Village, lineage and minority in the Pearl River Delta

Firstly, I provide some information that is necessary to support our discussion of this feud incident. This includes a description of the general condition of the study field and the hierarchical relationship between the lineage and the other residents in the minority formed in the history of development of the Pearl River Delta.

An overview of D village

D village, the scene of this averted feud incident, is situated in the southeastern part of Guangzhou City, located almost at the center of the Pearl River Delta. The main means of livelihood in the village used to be farming, mostly in rice production, but many have left farming for factory labor since the disbanding of people's communes and the commencement of the government's program to attract factories to the village and its surrounds from the first half of the 1980s.

While the village currently has a registered population of about 2,350, it has almost the same number of temporary residents who have migrated to the prosperous Pearl River Delta in droves from inland provinces such as Hunan and Sichuan. Let us look at the history of D village as an administrative village together with its population composition.

Before 1949 D village was inhabited by about 1,600 members of the Chens and about 100 members of the Xus and consisted of three subdistricts called Zhongyue, Xiyue and SC (Figure 4.1, left). After the founding of the People's Republic of China, D village, adjoining L village with about 400 members of the Zhuangs and about 400 boat dwellers living near D village were amalgamated to form D production brigade as part of the formation process of people's communes. The production brigade was comprised of subunits called production teams, with Teams 1 and 2 being located in L village, Teams 3 and 4 in SC, Teams 5 and 6 in Zhongyue, Teams 7 and 8 in Xiyue and Team 9 consisting of boat dwellers (Figure 4.1 right). In other words, production teams were formed in keeping with the preexisting boundaries of kinship and territorial relationships. As reported by other studies, the collectivization in D village was founded on the preexisting community framework, as was the case in other villages (Potter and Potter 1990: 265–267; Ishida 1996: 185–187; Han 2001: 208–209; Ruan 2005: 146–152).

After the dismantling of the commune system in the 1980s, the framework of the administrative unit was retained when D production

Figure 4.1 Pre-1949 villages and the formation of collectives

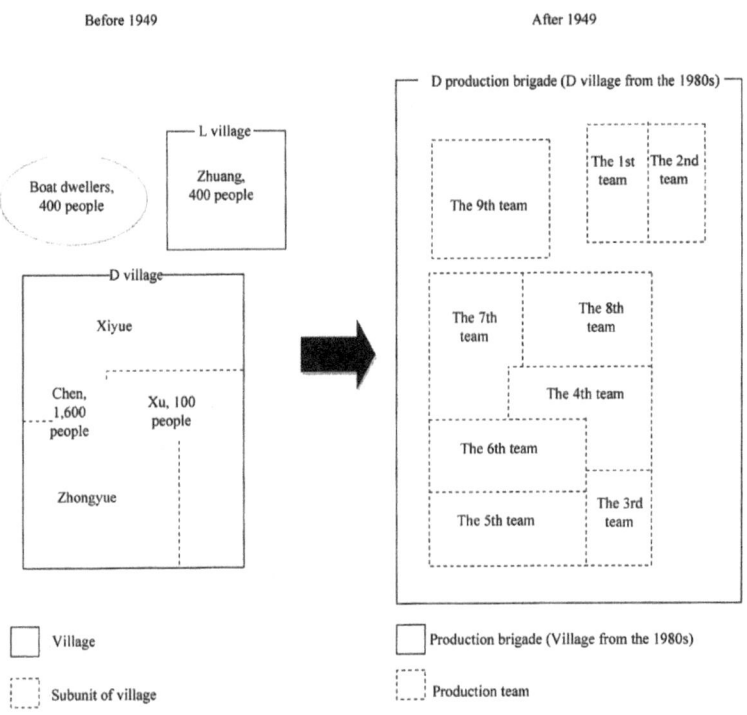

brigade simply became D village. Because production activity was back in the hands of individuals following the dismantling of the communes and most of the villagers in this area were no longer engaged in farming, the former production teams have all but lost their practical function in the local economy and production process.

Conversely, the locals still use the local place names of Xiyue, Zhongyue, SC and L on a daily basis today, even though they have been nonexistent as administrative units since 1949, and they still call the former boat dwellers' district SW. These districts were originally settlements based on territorial relationships as well as units delineated by kin relations and ethnic boundaries. The locals remain clearly aware of these boundaries largely because the production teams were built upon the social framework that existed prior to 1949.

Lineages and boat dwellers in the Pearl River Delta

What was the nature of the relationship between the Chen lineage of D village and the former boat dwellers who were parties to the incident, and how was the relationship formed? I now examine these questions by tracing back the history of the development of the Pearl River Delta, D village and the Chen lineage organization.

Regional development and lineage organization
Sometime after the fourteenth century, swampy plains began to appear in the expansive flats downstream of the Pearl River through the natural sedimentation of mud and sand as well as through artificial reclamation. Many people migrated to this region as reclamation works progressed and these new migrants carried out further reclamation works, extending the land area of the delta southward. D village was one of the communities formed in the delta's process of development.

The Chen lineage,[2] D village's overwhelming majority, claims their founder arrived from Nanxiong county in northern Guangdong province in 1131. They have genealogical records of the lineage reportedly handed down continuously from the time of the founder and, although they were forced to stop for a period under the policies of the Communist Party, they continue to build ancestral halls and worship the founder and other prominent ancestors and conduct memorial rituals for them.

Many lineages began to form in the Pearl River Delta, at the forefront of development, sometime after the fifteenth century. Settlers who were right in the middle of their struggle over land and resources found it necessary to rally around those who were gaining power.[3]

The Chens of D village gradually formed a lineage organization under such conditions. The lineage produced many members who passed the imperial examination for the mandarinate after having its first *juren* who passed the regional level examination in 1489 and a *jinshi* who passed the highest-level examination in 1508. These prominent members built ancestral halls to conduct ancestral rituals in the village to show off their success and prestige. A total of sixteen halls were built within the village area by the beginning of the twentieth century. The Chens of D village took advantage of its connection with the officialdom and the group's manpower to develop one tract of land after another and owned and managed them as the common property of the lineage. The land generated further wealth, which produced more elites, who in turn acquired more land. The Chen lineage continued to expand its power through this cycle and acquired more resources from the surrounding area.

Freedman, who pioneered the field of lineage studies in China, named Southeastern Chinese lineages that are characterized by several thousands members, asymmetrical internal segmentation and a small number of gentry elites who lead the rest of the membership politico-economically 'Z type' in his classification system (Freedman 1980[1958]). The Chens of D village was a large-scale powerful lineage that typically fit in this category. Those who migrated to the frontier of the Pearl River Delta at relatively early stages became the driving force behind regional development and proceeded to expand and own local resources through the formation of lineages, just as did the members of the Chens of D village.

The boat dwellers as the minority

While those who grouped themselves into lineages drove development to their advantage, those who were defeated by their competitors or arrived after all pieces of the pie had been taken by powerful lineages were unable to live in good areas and were denied access to resources. These people tried to find a niche on the lowlands at the mouth of the river under ongoing development and on the water.

There were those who lived on their boats or in simple thatched dwellings in the flats in the lower reaches of the Pearl River. Earlier settlers living on the long-dried land called them *dan* (蛋) or *danga* (蛋家) (*danjia* in Mandarin pronunciation). According to *Kangorin* (Chinese-Japanese dictionary), the bottom part of the character 蛋 means 'different races/ethnic groups', and the top part means 'the far corners of the earth'; the combined character signifies 'people of different ethnic backgrounds from the far corners of the earth' (Kamata and Yoneyama 1994: 964). The character 疍 is often used more recently, but both are derogatory words signifying 'outsiders'. Especially in Guangdong and Fujiang, *danjia* usually refers to boat or waterway dwellers. They normally lived on their boats and made a living through fishing or the waterway transportation of goods. *Danjia* also refers to those who lived in simple dwellings in low-lying wetlands and engaged in land reclamation works or tenant farming either permanently or seasonally.[4] Naganuma, who conducted a survey of boat dwellers in the Pearl River Delta, argues that *danjia* is merely a relative social category determined by their relationship with dry-land settlers they have actual contact with (Naganuma 2010). 'Dry-land settlers' here precisely indicates local majority groups who settled earlier and formed a lineage, such as the Chens of D village.

As mentioned earlier, the residents of a district of D village called SW used to live mostly on the water. According to members of the Chens, these people originally fished in rivers around D village, transported goods on the water, or worked on the land owned by the Chen lineage. In the process of the formation of people's communes after the founding of the People's Republic of China, these people were incorporated into D production brigade as one of its production teams. This collectivization prompted many members of this previously mobile population to settle down on the land. Very few of those simple thatched dwellings remain in the district as they were progressively replaced by brick and concrete houses from the latter half of the 1980s when economic conditions in the Pearl River Delta improved rapidly. Many now work in factories alongside the other residents of D village and very few people engage in primary industries such as fishing and farming. The term *danjia* is no longer used publicly as it is considered to be derogatory. Although there are no permanent boat dwellers, some households still own boats and catch fish or small shrimps in some seasons.

Lineages after 1949

The Chen lineage performed a major political and economic function in the village, but the situation changed dramatically from 1949. Having founded the People's Republic of China, the Communist Party began to severely clamp down on lineages and various religious observances, including ancestral rituals, because it regarded them as feudalistic and superstitious. Common property owned by lineages was distributed to the people and ancestral halls were either demolished or converted to other uses. Ancestral rituals were banned and the majority of lineage genealogies were destroyed. Lineages were unable to operate as groups and lost most of their social functions, at least on a visible level.

The circumstances surrounding lineages took another dramatic turn after the 1980s. After changing the state doctrine from the realization of communism to modernization based on economic development, the Communist Party began to show tolerance for the previously denounced cultures and religious beliefs, if they were now deemed beneficial for its policies. This change promoted the rebuilding of religious facilities and the resumption of religious observances in all parts of the country (Ashiwa 2000; Wank 2000; Chan 2005). There have been many reports on the revival of lineages (Ishida 1996; Han 2001; Pan 2002; Segawa 2004; Ruan 2005).

The Chens of D village in particular achieved a remarkable resurgence that could make it an interesting case to study.

The revival of the Chen lineage of D village was achieved by Hong Kong-based members who provided funds and lobbied the village administration. One member who migrated to Hong Kong to become a successful businessman in hardware retailing and a retired policeman who was a second-generation Chen born in Hong Kong formed a 'fundraising committee' at the beginning of the 1990s. They led a fundraising drive to collect more than 300,000 yuan from their fellow Hong Kong residents. This organization played the central role in promoting the revival of their lineage by not only raising funds but also conducting detailed negotiations with the village cadre.

Thus the Chens of D village completed the recompilation of the lineage genealogy in 1993 and the reconstruction of the main ancestral hall in 1999. The lineage genealogy has a total of 293 pages detailing the history of the Chen lineage, various epigraphs, the foreword from the previous edition of the genealogy and the family trees of its members, to flaunt its proud history by clearly declaring the authenticity of their ancestral origins and the prestige of the lineage which has produced many successful imperial examination candidates. The newly compiled genealogy is sold for 120

Photo 4.1 A reconstructed Chen lineage ancestral hall

yuan per copy, and one copy is permanently kept in the manager's office at the ancestral hall for viewing by the members who occasionally visit the hall. When lineage members or their descendants from Hong Kong or overseas visit the village after a long absence, this lineage genealogy is consulted before anything else to check their genealogical relationships. Besides being the venue for ancestral worship, the rebuilt ancestral hall is always open to visitors during the day and provides a gathering place for villagers to read newspapers, play mahjong or chat.

At the same time, the Chen lineage of D village has resumed the ancestral ritual of the Qingming festival at their ancestral tomb in the village. For the Chongyang Festival in autumn, they charter busses to visit their higher-order lineage ancestral tombs in northern Guangzhou to conduct ancestral rituals. They have rebuilt two more ancestral halls within the village area to date, and the village was given the national-level award of 'History and Culture Village' of 2008, recognizing the conservation of many historical buildings. The revival of lineages has been a widely observed phenomenon in this region over the last two decades or so, but the Chen lineage of D village can be regarded as an especially successful case.

The external recognition of the historical value of the lineage and the village inevitably influenced the consciousness of their members. A notable sign of this is the strong willingness on the part of D villagers to talk about the 'history' and 'culture' of their lineage and village. At the earliest stage in my research, the ancestral hall manager, to be mentioned later, readily agreed to my inspection of the hall and the lineage genealogy even though we had had no previous contact at all. It is generally very rare that a total stranger would be allowed to view a lineage genealogy. This was quite unexpected, because when I had visited ancestral halls in other villages I had been asked to present my ID or not to take photographs. Once I began a survey in D village, everyone I spoke to was willing to explain the village's ancestral halls and the tower and the bridge reportedly built during the Qing dynasty period or tell me that some journalists and academics had come to the village to take photos or that some tourists had come from Guangzhou. I asked the ancestral hall manager, who kindly told me many stories about the history of the Chen lineage of D village, why D village conserved so many old things. He replied, 'We in D village always considered our culture to be important'.

The resurgence of the lineage and the official recognition given to it by the outside world heightened the villagers' consciousness of it. Such a situation became the precursor of the incident in question, and their consciousness would rise to new heights in its wake. I shall discuss this later.

Common property and property rights of the lineage today
While lineage organizations are experiencing a revival after their decline under Communist Party policies, I must point out that they have not completely regained their pre-1949 status. First of all, today's lineages no longer serve a major function in the political and economic aspects of village administration to the extent that they did in the past. Village politics are controlled by the village council, and the Communist Party cadre and lineage organizations have no economic corporeality as their land and other common properties had been publicly owned. Instead, it is possible to point out that the main characteristic of today's lineages is to satisfy the membership's sense of identity through practical activities such as ancestral rituals and the compilation of genealogies.

The main issue for lineages in their pursuit of revival and various activities is funding. As mentioned above, lineages used to own land and other assets jointly, but it has been decades since they lost their common property due to land reforms. In the case of the Chen lineage of D village, rents paid by the factories established in the former ancestral gravesites at the invitation of the county government are applied to pay for its ancestral ritual observances. What we must remember here is that lineage members can no longer monopolize any parcels of land or profits from such land, because all lands in China have been publicly owned since 1949 and the ownership of buildings such as ancestral halls belongs to the village. Therefore, in principle, all villagers have the rights to use the ancestral halls and participate in any lineage events as long as they are operated with revenue from the village's land, even if they are not members of the lineage.

As far as Chen lineage members are concerned, on the other hand, the ancestral halls are consecrated to their own ancestors and the rituals for ancestor worship are still dedicated to their own ancestors. These aspects came to the surface in an acute form in the below incident.

The averted feud incident

A summary of the incident: 8 July

Now we move on to an account of the averted feud incident. It can be summarized thus. In the spring of 2002, a lane between Xiyue and SW was upgraded with funds donated by the expatriate members of the Chen lineage in Hong Kong. The residents of Xiyue installed a number of one-meter

Photo 4.2 Vehicle stoppers installed at the lane entrance

high concrete pillars at the entrance of the lane to block vehicle traffic in order to protect the lane. However, the blockade would force the residents of SW to take a long detour if they wanted to drive to and from the village; and the installation of the vehicle barriers was a decision unilaterally made by the residents of Xiyue alone. A quarrel broke out on the night of 8 July between angry SW residents and Xiyue residents. It gradually escalated to a near-brawl when both parties began to arm themselves with water pipes and other weapons. Fortunately, one of the residents called the police, and more than ten policemen from a nearby station rushed to the scene to prevent a violent clash from breaking out.

My informants told me about the incident the next morning; I was not at the scene on the night of the confrontation. As I witnessed the developments from that point, however, it became apparent to me that the relationship between the majority lineage and the minority boat dwellers that had been formed in the development process of the village was the background factor to the situation. As it manifests in the progress of the incident and through people's comments, I shall try to reconstruct the circumstances from 9 July, the day after the incident, as faithfully as possible.

Progress of the incident: 9 July

I headed to the ancestral hall in D village on the morning of 9 July. My fieldwork in D village usually involved talking to my two informants at the hall manager's office. These were an elderly man who managed the hall and a man who ran a health clinic in the village, and both were members of the Chen lineage.

The hall manager was a retired primary school teacher who took the manager's job when the ancestral hall was renovated. He manned the gate daily and looked after the hall manager's office during the day. Elderly residents of the village came to the hall to read newspapers or play mahjong. The manager collected fees for the use of mahjong pieces and tables or cups of tea and kept the hall clean. He sometimes made use of his well-developed writing skills as a former teacher by penning notices from the hall to residents or couplets to be posted in the hall for the Spring Festival. He had no political clout as he was not a party cadre, but he attracted a certain degree of respect from the villagers due to his education and unassuming personality.

The clinic operator was fifty-three years old at the time and was a so-called 'barefoot doctor' (*chijiao yisheng*). One barefoot doctor was posted in each production brigade under the party policy during the people's commune era so that each production brigade should have its own healthcare capacity. Now that the standards of healthcare and transport facilities have improved, the villagers usually go to a large hospital in the township but at the time some people still went to his clinic for simple treatment. As he had only a few patients per day, he often spent his time chatting with people at the ancestral hall.

On my way to the ancestral hall that morning, I noticed a gathering of about thirty people in front of the village council offices just before the hall. I was told that a meeting was taking place inside the offices. As I felt it would be impudent to intrude on the village council meeting, I proceeded to visit the ancestral hall as usual and listened to my two informants over a cup of tea. They told me about the incident of the previous day as summarized above.

The meeting finished sometime later and two men came to the hall manager's office. They were the leaders of the seventh and eighth production teams, i.e., the two production teams in the Xiyue district. They attended the meeting as representatives of the Xiyue residents who were party to the incident.

The hall manager offered them some cigarettes. They accepted and began to talk very indignantly:

'That lane was originally property of our ancestors!'
'If the SW fellows are taking this kind of stance, let's ban them from using the land in front of the ancestral hall!'

The doctor commented as if to agree:

'Well, we've been visiting the ancestor's tombs (in northern Guangzhou), using our funds for the ancestor's graves but somehow the SW fellows began to come with us'.

The two men followed:

'The banquet for the Qingming Festival too! They are our ancestors! If they say all villagers have the right to participate because the village is funding it, why don't we use our own money and we participate without them! The visit to the graves in Guangzhou too. We should hire cars by ourselves!'

The manager added in support:

'Since Xiyue has no more rice paddies, how about charging the SW fellows when they use the land in front of the ancestral hall (for sun-drying shrimps and chaffs)? One or two jiao per square meter? On the pretext of protecting the environment in front of the hall'.

When he finished his comment, he took a sheet of paper and began to write a notice.

As it was lunchtime, the two team leaders left the manager's office. The manager and the doctor conferred and decided to talk to the village head. After they rang the village head, three of us went to a local restaurant for lunch.

I shall summarize the argument made by the four men as follows. The lane in question, the former gravesite and the ancestral hall in the village were originally the property of the Chen lineage. The SW people had no claim on them to start with. If they were to resort to a high-handed approach like this, the argument followed that they should be excluded from various rights within the village.

We returned to the manager's office after lunch. They contemplated the contents of the notice they were trying to write over a cup of tea. The manager wrote the following down on a piece of paper.

Public notice

> It has been decided that a user pay system is introduced in order to protect the repaired ancestral hall floor. Those who wish to sun-dry their grains in the area from the foot of the bridge to the floor within the ancestral hall grounds must pay a fee. They need to pay two jiao per square meter per day from the day they bring grains in to the day they remove them. Before they can bring in grains, they must pay 100 yuan as a deposit. They must not leave any grains or other goods behind on the land in front of the hall or inside the hall. They must clean the floor at the end of use.
> This is an official announcement. From all the residents of Xiyue. 9 July 2002.

As soon as the manager finished writing, the village head entered. He was a Zhongyue resident in his early fifties whose surname was Chen and was a chain-smoker who spoke loudly in a hoarse voice. He generally came across as virile and energetic.

He repeated the line, 'This is really troublesome', a few times as he entered the room. The manager and the doctor explained to him that the two team leaders of Xiyue had visited earlier and after discussion with the two leaders it had been decided not to allow the SW residents to use the land in front of the ancestral hall. The village head stared at the notice for some time and said, 'The issuer of the notice should be the ancestral hall', and, 'Anyway, it's your issue. I have nothing to do with it'.

The three men began to discuss the incident again. During the conversation, the manager and the doctor agreed, 'If we post this, the situation may get worse. Even though we have decided on this earlier, should we smother it up?' The village head kept repeating that 'this is your issue after all' and said, 'There would have been fatalities if they actually came to blows last night. They had water pipes this thick', demonstrating a width of about ten centimeters with his fingers. When the doctor told him, 'You should be careful in the next few days', the village head snapped, 'Really troublesome. The village head is supposed to look after the economic side of the village'. Then he turned to me and said, 'The village head's job is really troublesome. Really troublesome, you know!'

The village head stayed and talked with the men for a long time as he continuously lit his cigarettes. His talk mostly consisted of his complaints, such as this incident being troublesome, and he did not make any specific suggestions towards resolution. When the manager and the doctor conveyed the wishes of the Xiyue team leaders to him, it was obvious that he did not wish to get involved in this matter.

The three men were Chen lineage members and lived in Zhongyue. Although they were naturally sympathetic to Xiyue residents who were members of the same Chen lineage, they were undeniably less committed than Xiyue people who were directly involved in this incident. The village head in particular seemed to be hoping to avoid taking sides with or committing himself to either party in consideration of his position. He said, 'This problem is beyond my control', several times during their discussion.

Indeed, the problem turned out to be unsolvable within the village as he predicted, and had to be referred to arbitration at the township level, an administrative unit above the village.

The resolution of the incident

In the end, the incident was considered by the township administration and resolved within several days. According to the decision handed down by the administration, the need for the installation of vehicle barriers for the purpose of protecting the repaired lane was recognized, but it was noted that they should be moveable so that emergency vehicles such as fire engines could drive through. It was indeed a neutral decision, accommodating the arguments of both parties to a certain extent.

The hall manager and the doctor told me that they had changed the contents of the notice after another discussion with the two team leaders and showed me the revised version, as below.

Announcement

> All rice paddies belonging to the seventh and eighth teams were converted to fish farming ponds earlier this year. From the eleventh day of this month, no one will be permitted to sun-dry grains on the land in front of the ancestral hall, which formerly belonged to the seventh and eighth teams, unless prior consent is obtained from the team leaders. People are requested to clean up any articles and litter they have left behind on the premises.
> From all village residents of the seventh and eighth teams. 10 July 2002.

The doctor explained as he showed me the announcement, 'We revised it this way after our last meeting because the previous version exhibited a strong "lineage sectarianism (*zongpai zhuyi*)." This land was vested in the seventh and eighth teams at the time of the land reform.'

The original notice was to be issued by 'Xiyue', and the village head suggested that it should be issued by the 'ancestral hall'. However, neither of them was the official owner of the land under today's law, and the issuing of such a notice by the ancestral hall or Chen lineage members living in Xiyue would not escape the charge of 'lineage sectarianism'. Because the seventh and eighth production teams had been the official owners of the said land since land reform, they named the two teams as the issuers of this announcement.

In reality, 'Xiyue' and the 'seventh and eighth teams' have the same members. While 'Xiyue' was a former subunit of D village and had no administrative existence since 1949, the 'seventh and eighth teams' were official units established at the time of formation of the people's commune. People of the Chen lineage revised their plan in order to achieve the goal of restricting SW residents' use of the ancestral hall land while avoiding the charge of 'lineage sectarianism'. Moreover, they made the contents of the announcement even more diplomatic by removing the requirement for the payment of fees and deposits.

There was a difference in attitude between Xiyue residents who displayed their majority consciousness from the start by excluding SW residents from village activities and people like the hall manager and the doctor, even though they were all members of the Chen lineage. The village head was simply apprehensive about aggravating the situation due to his official position. It is possible to say that the way these people in different situations reacted to the incident helped stop it from developing into a disaster.

The concept of death pollution and the funeral procession passage issue

Thus, the incident was more or less resolved, but as I gathered more information I came to realize very clearly that the underlying cause of this problem was deep-rooted and stemmed from a close link between the majority consciousness of the Chen lineage members and a sense of aversion to death held by the local people.

Figure 4.2 Funeral procession routes

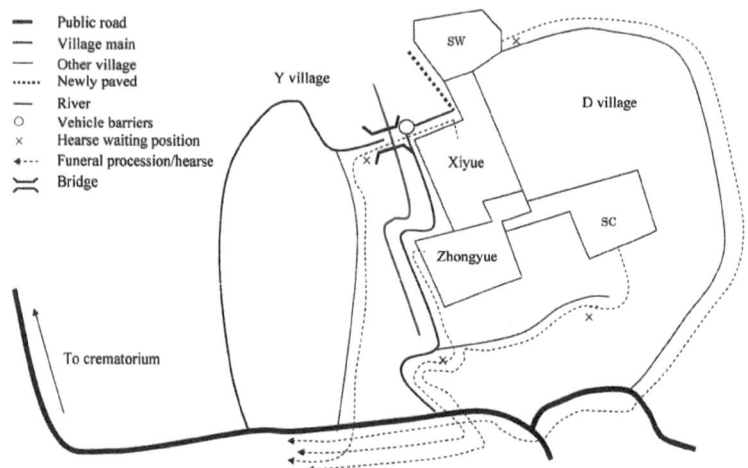

Aversion to death and funeral rites

At the time of the incident, it was explained that the vehicle barriers had been installed for the protection of the newly paved lane in Xiyue. While this explanation was not wrong, there had been disagreement between Xiyue residents and SW residents concerning the use of this lane even before it was paved. In another sense, it was about the passage of funeral processions of SW residents.

Chinese people, especially in Guangdong, have an intense feeling of aversion towards death. In particular, they have an abhorrence of coming close to or directly touching corpses. This is clearly observable in the way funeral rites are performed in this region. People rarely touch the dead body. They leave everything from dressing and transporting the deceased to placing the body in the coffin, carrying the coffin and burial to funeral professionals called *ngzonglou*. When the coffin containing the body is carried to the burial site, the procession is required to avoid residential areas as much as possible, and there is a strictly stipulated funeral procession route for each subdistrict within the village.[5]

Burial was banned and completely replaced by cremation from the latter half of the 1990s, and now the crematorium sends a hearse to the village to fetch the body. A funeral procession therefore marches to where the hearse is waiting instead of the cemetery on the hill. Although it is only to the waiting hearse, the procession must follow the stipulated route (Figure 4.2), and people still avoid touching the deceased during funeral rites despite the change to burial procedures. In short, people continue to have a strong abhorrence towards death today, and this was found to be the underlying cause of the incident in question.

A new conflict surrounding a funeral procession

Before cremation was imposed, the funeral processions of SW residents were able to travel to the burial site on the hill around the back of the village without passing down the main street. Once cremation had been introduced, the hearse from the crematorium now comes to the village and waits at the foot of the bridge or by the residential subdistrict of SW over the bridge. The funeral procession would march through Xiyue to reach the foot of the bridge in the former case, and the hearse carrying the deceased would drive through Xiyue in the latter case. The body would have to pass through Xiyue in either situation.

Xiyue residents were reportedly strenuously opposed to this. The hall manager and the doctor were not Xiyue residents, but both of them stated adamantly, 'It is absolutely impossible for SW bodies to pass through Xiyue', and added, 'We observe the time-honored customs of the village but SW has no history; it hasn't even reached 100 years'.

To solve the problem, the village council built a new road to allow access to SW from the back of the village. All vehicles, including the hearse from the crematorium, could use this road; so Xiyue residents installed vehicle barriers when the lane was paved. For Xiyue residents, this would not only protect the new pavement but also ensure that the hearse from the crematorium would never drive through their residential area. Conversely, SW residents were angered by the unilateral manner of banning even the passage of ordinary vehicles.

The attitude of the Xiyue residents who obstinately refused the passage of the funeral processions of SW residents displayed the blatant majority consciousness of Chen lineage members as well as the strength of their sense of death taboo today. What we see here is the majority claim of 'our village, our way' that no longer has official validity today, even though it is something that has been cultivated in the process of the development of the village.

Rising lineage consciousness

As we have seen so far, the majority consciousness of Chen lineage members with respect to the village was the underlying cause of the averted feud incident surrounding the installation of vehicle barriers. It came to be shared by members of the Chen lineage in the development process of the village and community and the incident led them to assert their lineage-consciousness in an even more acute manner.

It has been almost fifty years since lineages were denounced by the Communist Party and lost their common property. Yet, they continue to claim their rights to it. One of the reasons for this is arguably the historical fact that the people's commune regime was founded on the existing framework of kin and territorial relations. When the resurgence of lineages began, many researchers looked to structural continuity as a major factor. In other words, although the Communist Party overtly promoted the dismantling of lineages, the concept of patrilineal descent remained in people's consciousnesses because people's communes were organized according to the preexisting habitation units (Potter and Potter 1990: 265–267; Ishida 1996: 185–187; Han 2001: 208–209; Ruan 2005: 146–151). In D village, the production teams were organized in keeping with the frameworks of the pre-1949 village and its subunits as I mentioned earlier, and there is no doubt that this has been the structural background for the continuing significance of the boundary between the Chen lineage members and the minority.

However, the preservation of habitation units does not necessarily mean the preservation of the concept of patrilineal descent as it has been found that not all of formerly strong lineages have achieved revival (Siu 1989; Nie 1992). Nor does the preservation of the patrilineal descent concept directly lead to the manifestation of lineage consciousness. People may have an absolute awareness of their descent, but the state of consciousness and the manner of manifestation are extremely situation-dependent and constructional.

Shima argues in his essay about the compilation of lineage genealogies in the Korean Peninsula that what supports and actualizes the recognition of a genealogy are repetitive actions taken by living people (Shima 1997: 123). The intensification of the lineage consciousness among the Chens which served as the catalyst of the incident described above was triggered by the revival of the lineage driven from the 1990s by members living in Hong Kong. During the next decade or so, the Chen people of D village familiarized themselves with the recompiled lineage genealogy, some of them added their names to it, and they performed rituals at their ancestral tombs. Furthermore, the 'history' and 'culture' of D village and the Chen lineage acquired legitimacy by way of state recognition. The claim that land and buildings in the village and the village itself 'belonged to our ancestors' could not have come out of their mouths for the simple reason that they shared the essential notion of the genealogy and thus the kinship-based habitation patterns were maintained. Their intense majority consciousness has been heightened by their actual involvement in the lineage that has been revived and recognized as legitimate.

Conclusion

The claims made by the Chen lineage members that triggered the incident in question are thus invalid from the perspective of the village's present laws and institutions. They base their claims on the historically formed ethnic boundary and hierarchy and the majority-minority relationship. These factors are returning to the forefront of their consciousness thanks to the spectacular revival of lineage organization over the last two decades.

What we can glean from this phenomenon is the great significance people attach to 'culture' and 'tradition' grounded historically. While we understand that most of them actually are social constructs, the interested parties do not think so at all. They have produced many successful imperial examination candidates, built splendid ancestral halls and recorded them in the lineage genealogy; these are unmistakable 'essential facts' as far as they are concerned. Moreover, these histories and cultures are recognized for their essential value as tourism resources or grounds for national integration and 'Chineseness' in today's Chinese society. In this condition, lineage members are able to repair the gap in their history that occurred during the period of the Cultural Revolution and integrate their own existence into the continuity of Chinese history (Segawa 2004: 235). Needless to say, the imperial examination no longer exists and cadres and wealthy people cannot build ancestral halls named after them, no matter how successful they are. While there are 'invented traditions' (Hobsbawm and Ranger 1983), there are 'traditions that cannot be invented' as well.

Freedman, an eminent authority in the anthropological study of China, makes the following comment in his work, originally published some sixty years ago.

> The most obvious characteristic of a thoroughgoing unilineal system of kinship is the continuity it ensures between the past and the present… The ancestors worshipped by the Chinese in their halls were more than mere figures of history; they may be the religious correlates of a social structure achieving permanence through time. (Freedman 1980[1958]: 134)

At the same time, this continuity sometimes goes on to have great significance or sinks to the bottom of people's consciousnesses in response to constantly changing conditions. In contemporary Chinese society, the continuity between the past and the present is appreciated as 'history' or 'culture', and strongly appeals to the interested parties. The averted feud incident in question was caused by the consciousness of the majority group of the historically constructed ethnic boundary and hierarchical relationship.

5 Social Differences in an Emigrant Community in Modern China: A Case Study from Fuzhou City, Fujian Province

Itoe Kaneshiro

Introduction

The purpose of this chapter is to clarify the social differences that immigrants' 'success' and 'failure' bring to their native village in modern China. In order to do so, I first illustrate the situation surrounding migration in the surveyed area and then elucidate and analyze the image of 'successful' and 'unsuccessful' immigrants in the eyes of native villagers as well as the code of conduct expected from these immigrants. Through the discussion, I illustrate how symbolic capital, acquired using immigrants' economic capital, contributes through elevating the social prestige of immigrants and their families in the context of village society and examine how disparity emerges among the villagers.

'Symbolic capital' as referred to in this chapter derives from the concept introduced by Bourdieu. Symbolic capital signifies the non-economic resources that are not considered as 'capital' in the conventional sense, as in economic capital comprised of income and assets (Bourdieu 1980). As with the example of 'potlatch' cited by Bourdieu, symbolic capital can be acquired through the exchange of economic capital (offering of wealth and mass consumption), and the acquired symbolic capital allows the individual to gain and manifest a higher level of prestige within a particular social space. Such social space is comprised of several 'sites' constituted by members sharing the same values. It is at these sites that many of the actors engage in symbolic battles to differentiate themselves from others (Bourdieu 1980). In this chapter, we shall invoke the framework of a 'symbolic battle at the "sites"' outlined by Bourdieu, and discuss how the people in question attempt to transform economic capital (income acquired overseas) into various forms of symbolic capital (material/non-material) in order to differentiate themselves from others.

The target village of this study is the immigrants' native village known as 僑鄉 (Qiaoxiang) in Chinese. What I mean by 'emigrant community' here is one where many of the residents have migrated overseas. In southern China, Guangdong Province and Fujian Province are particularly well known for dispatching large numbers of immigrants overseas. These overseas immigrants are known as 華僑 (Hua-qiao) or 華人 (Hua-ren) and reside in various countries including South East Asia, the US, Europe and Japan.

Past studies on emigrant communities in South-Eastern China have mainly focused on social change, identifying the impacts that immigrants have had on the traditional social structures of the native villages and the process of how village societies have responded to such shifts (e.g., see Chen 1939, Watson 1995[1975]). As expected, immigrants have had an enormous influence on village economy and society. These effects are evident in the changes in the economy and traditional social structures of farming communities (e.g., Chen 1939). On the other hand, it was also noted that immigrants have become one of the forces maintaining the traditional social structures, and so called 'conservative transformations' (Watson 1995[1975]) have been observed.

The enormous wealth brought to the homeland was one of the direct causes that led to these changes. In South-Eastern China during the period between the end of the Qing dynasty and the Republic of China, especially in the Guangdong and Fujian societies, restoring and maintaining shrines, graves and village infrastructure with one's own funds was an important means to elevate one's social prestige. This measure continues to be adhered to by the many immigrants who follow the same path today.[1]

As we shall see through the discussion below, the influx of capital brought by the immigrants has changed the exterior look of native villages and contributed to creating an image of wealthy villages. However, when we look at what is occurring inside such villages, especially at the individual and family levels, we can observe disparities particularly in the level of financial income among families who have dispatched immigrants in the same manner.

While living in the village, I had many opportunities to hear about the financial situations of different households, which also often suggested the widening financial divide between 'successful' and 'unsuccessful' overseas immigrants. However, the villagers themselves rarely spoke directly of or compared each other's income or assets. In fact, the villagers' conversations suggested that their focus was more on how the acquired assets were consumed. Wealth was expended according to the village's internal cultural code. Indeed, how the capital was used was an indicator in terms of the creation of a 'successful' immigrant image.

Based on this view, in this chapter I illustrate how the wealth, acquired by the immigrants as economic capital, is consumed in the village's social life and then discuss how the residents attempt to differentiate themselves from others. To begin with, I present an overview of our survey area, Village X in Fuzhou City, Fujian Province. I then explain the background of why Village X began to dispatch immigrants, their destinations and the various situations surrounding immigrants, such as immigration methods. Based on this, I then focus on how the people remaining in the village, in other words, the constituents of the 'site', transform the economic capital into symbolic capital that denotes immigrants' success. At the same time, I point to the presence of the many immigrants who fail to achieve their goals and note the fact that the village is facing a situation that may be described as a monopoly of symbolic wealth.

Overview of the survey area

Fujian Province is located in the south-eastern part of China, bordering Zhejiang Province in the north, Guangdong Province in the southwest and Jiangxi Province in the west. Flat land is scarce in mountainous Fujian Province, but the coastal areas have flourished via domestic and overseas trading in the form of marine transport since the Song Dynasty. As farmland was limited, people did not hesitate to immigrate overseas to explore new opportunities when the population reached saturation point. The Min Nan region of southern Fujian Province was particularly active in dispatching many overseas immigrants to Taiwan and South East Asian countries from the end of the Qing Dynasty. It is due to this fact that Fujian Province is often referred to as the home of Chinese overseas immigrants.

Our survey area, Village X, is located in the township or *zhen* (鎮) T of Fuzhou City in the north eastern region of Fujian Province (Figure 5.1). Fuzhou City is the capital city of Fujian Province as well as its political and economic center. Fuzhou City is located in the coastal area and like many other cities, has flourished as a hub for marine transport trading. Village X is located near the mouth of Fujian Province's largest river, Min River (閩江). Village X has a population of 4,152 with 1,447 households (Editorial Committee of Zhen Journal of Village X 2010). However, this figure simply shows the number of people registered as residents. As most immigrants do not deregister when they go overseas, the number of residents actually living in the village would be much smaller. I estimate the number of villagers who actually reside in the village to be around 2,000 through my conversations with the villagers. The majority of residents are Han people and most speak the local dialect, Fuzhou language, but they also understand a certain amount of the standard Chinese known as Putonghua (普通語).

Figure 5.1 Location of Fuzhou City

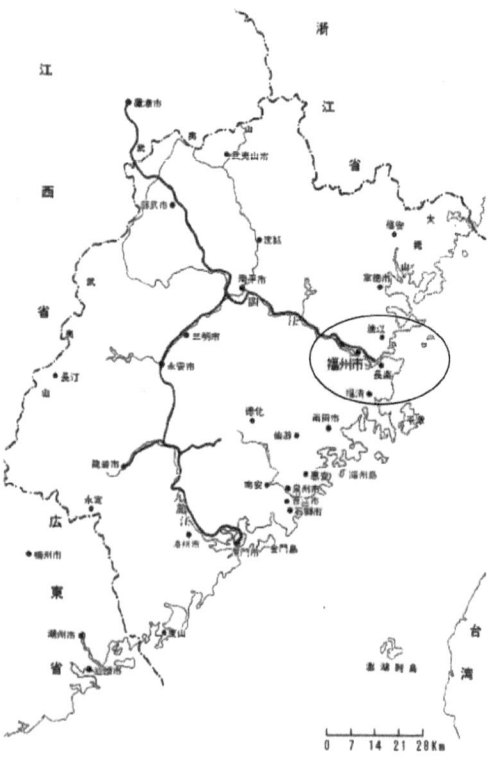

As described below, a large proportion of the residents of Village X have already left the village to work and live overseas or moved to other cities for job opportunities. The current population of Village X is mainly composed of the 'elderly',[2] women, children and migrant laborers from the inner regions of China known as Waidiren (外地人).[3] The village is equipped with a post office and banks offering foreign currency exchange services. The post office even has a small electronic bulletin board at the front where villagers can check the current exchange rate for US dollars. It is not rare to see people exiting with a large amount of yuan, which is another indication that the villagers' livelihoods have a close relationship with overseas remittance funds.

Being surrounded by mountains on three sides, Village X was not an ideal location for agriculture with limited arable land. However, it had the advantage of being connected to the cities via rivers and developed itself as a hub for long distance trade from the end of the Qing Dynasty to the Republic era, while it also functioned as a market town servicing surrounding villages. From 1949 onwards, policies to increase farming productivity were introduced but failed to bring intended outcomes. Instead, most people relied on natural resources from the mountain and engaged in stone material processing. Today, we hardly see any business activities in the village. Some people raise livestock such as ducks and chickens for their own consumption and grow vegetables in small plots; however, these endeavors do not seem to be contributing to their income. Instead, the unemployed, mostly comprised of the 'elderly', are busy with their 'consumption' lifestyles, spending time gambling and working on their hobbies.

Let us now review the situation surrounding immigrants in the Fuzhou region[4] since Chinese economic reform. According to Zhuang (庄) (2006), who studies post-reform policy overseas immigrants, the people of the Min Nan region of southern Fujian Province and Guangdong Province formed the main body of overseas immigrants prior to World War II. Then, after a period of 'national isolation', the number of overseas immigrants again soared due to the economic reform, but this time Fuzhou region of Fujian Province became one of the major sources of immigrants. The number of immigrants from the Fuzhou region from the reform period onwards amounted to some 700,000–800,000, of which approximately forty to fifty percent used illegal measures to leave the country. As Zhuang indicated, 'Fuzhou region was not an area traditionally known for dispatching immigrants but has managed to outnumber the traditional immigrant dispatching regions by successfully constructing a network which supported the dispatch in such a short period of time' (2006: 41). This should be noted as a characteristic of the immigration pattern in Fuzhou region.

The T zhen region, in which Village X is located, was no exception and has dispatched many immigrants to the US, Europe and Japan since the 1980s. Village X and many of the surrounding villages have sent out overseas immigrants in some form or another and they pride themselves as 'Qiaoxiang' (僑郷), the native villages of immigrants. Such Qiaoxiang villages are often viewed as being wealthy from the perspective of people of non-Qiaoxiang villages. For example, when I took a taxi from Fuzhou City to the bus terminal on route to Village X and informed the driver that I lived in that village the driver said, 'That village is rich. It is a "Qiaoxiang". Their funerals are so lavish and they give you money just to attend. I am always happy to attend (whenever I am invited)'. In reality, not all funerals are luxurious, but this shows how Qiaoxiang signifies 'a wealthy village' more than anything else by those from other regions.

All the villagers spoke of how the current standard of living was dramatically higher compared to the old days. According to the statistics, the average income per resident in Village X increased from 5,280 yuan in 2001 to 8,190 yuan in 2008 (Editorial Committee of Zhen Journal of Village X 2010). Considering the national average income for a 'farmer'[5] in 2008 was 4,760 yuan,[6] we can see how financially privileged they are. Taking this into account, we would now like to review the situation surrounding the immigrants in Village X.

The immigrants' situation in Village X

As previously stated, Village X has dispatched many overseas immigrants since the 1980s. There are two types of immigrants recognized in Village X: 'immigrants based on legal measures' and 'immigrants based on illegal measures'. The latter in particular are known as *toudu* (偷渡), and while their destinations spread to various regions of the world, in this paper I focus on immigrants to the US.

While I was conducting interviews on immigrants in Village X, someone mentioned the phrase 'Going (to the US) is stupid but not going is also stupid'. When I inquired what this meant, they told me that it was ironic that those who choose to spend a fortune to travel overseas are only met with tough days of hard labor. Then again, those who do not go when everyone else is going would lose face or *mei mianzi* (没面子). 'Those who choose hardship' referred to here indicates those who travel as *toudu* (偷渡), which are the majority of immigrants from Village X.

According to many informants, the reason why the residents of Village X began to aspire to go overseas was largely to do with poverty and conditions in the surrounding villages at the time. Following the socialistic policies enforced by the Chinese Communist Party since the founding of the People's Republic of China in 1949, Village X introduced various policies aimed at increasing agricultural productivity. However, they did not achieve a significant result as land was limited to begin with. The focus gradually shifted towards stone material processing, but people's lives remained very tough. The informants who reflected on those days all said, 'we did not have any possessions or food. We raised any livestock and cultivated any crops we could think of. Still, our life was really tough'.

Once the reform and open policy was introduced, people in the coastal area of Fuzhou region, including the T zhen (鎮) region, began migrating to developed countries such as the US, Japan and the EU. It is hard to say when, where and how this trend began, however, according to Zhuang, there seemed to have been several migration patterns at play.

The first pattern relied on the presence of two types of pioneers, the first of which refers to the small number of sailors who jumped ship (跳船) in the US from the 1940s and onwards, who after tough labor acquired a Green Card and settled into that country. The second refers to immigrants who migrated via Hong Kong after 1972. The Chinese Government allowed the residents of Qiaoxiang in Guangdong Province and Fujian Province to visit their relatives (探亲) in Hong Kong, Macau and other locations overseas, opening the door for many Fuzhou people to migrate to the US via Hong Kong (Zhuang 2006). Once these people acquired legitimate residential status in the US, they invited many others such as blood relatives and regional acquaintances, leading to a phenomenon that could be described as 'chain migration' (Zhuang 2006).

Then, the second pattern emerged with the gradual formation of illegal immigrants' networks. According to the people of Village X, most of the villagers did not have relatives in the US nor were they able to use systems such as overseas studies or investment immigration, so they paid large amounts of money to organize travel to the US. A male informant in his 60s spent USD 18,000 to send his son out of the country in the 1980s, and another male informant in the same age range spent approximately USD 60,000 in the 1990s, revealing how the fee increased over the years. As it was almost impossible for one household to cover the huge travel expense, they had to borrow money from relatives and friends. This meant that the family suffered significant financial losses when the immigrants lost their lives while overseas or before they even reached their destination. I have not encountered such a case in Village X, but I have heard of such stories being featured in the news. A few of the villagers in Village X still seemed to be wanting to leave the country and I heard rumors of some gathering money and information from those who have lived in the US.

So, what makes villagers want to leave the country with such burdens on their shoulders? Those who have immigrated in the past usually mention first and foremost that they sought to get out of their life of poverty, as described earlier. Some also said that hearing the success stories of immigrants from other villages or seeing how their fellow villagers became rich through illegal migration triggered them into leaving the country. Conversely, some cited 'being ashamed of not going (to the US)' as the reason for immigration. With these motives in mind, males in their twenties to thirties headed for the US in the 1980s to 1990s.

Years later, as the funds acquired by migrant workers gradually returned home, the infrastructure of the village was upgraded and luxurious common facilities and houses were built, giving the village a modern look. When one visits the villagers, one can see that not only are most households equipped with electrical appliances such as televisions: most elders use mobile phones and many even own personal computers. A lot of the elders seem to be communicating with their children and grandchildren in the US via the Internet and spend their leisure time gambling, playing mah-jong and cards, watching TV and chatting on the street. Households comprised of only elderly members often hire helpers called *baomu* (保姆)[7] to do the household chores such as cooking and washing. This is why outsiders see the village as a 'wealthy village'.

However, as the survey progressed, it became evident that not all immigrants who left the village were 'successful'. When the residents of Village X talk about the success of immigrants, there seem to be a number of criteria. These are not simply about how financially successful the immigrants are but also relate to how the acquired wealth is consumed. We shall look at the details below.

The borderline between 'successful' and 'unsuccessful' immigrants

Conditions for 'success': Repayment of debt, remittance, 'legitimate status' and homecoming

The first determining factor is whether or not immigrants are financially stable. More specifically, have they repaid their travel expense debt and are they able to remit money back home? As we saw above, in many cases the purpose of immigration is to find means to alleviate poverty, so most villagers are not capable of saving the travel expenses themselves. In such cases, they borrow money from friends and relatives and repay the debt from the salary they earn at their destination. Most people begin by working in China Town in New York City, and informants say that they can usually repay the travel debt within the first four years. Whilst repaying the debt, they start sending small sums back home once they begin accumulating surplus. The average sum or frequency of remittance in Village X is hard to grasp. Some seem to be making regular remittance while others send money only when it is needed for a particular purpose. The situation seems to vary on an individual basis.

The next important factor to take into account when determining whether or not the immigrant is successful is the immigrants' 'status'. When the villagers talk about immigrants, the presence or absence of a Green Card is the most frequently mentioned issue. Generally speaking, the residents of Village X immigrate through illegal measures, so they start off their lives in the US as illegal immigrants. Once they arrive in the US, they strive to achieve financial stability and to acquire a Green Card. Once they successfully acquire this certification, they can be freed from psychological and legal instability and as Shen indicates, the possibility of achieving financial security will increase as this brings many benefits such as greater occupational opportunities (Shen 2004). At the same time, the acquisition of a Green Card means that they can now return home. As explained later, the immigrants can show off their success on their first homecoming by inviting friends and relatives to a spectacular feast and offering various gifts.

If the immigrants cannot acquire a Green Card, they cannot return home and this may cause potential problems in various situations. Let us look at funerals by way of example. From what I have observed regarding funeral rites in Village X, when a husband passes away, his wife cannot attend the funeral as she must remain in the house in mourning.[8] Instead, it is the son who is expected to act as the host of the funeral. A son who is unable to attend his parent's funeral is regarded as 'undutiful', and this is unfavorable from the elders' point of view. Some elders even say that 'the funeral cannot be held until the son comes home', which indicates the importance of the male descendant's role in the funeral rites. In a case that I observed, the son came home from the US two days after receiving news of the death, and the funeral was held upon his arrival.[9] According to the informants, sons who have not acquired a Green Card or cannot attend a funeral due to work commitments attempt to settle the matter by sending enough money to compensate for non-attendance. However, people remaining in the village still tend to think that a son should come home to attend a funeral, and those who have managed to return are afforded a certain level of recognition.

A few years after acquiring a Green Card, immigrants can sit a test to obtain citizenship. Immigration of their families becomes significantly easier once they acquire US citizenship, so most people sit the test. When they successfully pass, not only do they acquire 'American citizenship', but also bestow a great honor on the family who has produced an immigrant of the highest 'status'.

Actions expected from a successful immigrant

As we have seen above, immigrants' success can first be confirmed through their financial stability and acquisition of status and it is considered ideal if their status allows them to return home or move without restrictions. From then on, there are a few actions that need to be taken to accentuate their success in the village. Let us now look at these measures.

The feast to be held upon their first homecoming
The immigrants who left the village between the 1980s and 1990s usually took more than five years to return home. Back then, they were not even sure if they would reach their destination safely. Therefore, news of safe arrival was greeted with great delight, worthy enough to take action such as the dedication of a theatrical play to the shrine. Also, when returning home, immigrants had to prepare various gifts in addition to paying for the return airfare. As returning home alone required large amounts of money, to be able to afford this was enough of an indicator to show that one had become fairly wealthy.

For example, Informant C (sixties, male) said:

> When someone returned home in the 80s and the 90s, we used to have spectacular feasts. The immigrant himself acted as the host and invited friends and relatives to enjoy the reunion. He brought gifts from the US, such as Western liquor (whisky and wine) and tobacco. Sometimes cash was given out, not in yuan but, say, a $100 note in a little envelope. But homecoming had become quite common by the 2000s, especially in the last five to six years. People no longer have special feasts at homes but they still invite friends and relatives to a restaurant in a nearby town and offer gifts. These days, they bring us American medicine and household goods.

We can see here that homecoming required significant preparation and cost a lot of money. As this informant said, homecoming had become such a common event by the 2000s that people no longer went to the trouble of hosting a large feast at home. However, they still invited their close friends and relatives to restaurants or offered various gifts.

Home renovation
As Watson (1995) has pointed out, one of the immigrants' most clear-cut manifestations of wealth has been home renovation. The renovated houses look different from the conventional style, arranged with a 'modern' and 'Western' design, and this trend goes for Village X as well.

Between the 1980s and the 1990s, Village X underwent a construction boom. Those who accumulated wealth by working overseas raced to spend their assets on housing construction. Until then, houses in Village X were built of wood or bricks, but from the late 1980s to the 1990s, four to five story houses made of concrete, with colorful tiles on the exterior walls, were built one by one (Photo 5.1). The informants say that there was a competitive atmosphere symbolized by the phrase, 'If you build, I build too!' (你盖，我盖！) The higher the house, the better it was. People also paid great attention to the interior design, which attracted the eyes of visitors and became a point of differentiation. Many of the houses I visited featured huge chandeliers at the entrance hall and a TV surrounded by sofas in the living room.

It is said that the immigrants themselves hardly ever return home to live in the luxurious houses. Instead they were usually occupied by family members left in the village, often the elderly couple or sometimes an elder by themselves, or they were left completely empty. Needless to say, it was not possible for the older generation to use all the space in the house by themselves, which meant a lot of the space simply remained closed. In many cases, the houses were maintained with outside help such as relatives visiting for regular cleanups or by casual cleaners. This is one of the facts that indicated that people were no longer trying to build a house to fulfil a comfortable and functional 'modern' lifestyle, but more as a symbol to show the level of success achieved by working overseas.

However, the trend of home renovation became obsolete by 2000 as more and more people began to choose to migrate to nearby cities. The reasons behind this migration requires further discussions, but people often cited purchasing an apartment in the city as an investment property given the soaring real estate values in the city area or being able to enjoy advanced services such as access to hospitals and schools. Even then, these people usually do not sell their old or renovated houses.

Photo 5.1 Western style houses built in the 1990s

Donations and contributions to the shrine

Village X has a shrine that village members are deeply devoted to, especially the immigrants. Many pray for their safe journey and the success of their business before departing, and once their prayers are answered, they present offerings to thank the gods, often in the form of plays and movies (Photo 5.2).

Photo 5.2 *Offering of a play*

Photo 5.3 *Notice of the play performance*

When a play is to be offered, the sponsor invites a theatrical company that specializes in this field and offers performances day and night. Prior to this, it is customary to post a notice, in red paper, on the village bulletin board indicating the details of the play such as who invited the company, when and for what reasons (Photo 5.3). Being able to enjoy a play is one of the very few entertainments available for the elderly in the village, so when the day arrives, they all flock to the theater.

The quality of theatre companies varies, as does the cost involved in inviting them. For example, if one wishes to invite a company from the provincial theatre school, it would cost about 10,000 yuan, but one may get away with spending 2,000 to 3,000 yuan for a local company. Given that the villagers are aware of the cost and quality of each company from their past experiences as audiences and knowledge gained from those who have actually invited companies in the past, the performance tends to have a significant influence on the appraisal of the host. Generally, it is regarded that the larger the audience the better, so the host often gets creative in trying to attract more people to attend the play. Some may even add sentences such as 'it is going to be really enjoyable so please make sure you come' to the bulletin board. At the end of the day, when choosing the company, the hosts need to carefully balance the budget and the quality of the company in order to ensure attendance and to save face.

Contribution to public works projects

In Village X, the 'Public Service Works Foundation' (公益事業基金会) was established in 2000. It is an organization whose purpose is to accept donations from overseas immigrants and is managed by the board members of the Elders Society. 'Public service works' refers to projects that benefit the whole village such as the construction of public facilities or maintenance of roads. This is the most visible form of contribution to the hometown and such acts are often realized by individuals donating a large amount of

Photo 5.4 Recognition of contributors through a photo display

funds. Let us look at the case of Mr. R, one of the most prominent overseas immigrants of Village X. Mr. R went to the US in the 1940s where he succeeded in his restaurant and real estate business and became one of the wealthiest immigrants in Village X. He made a contribution of more than 100,000 yuan in total and these funds were used for the construction of the primary school and public entertainment facilities, such as the 'respect-for-the-aged facility', as well as for the reconstruction of the shrine. Monuments with inscriptions of R's name can be seen in various parts of the village. R passed away in the US in 2008, but his ashes were brought home and laid to rest in a pre-prepared grave. The scale of his funeral and the number of guests invited were so phenomenal that people still talk of the outstanding ceremony today.

In 2011, the respect-for-the-aged facility opened a new section to commemorate its contributors in celebration of its tenth anniversary (Photo 5.4). Here, the photos of the contributors are framed and adorned on the wall, each with the sum of donation stated at the bottom. The photos are laid out in the shape of a pyramid where the positions of the contributors are determined by the amount of donations – the higher the contribution, the higher the contributor's photo. We can see here how donation has become a representative tool to elevate one's reputation in the village, as an individual's prestige can be clearly recognized through this highly public display.

Lavish rites of passage

Photo 5.5 Funeral procession marching through the village

Among the four acts cited thus far, the first and second reached their peaks in the 1980s through to the 1990s among the early immigrants and have since downgraded in scale or have taken different forms while maintaining the same context. The third and fourth are basically still conducted in the same way as the early days, recognizing the contributors by publically releasing names, images and the amount of donations. The next act has also been conducted continuously for many years but is rapidly expanding and has now become the most prominent occasion for the host to show off their wealth in Village X.

While conducting fieldwork in Village X, I once encountered a magnificent funeral procession featuring several bands and groups of dancers marching through the village (Photo 5.5). According to the villagers, from around the 1990s funeral processions for burial became a trend, headed by bands and dancers and followed by families and attendees, and a large-scale feast was held after the burial.

From previous studies it was found that the basic structure of the funeral rites of Han people is generally uniform from death to the departure of the casket, but the ritual expressions seen in this process and those conducted at the burial and afterwards are quite diverse (Watson 1994). In the case of Village X, people obediently follow the legitimate ritual processes but also focus on how extravagant the funerals can become in areas where arrangements are allowed.

This can be observed most prominently in the feast following the burial. The family of the deceased who hosts the rituals usually invites 200–300 guests to the funeral.[10] All guests are then invited to the feast held after the burial where they are treated with sumptuous food and gifts of household items such as oil, drinks, fruits and even cash. Here, wealth is consumed competitively. In the case of cash, it is common to give out 300–500 yuan per guest, but there are cases when USD 100 notes have been handed out. People will start talking about the contents of the gifts and the amount of cash distributed straight after the feast and the more money spent at the feast, the more envious people become.

The image of the 'unsuccessful' projected from that of the 'successful'

Thus far we have looked at the image of 'successful' immigrants, but those who lie at the opposite pole would be the 'unsuccessful' ones. In the interviews, the villagers hinted at the presence of immigrants who do not reach their 'ideal'. In brief, these are people who do not conform to the conditions for success we have discussed so far, that is, those who have not repaid their debts, have not begun remittance, have not acquired a legitimate 'status' and have not returned home. People rarely speak directly of these cases, but rumors about them often spread through the village.

In reality, immigrants' financial failure greatly affects their family's finances. For example, while interviewing about immigrants' financial support for their family, Informant A (seventies, female) told me about her daughter and her nephew (A's younger brother's son).

> My daughter went to the US more than ten years ago and sends me money once in a while. Besides money, she has brought me gifts such as platinum necklaces but now that the US economy is not doing so well, she does not come home every year. My nephew also went to the US but he, on the other hand, has never sent his parents any money. I lent him more than 20,000 yuan for the opening of his restaurant in the US but there is no sign that the money will ever be repaid. He owes so much money to everyone. The family has no money and are struggling just to survive in this village so I sometimes give them (my brother and his wife who live in the village) money.

From here, we can see how those who are not financially stable, cannot repay their debt or remit money are generally portrayed in a negative manner, regardless of their circumstances.

Not having 'legitimate status' is also often viewed negatively and has become a major barometer in determining the success of the immigrant in the village. This is a major issue, not only for those who remain in the village but also for the immigrants themselves. An informant who just returned from the US (forties, male) told me his story.

> Life in the US is really tough. You have to work all day, from morning to evening, and have no peace of mind until you acquire "legitimate status". I applied (for a Green Card) many times but, for some reason, was never accepted. Eventually, I became sick and the immigration officials caught me and sent me home. I could not do anything but tell myself that I was out of luck. Whether or not you have "legitimate status" is such an important factor.

We can tell from the above story that having a 'status' or not is also an important issue for the immigrants themselves. Needless to say, an immigrant who cannot acquire the 'status' for a prolonged period is a source of worry for their family as they cannot hope for an increase in income while the range of occupations in the US remains limited. Eventually people start judging the immigrant, saying 'what was the point of the immigration?'

As we have seen so far, based on the fact that the standard of the immigrants' 'success' in the immigrants' native village depends on financial and social stability, we can see how difficult it is for 'unsuccessful' immigrants to perform acts that are categorized as 'successful'. The distance between the 'successful' and 'unsuccessful' is expected only to grow wider.

Conclusion

In this chapter, I have reviewed the images and codes of conduct expected of 'successful' and 'unsuccessful' immigrants, as seen from the eyes of the residents left in the village, in order to clarify the social disparities these immigrants have brought to modern China's immigrants' native villages. What we have seen in the 'sites' of the immigrants' native village is the 'symbolic contention' of people who struggle to differentiate themselves from others by manifesting their 'success' through the exchange of financial capital gained while working as an immigrant into symbolic capital through various consumption methods. Now, let us review our discussion.

In Village X, financial stability and the acquisition of 'legitimate status' are highly valued as the basic conditions for immigrants' 'success'. In addition, it became evident that there are certain tools that manifest the 'success' of immigrants and these social acts can only be achieved by those who have fulfilled the basic conditions. In the case of Village X, the homecoming, the feast and home renovations were considered the barometers of 'success' in the early days of immigration from the 1980s to the 1990s. However, by the 2000s, such acts became outdated as homecoming became quite a common event and more people felt that buying a new apartment in the city was more profitable than renovating their homes in the village.

Provision of funds still continues today in the form of donations and offerings of plays to the shrine and donations to fund the village's public service projects. Those who make donations are recognized through having their names engraved or having a color photo displayed in public. In other words, these acts of donation are methods to visibly elevate an individual's social prestige through recognition in highly public open spaces.

In addition, the display of wealth, as seen in lavish funerals, has provided a new 'contention ground' for successful immigrants to boost social dignity in the village society. The mass consumption of wealth at feasts and through funeral processions are not only easy ways to gain recognition but also allow them to maintain their dignity for many years to come through talk and gossip in the village.

It is also characteristic that the various forms of displays of wealth are all targeted toward those who remain in the village. The methods of consuming wealth, essentially the 'weapon' at the contention ground, are based on the cultural code shared within the village society and are regarded as indicators in the creation of a 'successful' immigrant image.

Furthermore, the series of phenomenon in the native village of modern China may be interpreted as the revival of accumulation and show of personal wealth that had once been denied by socialism. In other words, the social hierarchy that was equalized by the socialist policies is once again seeing disparities among the villagers who acquired the opportunity to elevate themselves financially through immigration. In this regards, it can be said that the quantity of wealth still remains an important factor in the manifestation of social status.

However, while there are successful immigrants who achieve their cultural ideals, there are also many unsuccessful ones who fail to achieve their goals. The disparity between the 'successful' and the 'unsuccessful' is clearly evident. I would like to end the discussion here by saying that the oligopoly of wealth may generate a renewed level of social inequality.

6 Social Change and Transformation in Toba Batak Ethnic Associations in Medan, Sumatra

Toshiaki Kimura

Introduction

In this chapter, I address the ethnic associations formed by Toba Batak migrants living in the multiethnic city of Medan on the Indonesian island of Sumatra. Toba Batak ethnic associations are well known, having been the subject of a classical contribution to urban anthropology – the research of E. Bruner (1961, 1972). While based on surveys in the 1950s, Bruner described how the Toba Batak, an urban minority, did not discard their traditional worldview and values, but rather utilized them in forming a community based on mutual assistance.

More than half a century has elapsed since then. During that time, Indonesian society achieved rapid economic growth under the Suharto regime, leading to further migration from the countryside to the cities. The social conditions around Toba Batak immigrants in Medan also have changed drastically through the period. Do these changes have any influence on the function of the ethnic association that Brunner recorded? If so, then how? In this paper, I try to consider this problem by examining the constitution of several Toba Batak ethnic associations in Medan.

A short history of Medan and the Toba Batak

The Toba Batak people

The original dwelling-place of the people called the 'Toba Batak' was located around a crater lake called Lake Toba in the highlands of inland Sumatra. The Toba language is their common tongue, and they maintain a lineage linked to a common ancestor, Si Raja Batak. These aspects have important significance in the formation of their sense of belonging.

The most vital unit constituting their society is the clan, called *marga*. Members of each clan are believed to have a common ancestor, and the family line from that ancestor is handed down by respective clans. Moreover, the element that ties these clans together and serves as a thread weaving Toba Batak society into something cohesive is relationships bound by marriage. In Toba Batak society, which follows exogamous marriage regulations with one *marga* or a combination of several *marga* serving as a unit, marriage always takes place between men and women from different clans, with an asymmetric relationship governing the movement of women. This relationship, often expressed by the phrase '*dalihan na tolu*', can be further classified into a relationship with the *hula-hula*, a group that gives women to another group, and a relationship with the *boru*, a group that takes women from another group. One should always be respectful and meek in one's dealings with a *hula-hula*. As evidenced by the existence of a proverb that states '*Hula-hula* are gods visible to the eye', people who do not cherish their own *hula-hula* are believed to be punished by *hula-hula*'s '*sahala*' (spiritual power). By contrast, Toba Batak can demand a respectful and obedient attitude from their *boru*. Of course, this means that they will use their *sahala* to protect their *boru* in return.

These kinship relations are the most important category controlling Toba Batak social life, especially in settlements. A new settlement is established by members of a single clan, and they maintain some special economic and political privileges as the settlement's founding clan, the Siswan Buru (the people who planted the bamboo fence). Usually it is only the members of the Siswan Buru clan that are deemed to have rights relating to land use, as well. It often happens that some men who have taken women from a clan, and who themselves are from a different clan, reside in a particular village as *boru*. They dwell there, having been granted restricted land rights, but they naturally occupy a low position in the village in terms of their status in customary law. As this situation in the settlement is important, let me quote from a certain sermon. This is something that I recorded at a prayer meeting of an ethnic association, which I will describe later.

> My village was built by the Sitompul Clan that came from Tarutung[1].
> We [the preacher's family] were in business there, but the Siswan Buru were the Sitompul Clan. There were only a few clans living in the village; and because the other clans (not of the Sitompul Clan) were their *boru*, the Sitompul Clan were like kings. The reason for this was that *boru* had to respect their *hula-hula*. I thought that the Sitompul Clan was the biggest clan in the world. (3 October 2004, Sitompul Sirinkiron Clan prayer meeting)

The preacher who gave this sermon was a man from the Siagian Clan living in Medan, but he was born as a *boru* in a Sitonpul Clan village, and spent his boyhood there. It is precisely because he grew up in such an environment that he could feel that the Sitompul Clan, the pioneering clan in the village, were like 'kings', and think that they were 'the biggest clan in the world'.

The customary law rituals of the Toba Batak can truly be said to be a concentration of these social relations. At a wide variety of occasions, including births, baptisms, weddings, funerals, reburials, construction and so on, the Toba Batak conduct rituals, but the basic structure of these rituals is almost identical. Confronted by life's rites of passage or major events, all Toba Batak aim to have blessings given through the power of the *hula-hula* group's *sahala*. To that end, the organizing group itself, while depending upon the cooperation of their own *boru* group, invite the *hula-hula* group to the ceremony, and as well as showing them respect by means of speeches and dances, they give them prescribed gifts. By way of response to this, the *hula-hula* group give blessings to the organizers through speeches, dances and gifts. In particular, the *magulosi*, in which a cloth called *ulos* is placed on the shoulders of the organizer, is conducted in concert with words of blessing and dancing, and forms the highlight of the ceremony. In this manner, in customary law rituals, the fundamental principles that constitute settlement society are expressed in a condensed form through various physical movements, symbolic assets, and the like.

Conversely, Toba Batak are also known as followers of Protestant Christianity. The HKBP (Protestant Batak Christian Church), of which the majority of Toba Batak are devotees, is one of the foremost Protestant denominations in Indonesia, with 3,017 churches and more than three million members as of 2003,[2] and 103 churches in Medan (HKBP 1998). Among the Toba Batak, it was the German Rheinische Missions-Gesellschaft (Rheinish Mission Board) that succeeded in Christian evangelism, where others had repeatedly failed. Its missionary work, which began in 1861, is thought to have succeeded through making practical use of Toba language and customs. In particular, the way the missionaries transitioned the villagers into an organization of believers without disrupting village order by means of first converting a person of influence, such as the chieftain, and making them into a church official before Christianizing the entire village, is said to have been a contributing factor to the large volume of converts over a comparatively short space of time (Pederson 1970: 63). Churches belonging to HKBP, which is descended from this Rheinische Missions-Gesellschaft, have been erected all over Indonesia following Toba Batak migration, and can now be seen in nearly all cities. As most of its churches use Toba language bibles and hymns and conduct their Sunday worship services in Toba, their devotees are almost solely restricted to Toba Batak. If anything, HKBP often emphasizes the fact that it itself is a 'guardian of the customary law' of the Toba Batak, and is considered to have actively taken on a role as the bastion of Toba Batak identity as their 'ethnic church' (Bruner 1972; Kimura 2005).

Medan and Toba Batak immigrants

Medan, located on the eastern coast of Sumatra in the Republic of Indonesia, is the island's largest city. With a population of about two million,[3] it is both the capital of the state of North Sumatra and a thriving commercial centre, boasting a fine port in Belawan facing the Straits of Malacca.

Once nothing but a small village occupied by Malays, Medan underwent rapid expansion after Jacob Nienhuys of the Netherlands founded a company called Deli Maatschappij in 1869 and promoted the development of tobacco plantations in that area, growing to become the economic and political centre of North Sumatra. In the 1950s, and particularly following independence, Medan attracted migration from other areas, and has developed into one of the foremost multiethnic cities in Indonesia.

Toba Batak migration to Medan was triggered by the hiring of 132 Toba Batak by an opium company that opened for business in 1912 (Hasselgren 2000: 141). Though their number was not very great,[4] in recent years it has been the dominant view that their experience as a Christian minority in the locality of Medan, under the control of a Muslim sultan, provided a strong driving force behind Toba Batak ethnic formation.

Toba Batak migration rapidly increased from the 1950s onwards. Over this period, migrants from all over the island of Sumatra set their sights on Medan, but even among these, Toba Batak migrants showed a pronounced increase. What Figure 6.1 shows is the population composition of Medan in 1930 and in 1981. The way the Toba Batak, who accounted for a mere one percent of the population in 1930, had grown to become Medan's second largest ethnic group in the 1980s is clearly exhibited in this figure.

Figure 6.1 Ethnic composition of Medan City

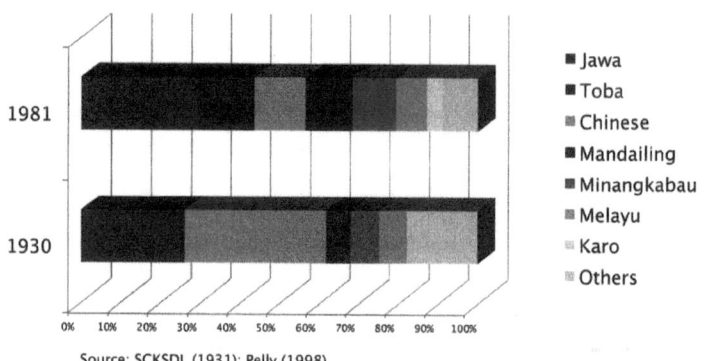

Source: SCKSDL (1931); Pelly (1998).

Toba Batak ethnic associations in Medan

The ethnic associations that form the focus of this chapter – mutual-aid bodies – play a vital role in the social life of Toba Batak living in Medan. As Bruner points out, such organizations are not seen in the villages around Lake Toba, and are specific to urban migrant society (1972: 208). In other words, they came into being through the transplantation to the city of the worldview and values of village society embodying an order dictated by bloodline and marriage. It is usual for Toba Batak residing in Medan to join this kind of mutual-aid organization and attend the prayer-cum-association meetings that they regularly conduct.

There are two broad categories of Toba Batak ethnic associations evident in Medan, namely, the district association (STM = Serikat Tolong Menolong) based on territorial bonds, and the clan association, united by ties of blood. The former, in simple terms, is an ethnic association formed by Toba Batak living in adjacent areas in order to offer mutual aid and to resolve issues in the local community, and it is typical for a prayer-cum-association meeting to be held about twice monthly at the home of an association member. The latter clan association is, as the name suggests, an organization of people with the same patrilineal clan (*marga*), the axis around which Toba Batak interpersonal relationships revolve. It is common practice in the households of Toba Batak living in Medan to belong to two different clan associations, one on the father's side and one on the mother's side. In the case of even larger-scale clans, these are frequently divided into several sub-clans, and in such cases this involves participating in a sub-clan's clan association in addition to that of the main clan.

Prayer meetings are held on a rotating basis at members' homes. In brief, these usually take the form of a sermon given by one pre-determined person as the main event, with the addition of prayers by several others chosen on the spot and the choral singing of hymns. The prayers, entitled 'Start of meeting', 'Open the sermon', 'Close the sermon', 'People who have come', 'Owner of the house', 'Close of meeting' and so on, are assigned to appropriate persons. I have also heard it said that care is taken to ensure that it is not the same person who always prays, and that people who are skilled at giving prayers are teamed with those who are not. As the number of participants in prayer meetings can range from less than twenty to about sixty, even if each participant's turn to lead prayers does not come about frequently, being occasionally called upon to perform this task could be termed an inescapable duty. Moreover, being skilful at leading prayers is an important matter that can impact on an individual's social evaluation, and one often hears amusing tales of people who were unable to produce a suitable prayer.[5]

Previous studies

There have been several prior studies of Toba Batak ethnic associations. In conducting an examination of the Toba Batak community in Medan prior to Indonesian independence, Hasselgren (2000) points out the important role fulfilled by ethnic associations in the formation of identity as Toba Batak. Bruner, on the other hand, as well as conducting ethnographies of Toba Batak ethnic associations in the 1950s when Toba Batak migration rapidly increased, viewed them as an adaptive strategy that attempted to provide a new understanding to their own worldview and values in the context of urban society (1961, 1972).

This research can be said to have focused on the role played by Toba Batak ethnic associations in the process of migrating from regional areas to the city and establishing a footing there. Figure 6.2 shows population changes in Medan, and it is evident that the 1950s, with which Bruner dealt, were indeed the first period when the population of Medan began to increase. In that sense, Bruner's research is a valuable record of the Toba Batak migrants who initially set foot in Medan, with almost no basis for a livelihood nor any established networks.

However, what can be appreciated from the figure is that an even steeper rise occurred after 1965, especially in the 1970s. That period roughly coincides with the establishment of Suharto's 'New Order' (*Orde Baru*) and the subsequent firming of the foundations for long-term rule. The Suharto regime promoted such slogans as 'progress' and 'nation-building', actively

Figure 6.2 Population growth in Medan

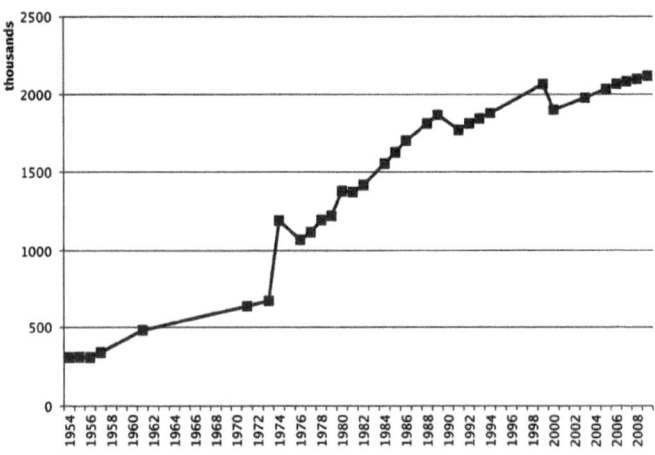

Source: SCKDSL (1931); Pelly (1998); BPS SUMUT (2009).

solicited investment from overseas and fostered Indonesia's dramatic economic growth. This kind of growth underpinned the explosive increase in Medan's population. Many of the ethnic associations that continue to this day were those established during this period.

What is more, it would not be surprising if the significance and function of ethnic associations were to have undergone transformation, since nearly fifty years have passed since the migration boom. Many Batak living in urban areas in the 1950s were born in the Toba region and later moved to cities including Medan in search of opportunities for education and employment. Now, however, there is an increasing number of second- and third-generation Medan-born Batak, and generations that feel a greater degree of familiarity with the lingua franca of Bahasa Indonesia than the Toba language are on the increase. For such people, what might the meaning of the ethnic associations be?

Below, I examine the changes in function of the Toba Batak ethnic associations in Medan, comparing three examples. Firstly, as an ethnic association from the first period of migration in the 1950s, I examine the case of the Simanjuntak Clan through material from Bruner's ethnography, as mentioned above. Next, in order to trace the changes from that time until the present, I take one example each of a neighborhood association and clan association and analyze their 'constitutions'. In these ethnic associations, amendments to constitutions have been effected, and I wish to move forward with my consideration in light of these points of amendment.

Case studies of association functions

Ethnic associations in 1950

The ethnic association analyzed by Bruner as an example of those in Medan belongs to the Simanjuntak Clan, many of whose members are economically successful. People of the Simanjuntak Clan who migrated to Medan initially established an association in 1934 along with the Siahaan and Hutagaol Clans, it being believed that their ancestors were brothers. Due to a subsequent increase in clan membership, however, an association solely for the Simanjuntak Clan was formed in 1942. According to Hasselgren (2000), this was the first clan association established by the Toba Batak in Medan.

Bruner (1961) conducted a survey of this Simanjuntak Clan in the 1950s and described its functions. Primarily, the association extended financial aid when its members held funeral ceremonies. The amount of aid given was 300 rupiah in the case of an elderly person who had grandchildren, but in line with Batak custom, when the deceased was younger and with fewer descendants, the sum was less. The assistance was not only monetary as it was also an important function of the association's membership to attend members' funerals and other rites of passage and to fulfill the roles that kin ought to perform in these ceremonies. According to Bruner, as the Medan Toba Batak community grew, the question arose as to what to do about funerals and weddings. In the beginning, on the occasion of such rites of passage, the migrants would return to their own villages and hold the ceremonies there, as it was difficult to conduct rituals in the city where they were unable to obtain aid for preparing and conducting the ceremonies. As the Toba Batak community burgeoned and there was also an increase in people from the same clan, however, momentum arose to help each other and hold rituals in Medan. In such circumstances, ethnic associations fulfilled the function of supporting ceremonies in place of villages.

Yet, according to Bruner's reports, ethnic associations in the 1950s also played roles apart from fulfilling functions to facilitate rituals. One of these was to offer revolving loans called *arisan*, which are widely seen in Indonesia. Bruner does not elaborate, but in general, the way these work is that members each contribute a set amount monthly, with one individual in turn, determined by drawing lots or the like, receiving the entire sum. In this way members accommodate each other with lump sums. During this time, associations also offered scholarships for members' children or relatives to attend school. Ethnic associations of the 1950s thus also fulfilled the role of providing necessary aid for newly arrived Toba Batak migrants to build a foundation for their livelihoods in Medan.

Neighborhood associations

Next, I look at an example of a neighborhood association, based on my own surveys. I examine the association in S. Avenue's U. District, which is a residential area in northwest Medan. Until the 1960s, this vicinity comprised paddy fields owned by Javanese, but as the urban area of Medan expanded it changed into a residential district. When a permanent market was constructed at the eastern end of S. Avenue, Toba Batak who operated small-scale retail activities there gradually came to reside in U. District in a concentrated manner. This culminated in the establishment in 1969 of 'STM Tapian Nauli',[6] the district's Toba Batak neighborhood association. From around this time, U. District began to attract attention as a residential area that was comparatively close to the city, and middle-class Toba Batak such as civil servants and company employees started to migrate there. Table 6.1 below shows a list of occupations of Toba Batak residing in U. district. It is evident that in addition to the retailers who were the initial residents, the white-collar cohort comprising civil servants and the like came to occupy a fairly large proportion. Based on their economic clout, a Toba Batak ethnic church, HKBP M. Church, was built in this district in 1976. In addition, business people who noted the growth of this area's Toba Batak community constructed a Toba Batak wedding hall next to the church in 1987. In this way, as some parts of the neighborhood association's constitution that did not align with the current situation emerged, along with the maturation of the U. district Toba Batak community, revision of the neighborhood association's constitution was carried out in 1996, a quarter-century after its formation.

Table 6.1. The residents in U District according to their occupations

Occupation	Number	
Civil servant	12	
Commercial	11	
Teacher	4	
Self-employed	4	
Military	2	
Driver	2	
Plantation owner	2	
Priest	2	
Others	3	Lawyer, construction laborer etc.

Though U. District arguably has a comparative concentration of Toba Batak residents, it must be noted that the community in question has a completely different structure from the villages. Table 6.2 shows the number of households resident in U. District, classified by clan. The largest clan, Sitanggan, is one of those that first began to live in this area, and because its members later invited their relatives and such, four households now reside here. However, even the Sitanggan Clan has a completely different status from one such as that of the core clan in a village, there being a whopping thirty-six clans dwelling in U. District overall.

Table 6.2 The households in U District according to clan membership

Number of Households	Clan
4	Sitanggan
3	Sihombing, Simanjuntak, Simarmata, Simbolon, Siregar
2	Butarbutar, Hutahean, Lubis, Manalu, Napitupulu, Pasaribu, Siahaan
1	Aritonang, Bangun, Batubara, Hasibuan, Hutapea, Hutasoit, Manik, Manullang, Manurung, Naibaho, Pandiangan, Panggabean, Panjaitan, Pardede, Purba, Siagian, Silaban, Silaen, Simamora, Simaremare, Sinaga, Sitindaon, Siahaan

From the rules and regulations instituted in 1969 when the neighborhood association was established in this district, it can be seen that this association also deems cooperation in members' rituals to be its main function. Firstly, when funerals are held, members of the district's association can receive aid from the organization. In the case of the death of an adult member, the substance of that aid constitutes something like: 1) a coffin; 2) the burial; 3) an ambulance; 4) an accompanying motor vehicle, restricted to the Medan city limits; 5) three kg of beef from water buffalo or cattle; 6) three kg of sugar; 7) two kg of coffee; and 8) one kg of rice from each member. In regards to items 5–8, however, differences in quantity in accordance with the status of the deceased can be observed (see Table 6.3 below). As can be seen in the table, in the STM association rules, there is division into five different cases, with the amount of goods to be distributed according to whether the deceased was an adult member (= married person), their child (= unmarried person), their parent, or an adult or child staying with them as a guest. This difference is based upon Toba Batak custom. While a married person's funeral is conducted in grand style over several days, in the case of an unmarried person, the body is buried after only a simple funeral (Siahaan 1982: 99). Such ranking of funerals is reflected in the quantity of goods given as aid.

Table 6.3 Aid by STM on the occasion of a funeral

	Adult	Child	Parent	Guest (adult)	Guest (child)
Water buffalo meat/beef	3kg	2kg	3kg	1.5kg	1kg
Sugar	3kg	2kg	3kg	1.5kg	1kg
Coffee	2kg	1kg	2kg	1kg	0.5kg
Rice (from each member)	1kg	1kg	1kg	0.5kg	0.5kg

In the constitution, when a member's child marries, it is customary for the neighborhood association to give stipulated aid. If the child is female, one piece of ceremonial shoulder-wrap cloth (*ulos ragi hotang*) is given, while if the child is male, a monetary gift (*tumpak*) of the same value as the cloth is bestowed. In Toba Batak custom, invited guests on the bride's side give the newlyweds ceremonial cloth, while conversely, invited guests on the groom's side hand monetary gifts to the newlyweds; thus these rules could be said to be based on regulations in the constitution.

What also cannot be overlooked is that on the occasion of rituals such as funerals or weddings, this neighborhood association does not merely extend material aid, but also provides the personnel essential for running the ceremony. In Article Nine of the constitution on the obligations of members, Items One to Three are stipulated as follows:

1. When a member is holding a ceremony, each member is to respond to a call in the following manner:

2. To help in the execution of the ceremony in accordance with Tonggo Raja;

3. To give a congratulatory or memorial speech on the occasion of the ceremony.

In Toba Batak *adat* (customary law), the cooperation of people called *Dongan Sahuta* (people of the same village) is essential in the preparations for and running of ceremonies. The above-mentioned *Tonggo Raja* was also originally a site where *Dongan Sahuta* would gather to discuss the carrying-out of ceremonies, but in cities like Medan, it is usual for neighborhood associations to perform the role in its place. Moreover, as in Item Three, the neighborhood association has assumed the role of making a congratulatory speech or memorial address during ceremonies as *Dongan Sahuta*. This simultaneously means that the neighborhood association has certain rights within the ceremony, and at such times as the distribution of meat and money, people from the neighborhood association can receive a fixed share. As such, the neighborhood association fulfils a function as a fictive 'village' in Medan City in the *adat*-like rituals of local Toba Batak.

As previously stated, however, this U. District neighborhood association implemented a revision of its constitution in 1996. What was amended was the content of the aid vis-à-vis rituals. Firstly, in the case of a funeral, aid that was originally in the form of tangible goods such as water buffalo meat, sugar, coffee and rice was changed to involve the exchange of cash. The monetary amount was 200,000 rupiah in the case of an adult member, with the sum being reduced accordingly in the case of a child, a guest or the like. It was a similar case with weddings, and it was decided to give aid in the form of 30,000 rupiah in cash instead of ceremonial cloth. In this manner, although the framework of giving aid in ritual settings is being preserved, the substance of the assistance has shifted from tangible goods to cash. If we bear in mind that these goods, especially the ceremonial cloth and such things as meat and rice, are not mere consumer goods in Toba Batak rituals, but are symbolic assets, then we can perhaps regard the neighborhood association as on a path of departure from the worldview of customary law.

Clan associations

Next, I will deal with Ijolma Clan's association as an example of such. Clan associations are those formed by members of the same clan who live in close proximity. The significance of the clan to the Toba Batak is as I have already described, and in Medan, most of the major clans have such associations.

Strictly speaking, Ijolma Clan, which I discuss here, is one of the branch clans of the Batubara Clan. Members of Ijolma Branch Clan usually claim Batubara as their family name, and are also members of Batubara clan associations. According to Toba Batak genealogy (Tarombo), the Batubara Clan are a group deemed to be descendents of Datubara, the seventh generation[7] after Si Raja Batak, who is taken to be the common ancestor of the Toba Batak.[8] Around the beginning of the 1980s, however, due to resistance towards using the word *datu*, meaning 'shaman' or 'witch doctor', as the clan's name, the clan as a whole changed its surname from Datubara to Batubara, and now all members, bar a small number of exceptions, identify themselves as Batubara. This Batubara Clan established a clan association in Medan in the 1960s, before the others. The people of Ijolma Branch Clan also joined this Batubara Clan Association and engaged in its activities.

Ijolma Branch Clan is a group of people who claim Ijolma, six generations after the Datubara in question, as their common ancestor. However, Ijolma Branch Clan maintains the legend that their ancestor Ijolma was murdered and buried by his brothers out of jealousy over his skills in sorcery, and so they harbor complex feelings towards other Batubara Clan members, especially the descendents of those siblings. Such rivalry was at work behind the establishment in 1983 of an exclusive Ijolma Branch Clan Association in Medan. One can clearly see this awareness in construction projects for monuments to ancestors. After Independence, among Toba Batak clans it began to be popular to trumpet the clan's prosperity by erecting monuments to its pioneers. In such cases, moreover, it often happened that clan associations in Medan, which had more economic power than the villages, played an important role as sponsors. A Batubara monument was also built in 1966 on the initiative of their clan association in Medan. The people of Ijolma Branch Clan also contributed in various ways to the construction of this monument. On the other hand, an incident occurred in 1989 involving the appearance of Ijolma in the dream of a certain female member instructing her to find his bones and erect a monument. As a result of consultation, the people of Ijolma Branch Clan acted in accordance with this instruction, exhuming Ijolma's remains and interring his bones in a reburial grave constructed in his homeland of Banuarea. The Ijolma Clan Association in Medan that I am discussing here provided financial backing for this ritual.

An examination of the constitution set down in 1983 will show that this ethnic association, too, prioritized giving aid on ceremonial occasions as their principal aim. Firstly, when a funeral was held, the association gave 100,000 rupiah in aid for a member's funeral, or 50,000 rupiah for that of a member's child. In the case of a wedding ceremony, it was stipulated that one piece of ceremonial cloth (*ulos ragi hotang*), or 35,000 rupiah, was to be given. Even in cases of other rituals hosted by members, association officials discuss among themselves and give an appropriate sum of monetary aid, and so even more nuanced aid is extended by neighborhood associations. Of course, their participation is essential for carrying out Toba Batak rituals in the city, given the importance they attach to their clans. Even in associations' constitutions, attendance at members' life rituals is demanded.

Interestingly, this ethnic association, formed in the 1980s, has new functions that are not observed in other ethnic associations. Primarily, it pays 50,000 rupiah to any member who has met with a natural disaster. Similarly, in a case where a member is hospitalized for five or more days, it pays them 25,000 rupiah. Having such a compensatory function vis-à-vis calamities is a new aspect not seen in previous examples.

Conclusion

From the three examples of ethnic associations discussed above, we have been able to find commonalities and disparities in their functions. Arguably, the point that has not changed is the fact that these associations have as their greatest objective the provision of aid for rituals such as members' weddings or funerals. As I stated at the beginning, Toba Batak rituals have at their essence the receipt of the power of blessings through exchange of stipulated symbolic assets with members of their mother's and grandmother's clans. As villages are composed of clans as their unit, it is not difficult to invite such relatives, it merely being necessary to invite people who hail from one's mother's or grandmother's village. For Toba Batak migrants who have left their villages and live in Medan, however, it is no simple matter to find kin with whom to exchange symbolic assets. It is the ethnic associations that facilitate this exchange. In actuality, when quizzed as to their reason for participating in an ethnic association, many informants replied that it is so that people will come along when a ceremony is held. Conversely, one often hears small-talk to the effect that there were scarcely any attendees at the wedding of someone who usually showed little zeal for their ethnic association, and that their wedding was thus a very forlorn affair.

It is not that there has been no change in the function of ethnic associations in relation to rituals, either. The example of the neighborhood association in U. District is worthy of note in this regard. In the initial stage after its establishment in 1969, this association provided such necessary things as labor and goods, foodstuffs and symbolic assets for members' rituals. As I have stated above, aid was listed in concrete detail in the constitution, comprising a coffin, ambulance, the task of burial, meat, rice and so on. Through a 1996 amendment to the constitution, however, these kinds of assistance were changed to aid in the form of cash. Though differences in the monetary amount according to the attributes of the deceased were maintained, all other specificity of the aid was lost, and the requirement to donate effort and time also disappeared. In the examples of clan associations introduced by Bruner, aid in the form of cash was being implemented in the 1950s, and it is exceptional for this neighborhood association to have carried out the kind of concrete aid that would also be applicable to village society; but that, too, has been gradually lost.

The revolving loan function reported by Bruner on the 1950s was not seen in the other examples I have dealt with in this chapter. Even in my own interview surveys, I did hear of several clan and neighborhood associations having once operated revolving loans, but I do not know of any cases in which these are continuing at present. I have heard that the reasons for stopping the practice were that though revolving loans had once been effective as capital for starting up businesses, including sole trading, there was a gradual intensification of entertainments such as gambling, and there was trouble in the form of people 'making off with the winnings' by quitting the association without making further contributions, and so on. Nobody in present-day ethnic associations has heard of the scholarship reported by Bruner, either. Their point in common was that associations were bodies fulfilling the function of assisting migrants without a base for their livelihood in Medan by supplying part of the funds needed for them to establish such a foundation. Nowadays, when a half-century has passed since the migration boom and second- and third-generation Toba Batak have grown in number, the associations perhaps can be said to have finished with that role.

Conversely, the Ijolma Clan Association, established in the 1980s, had a function that had previously not been seen, namely, a mechanism for giving aid in times of natural disaster or hospitalization due to illness. Here, it could be said that they focus the content of their mutual aid on insurance against the risks that rain down in life. This does not mean that such aid can be observed in all associations, but it could be argued that a transformation in the migrant community as previously described is behind this kind of change that has taken place in the content of 'mutual aid' in associations.

7 The Dynamics of Household Rituals in Mongolia: After undergoing Religious Control under the Socialist Regime

Katsuhiko Takizawa

The religious situation in Mongolia has undergone drastic changes since the collapse of socialism in 1990. During the socialist era, virtually all religious activities were banned, however, as the country democratized, Buddhism and Shamanism which had been suppressed were revived and foreign creeds such as Christianity have shown remarkable development.

Looking at this phenomenon from the religious group level, it may be defined as the 'revival of religion'. However, religions had, in fact, remained very much alive throughout the socialist era at a more personal level. In this chapter, we focus on 'household rituals', or ritual expressions at the household level, as a framework that allows us to examine the phenomenon through and after the socialist era and analyze the dynamics, drawing on field research.

Household rituals were not practiced simply as the remnants of customs from the pre-socialist era. As religions were ousted from the public arena through purging and socialistic regimentation, 'household' became an important locus for religious expression. While adapting to changes in the social environment such as settlement, these ritual practices contributed to the promotion of individualization and the diversification of religions.

Introduction

Mongolia (the Mongolian People's Republic until 1992) was governed by a socialist regime from 1924 to 1990. The period, lasting almost seventy years, was an era of religious control. The move was intensified during the purge that began in 1937, through which the country's 800 or so Buddhist temples were all destroyed or closed down. Then, for the fifty years that followed, almost all religious activities were officially banned.

The transition into capitalism, beginning in 1990, brought the liberalization of religion along with the liberalization of the economy, and the situation surrounding religiosity has developed intensively and diversely ever since. While existing religions such as Buddhism, Islam and Shamanism revived, foreign creeds such as Christianity and Bahaism also gained popularity and increased their followers. For example, the number of Buddhist temples surged from only one to ninety-three up to 1992 (Tsedendamba 2003: 67) and the number of Shamans in eastern Mongolia is also showing a steep rise (Shimamura 2002: 90). The number of Protestant churches is now in excess of 200, with followers amounting to one to two percent of the nation's population, even at a modest estimate.[1]

We must, without any doubt, regard this phenomenon as the 'revival of religion' and record such developments in the annals of history, but this is not the only element that explains the current religious situation.[2] If we discussed this purely at the religious group level, we would be ignoring the existence of religions for the fifty-year period following the purge. The truth is that religion continued at a personal level, reproducing itself through daily religious rituals, and remained deeply embedded in people's minds as a framework through which to interpret and express experiences such as death. 'Household' was a territory that played a particularly important role in confronting the forces of external religious control and, while absorbing the changes in the social environment such as collectivization and settlement, it became the locale where religious customs and ideas were maintained and developed. In this chapter, we shall focus on the importance of 'household rituals' as a framework that allows us to capture the religious situation in Mongolia during socialism and post-democratization on a continuous timeline and analyze the dynamics through locally-based fieldwork.

Socialism and religions in Mongolia

Often mocked as 'the sixteenth republic of the Soviet', the political autonomy of the Mongolian People's Republic was fragile and its religious policy interlocked closely with Soviet policy and international relations. As such, when the socialist system was established, anti-religious policy was also adopted in Mongolia. However, until the early 1930s, the policy focused more on legal measures, such as excluding religion from education or taxing religious groups. This changed when the purge began in 1937 where hard-line measures did not falter. According to Fukuda:

> [I]n the Soviet Union, religious issues were entwined with ethnic issues. The Soviets were afraid that the connection with the outside world would weaken the Soviet system and therefore Islam among the Asian ethnic groups and the Catholic Church in Lithuania were regarded as threats. (1998: 55)

The situation was no better for Buddhists. In fact, these people 'faced the severest situation of all cultural and religious groups among the citizens of the Soviet Union' (Kolarz 1961: 449). One of the reasons behind this was the geopolitical situation of the time. Tensions were rising in Europe and the Soviets needed to resolve the issues in the Far East as quickly as possible. Given the situation, Buddhists were looked upon with hostility as dangerous elements that could potentially collaborate with Japan. By eradicating Buddhism, a remnant of the old regime, the Soviet Union also managed to conclusively strengthen its influence in Mongolia. The religious oppression in Mongolia was far more intense than the situation in the Soviet Union. More than 17,000 monks were executed during the purge that took place mainly around 1937.[3] These monks would have constituted a significant proportion of the adult males in Mongolia, considering that the population was only 738,000 at the time (1935) (Tanaka 1992: 263–264). In addition, the 800 or so temples that existed at the time were all destroyed or closed down by 1940 and almost all the lamas, who constituted a third of the adult males of the country, returned to their secular lives.[4] In 1944, the Gandan Temple of Ulan Bator, the head temple of Mongolian Buddhism, was restored but members were kept under strict surveillance by the government and their range of activities was strictly limited. For the fifty years following that time, almost all religious activities were publically banned.

The religious policy of Soviet socialism was based on scientific atheism and was in effect 'an experiment to see if religion could be excluded from a nation or a society' (Fukuda 1998: 47). In principle, the individuals' freedom of religion was guaranteed even if the nation and religion were to be separated. However, in reality, the ultimate goal was to eliminate religion from the minds of the people. The ideology of scientific atheism was to replace the interpretive framework of the world that religion had provided to the people. It is clear that such substitution of worldview ended in failure, evident in the religious consciousness survey conducted after the collapse of the socialist regime.[5] The most decisive aspect of this failure was, as Froese notes, that 'scientific atheists were not aware of the non-empirical essence of the religious concepts and stories' (2004: 47). At the end of the day, scientific atheists could not assemble an ideological system that could replace religion. On the contrary, as it is often pointed out, atheism became more quasi-religious as time passed (Lewis 2000: 16; Froese 2004: 43).

So, the attempt to create a new worldview of scientific atheism did not succeed. However, the effort to exclude the conventional religious worldview may have succeeded to a certain extent through the indirect means of suppressing religious activities. The loss of the religious worldview deprived people of the framework and language that allowed them to interpret and express death and religious experiences (Lewis 2000:

14). To explain the diversification of religions and the trend of cults after the collapse of socialism from this perspective (Fukuda 1998: 57–58) would be a valid approach to understanding religiosity during and after socialism in a continuous timeline. However, if the process of the loss of religious perspectives and the search for a new framework were to be reduced to a personal concern, the majority of the historical and social aspects of socialism would be abstracted. It is therefore important to emphasize at this stage that for many ethnic and religious groups, anti-religious policies were often imposed upon the people by external forces. This is due to the fact that between external pressures and individuals there always exists some form of social organization that acts as a buffer system. In reality, this was exactly why the destruction of these social organizations became the next agenda for the Soviets. In other words, in order to reform the religious worldview, they had to reform the social structure that supported such perspectives.

In the next section, we will present an overview of the relationship between the socialistic reform process of these social organizations and the religious policies in Mongolia in order to accentuate the profile of the 'household rituals' to be discussed in this chapter.

Social structure of nomadic society and change

The nomadic society was a major impediment in terms of the establishment of the Soviet's socialist regime. This was because the existing power structure was closely associated with nomadic social organizations, and these could not easily be controlled through colonization, as was the case with the settled society. The ideology behind the settlement and collectivization of the nomadic society was 'to modernize the backward, unproductive and old fashioned nomadic style of economy by the economy of the settled society' (Kimura 1999: 175). However, this endeavor was inevitably connected to another goal, which was to disaggregate the existing social structures.

For this very reason, settlement and collectivization were met with fierce resistance from the existing social structures. For example, in Central Asia, the tribal bonding of nomadic societies became an obstacle.[6] Given the situation, the Soviet had to compromise to a certain extent in order to advance with the socialistic systematization.[7] Consequently, even in the cases of successful settlement, existing social structures were strongly reflected in aspects such as residential pattern. For example, in the case of a kolkhoz in Kyrgyzstan, groups with the same paternal line 'tended to live as a unit or within several neighboring street regions, with relatives from the paternal line also living close by' (Yoshida 1999: 154) even after settling down. In such cases, the street was often known by the group's family name and played an important role even in the post-settlement society.

As we have seen, the existing social structures could not be totally dismantled in the nomadic society of Central Asia and became a serious impediment for the Soviet's religious policies. This was because these social structures functioned as a buffer system that stood between the external forces, i.e., the religious policies and the individuals, in addition to becoming an important foundation for the reproduction of religious customs. Bearing these issues in mind, let us now look at the social structure of the nomadic society of Mongolia and the historical changes it underwent.

The smallest unit for residence and travel in the Mongolian nomadic society was the yurt. Yurts often got together to form a small group called *hot ail* (хот айл) to collectively perform seasonal pastoral activities (grazing, traveling, felt making, shearing, etc.). *Hot ails* were often formed with parents, sons and relatives but there were no rules maintaining them, so people were free to form *hot ails* with anyone depending on the needs of their lives or livelihood.[8] One of the largest factors that affected the formation of *hot ail* was the pressure of grazing in the grassland, in other words, the number of livestock. The grazing pressure was influenced by the state of the grassland or abundance of water, so the formation of yurts in a *hot ail* changed seasonally and the pattern was not necessarily the same every year. Such gathering and dispersal of *hot ails* were observed both prior to the socialistic collectivization as well as after the collapse of socialism (Sneath 1999: 174; Kazato 1999: 38).

In Mongolian nomadic society, categories for residence and social structures need to be considered separately. Yurts and *hot ails* can be classified in the residential category, but there is no equivalent social structure with a clear boundary at this level. 'Mongolian terms for family groups,' such as brothers (ах дүү) and relatives (хамаатан), 'refers to domains centering around the interviewee with no set boundaries' (Sneath 1999: 139). To a certain degree, a group living in the same yurt, or a household (өрх), may be considered as a basic unit of the social structure. However, while the households are mainly comprised of nuclear families, their structure varies from extended and multiple families to single parents with children or grandparents and grandchildren, and it is also not uncommon for non-family members to live inside a yurt. As we can see from here, the connection between residential group and social organization is rather fluid. The nomadic society is basically constituted of un-territorial networks of relatives, with the parents and children, brothers and married partners at the center, as well as acquaintances (танил). The residential group is merely a partial and fluid form of social organization that becomes visible by giving it a spatial boundary (Sneath 1999: 139). However, the fluidity of the residential group also allows for opportunities to reproduce the social network and in that regard, the formation of *hot ails* with various households can be used as a strategy to expand the network (Kazato 1999: 41).

In the pre-socialist era, there were higher-level social organization categories to which people identified themselves with to a certain degree. These were organizations based on blood relationships,[10] such as through lineages and clans as well as regional organizations where blood related organizations loosely collaborated within certain administrative regions. These organizations formed local authorities, headed by the aristocrats, and in the pre-socialist era, functioned as a buffer system against the higher governing system, contributing in terms of general social logistics such as the distribution of taxes and providing relief to the underprivileged (Oka 2002: 230–231). Such organizations had their own temples and worshiped their own *oboos* (овоо = build by stacking up stones) and were united in their religious solidarity.

These regional organizations could have acted as a buffer system against the anti-religious policies, as was the case in the Turk Muslim nomadic society of Central Asia. However, the exhaustive purge of the late 1930s not only wiped out the religious aspects of the regional organizations, namely the temples and *oboo* rituals, but also totally dismantled the existing authority system headed by the chiefs.

Collectivization

The next stage involved socialistic systematization through collectivization and settlement. Collectivization began in the 1930s, but proceeded rigorously through forceful measures such as a tax hike for self-employed farmers after the adoption of the Model Article of Incorporation for Agricultural and Stock Farm Cooperatives in March 1955. By 1959, virtually all pastoral people were integrated into *negdels* (хөдөө аж ахуйн нэгдэл)[11] (Onuki 1993: 231–235). This collectivization brought significant changes to the existing stock farming organization of *hot ails*. In the *negdel* system, *hot ails* were reorganized into stock farming units called *sori* (суурь). The formation of *sori* and the pastoral field assigned for each was designated by the *negdel*, and each *sori* had the responsibility of taking part in grazing the livestock owned by the cooperative.[12] Here, the free formation principle of *hot ails* was put to an end. Furthermore, many pastoral people who despised collectivization headed for the cities and this lead to a massive decline in the percentage of livestock farmers within the population. This also meant a surge in the number of animals each household had to care for and in order to cope with the grazing pressure, households became more and more isolated from each other.[13]

As above, the existing nomadic social structures were reorganized dramatically due to the purge and collectivization and were heading towards dismantlement and dispersal as a whole. However, with the democratization in 1990, *negdels* were disbanded and livestock were gradually privatized. With this, *hot ails* experienced a revival. In fact, while people still followed the general framework of the designated administrative regions, the level of freedom for the gathering and dispersal of *hot ails* increased more than ever with the collapse of family, regional or socialistic social structures in the higher order. This, as previously mentioned, can also be regarded as an attempt to restore the network through the formation of *hot ails* with various households.

There have also been movements to recognize the traditional family and regional organizations.[14] This is evident specifically in the revival of *oboo* rituals.[15] Each *oboo* is related to a specific regional organization and thus performing a ritual inevitably provokes a sense of affiliation with the relevant organization. Large-scale joint celebrations of *oboos* that took place at certain times of the year were also revived, often in conjunction with the regional Naadam (наадам: festival featuring horse racing and a sumo contest), with the intention to revive the pre-socialistic style as 'tradition'. However, the 'revival of traditions' in *oboo* rituals was often associated with the various interests of sponsors and participants and was not always all about the reproduction of regional affiliation (Ozaki 2002: 109–110). Humphrey compared the joint *oboo* rituals in ten regions and pointed out the diversity of the hosts or sponsors (1999: 125). For example, in regions where minority tribes live in close proximity and people have a relatively strong sense of affiliation to the family or region, we may see *oboo* rituals that contribute to the reproduction of regional and family identities. However, in a case the author surveyed in Zavhan *sum* (district) in Uvs Province, a native of the district who lived in Ulan Bator at the time built an *oboo* in 1991 based on what the elders told him about *oboos* from the old days, invited priests from Gandan Temple to conduct the ritual and hosted a Naadam. This massive joint ritual was never to be repeated again but even so, the recreated *oboo* was treated as the *oboo* of the regional organization[16] to which the man belonged and became a personal focus of worship.[17] This indicates that the current *oboo* rites have basically become quite personalized.

Settlement

Settlement was advanced in conjunction with collectivization. The public office of the district or *sum* (сум) that once moved with the nomadic migration was settled in the 1950s. The administrative center of the *sum* became the center for the *negdel* and settlement district with schools, hospitals and food factories etc. built around them. The same went for the centers of the *heseg* (хэсэг), the subordinate production organization of *negdel*, where a smaller scale of settlement district was formed (Onuki 1993: 241).

In Mongolia, the settlement process rarely reflected family and regional social organizations in terms of residential distribution. For example, in Hovd City, there are regions such as that commonly known as Oold (Өөлд), named after a tribe's name, but its boundary is not necessarily clear nor exclusive. Spatially demarcated administrative units such as street districts (гудамж) were more significant as the basis for socialistic systematization and advertisement, through which public activities (such as street cleaning and tree planting) known as Subbotnik, residents' meetings and lectures on scientific atheism were conducted.

The important point to note in the settlement process of Mongolia is the influence of nomadic residential style. There were two types of permanent residence, namely the apartment and *hashaa* (хашаа). *Hashaa* actually means 'fence' for livestock and, in the settlement situation, represented the wooden wall (or block wall) and the twenty m^2 area surrounded by this wall. The residential area was separated from the outside world by *hashaa*, two meter high boards closely lined up together, and in many cases, multiple yurts or independent houses were built inside. Each residence was occupied by a separate household and the composition of *hashaa* was extremely fluid. For example, according to a survey conducted by the author in the spring of 2004 (refer to Tables 7.1 and 7.2), the households of Interviewees 28, 49 and 51 lived in temporarily built yurts in the *hashaa* of their relatives or brothers during the winter seasons. As such, households often move between *hashaas*. When Interviewee 26 bought the *hashaa* where he now resides, he let a student, who lived in a yurt in this *hashaa* with the previous owner, stay on. As can be seen from this example, there are no strict restrictions as to who households chose to live with in the *hashaa*. In other words, we can say that *hashaa* residence is equivalent to the '*hot ail* in the settlement area' and wood walls would be equivalent to the grassland between the *hot ails*. In a relatively confined settlement area, concentrated living in areas such as street districts did not have much significance. The foundation of social networks manifest in the form of *hashaa* residence was an 'invisible' and unterritorial network of relatives and acquaintances, just like in *hot ails*. People knew where lamas (people who used to be lamas) lived even during the socialist era and visited them when their loved ones passed away or were sick, and this was made possible through such 'invisible' networks. Conversely, as previously described, the 'visible' territorial street districts functioned as units for socialistic systematization and anti-religious advertisement. These two layers of 'social relationships' each corresponded to the 'inside' and 'outside' of the house and dealt with the reality and principle of religion respectively.

As above, while the family and regional social organizations were dismantled and dispersed in the nomadic regions, settlement regions were reorganized into administrative units that were in principle anti-religious and as a result of all this, religions were excluded from public spaces. On the other hand, 'houses' (гэр: residence including yurts, independent houses and apartments) began to play an important role as the space for the maintenance and transformation of religions.[18] In the next section, let us define 'household ritual' as religious practice performed in the residential space called the 'house' by members who live in the same 'house' and examine its dynamics through reference to case studies.

Dynamics of household rituals

The specific case studies regarding the dynamics of household rituals described in this section are based on the results of a survey conducted by the author from January to March 2004 in the capital city Ulan Bator and Hovd City, the core city of the western region (refer to Tables 7.1 and 7.2).[19]

In the pre-socialist era, there were a number of rituals customarily performed in yurts. The household wife's daily ritual was to boil tea (tea with milk) and offer this to the Buddha (statue or picture of Buddha) or the god of the hearth-fire. She would then go outside and offer the tea to the heavens and earth or the sacred mountain. Traditionally, when offering tea outside, a special spoon called *tsatsal* was used and tea was offered in all four directions as the lady rotated in a circle. Where the families had strong faith, every night the head of the household would light the sacred light, burn incense and read Scripture and mantra to the Buddha. As a monthly ritual, the head of the household observed a certain day of the lunar calendar as a cleansing day (мацаг өдөр) and offered sacred light and incense in worship. As an annual ritual, the household lit the sacred light continuously from New Year's Eve to the Lunar New Year Day and invited the lama within fifteen days of the New Year to hold an auspicious service.

Table 7.1 Overview of the survey on household rituals in Ulaanbaatar

Interviewee number	The year interviewee was born in	Type of residence	About the Buddha images from the parents' generation	About the Buddha images currently in possession			Photo of the deceased	Offering of sacred fire	Offering of tea	
				Present or not, new or old	When they were acquired	Why were they acquired			To *hoimor*	Outside
1	1921	Yurt	There were not any	None	—	—	Yes	o	o	o
2	1925	House	Disposed in late 1930s	New	After democratization	Death of husband	Yes	o	o	?
3	1927	House	Eldest brother inherited	New	1986	Retirement	No	o	o	o
4	1930	Yurt	Interviewee inherited	Old	—	—	Yes	×	?	?
5	1930	Yurt	Interviewee inherited	Old	—	—	No	?	o	o
6	1938	Yurt	Eldest brother inherited	None	—	—	No	o	×	o
7	1943	House	There were not any	New	After 2000	?	Yes	o	o	o
8	1947	House	Disposed in 1973 after father's death	None	—	—	No	o	×	o
9	1947	Yurt	Younger brother inherited	None	—	—	Yes	o	×	o
10	1947	House	?	New	1970s and recent	?	Yes	o	o	o
11	1948	Yurt	Brother inherited	None	—	—	Yes	o	o	o
12	1950	Yurt	Disposed at the end of 1950s	None	—	—	No	×	×	×
13	1951	Yurt	Offered to Gandan Temple in 1977 after father's death	New	1995 and 1996	Child's sickness	No	o	o	o
14	1951	Yurt	?	New	More than ten years ago	?	?	?	o	o
15	1952	House	Interviewee inherited	Old	—	—	Yes	×	?	?
16	1956	Yurt	Destroyed during revolution	None	—	—	No	×	?	?
17	1956	House	?	Old and New	?	?	Yes	×	?	?
18	1959	House	?	New	Recent	Death of husband	Yes	o	o	×
19	1960	Yurt	There were not any	None	—	—	No	o	×	o
20	1961	House	Younger brother inherited	None	—	—	?	×	×	o
21	1962	Yurt	There were not any	New	After 1999	Advised by lama	No	o	×	o
22	1963	Yurt	?	None	—	—	No	×	?	?
23	1964	Yurt	?	New	1983	Marriage	No	o	o	o
24	1964	House	?	New	After democratization	Could not conveive a child	?	o	o	o
25	1965	Yurt	There were not any	None	—	—	No	×	×	×
26	1965	House	Still at parents' house	None	—	—	Yes	o	o	×
27	1965	Yurt	Offered to Gandan Temple after becoming a Christian	None	—	—	Yes	×	?	?
28	1967	Yurt	Still at parents' house	New	Around 1996	Purchasing livestock	No	o	×	o
29	1970	Yurt	Still at parents' house	None	—	—	No	×	×	o
30	1971	Yurt	Uncle inherited	None	—	—	No	o	×	o
31	1972	Yurt	?	None	—	—	?	×	o	o
32	1974	Yurt	There were not any	None	—	—	Yes	o	o	o
33	1974	House	Went missing	None	—	—	No	×	×	×
34	1974	Yurt	There were not any	None	—	—	No	×	?	?
35	1974	Yurt	Destroyed in interviewee's lifetime	None	—	—	Yes	o	o	o
36	1975	House	There were not any	None	—	—	No	o	×	×
37	1976	Yurt	There were not any	None	—	—	Yes	×	o	o
38	1977	House	There were not any	None	—	—	No	o	?	?
39	1978	Yurt	Still at home in the country	None	—	—	No	o	o	o

Notes: 1. 'Old' means that the interviewee has Buddha statues inherited from their parents; 'new' means interviewee has statues they acquired themselves.

2. Interviewees 7, 12, 20, 25, 27, 39 are Christians.

3. All information is as of the survey time, conducted from January to March 2004.

The Dynamics of Household Rituals in Mongolia

Table 7.2 Overview of the survey on household rituals in Hovd

Interviewee number	The year interviewee was born in	Type of residence	About the Buddha images from the parents' generation	About the Buddha images currently in posession			Photo of the deceased	Offering of sacred fire	Offering of tea	
				Present or not, new or old	When they were acquired	Why were they acquired			To *hoimor*	Outside
40	1929	Yurt	Disposed in 1954	None	—	—	No	o	x	o
41	1931	Yurt	Interviewee inherited	Old	—	—	Yes	o	o	o
42	1934	Yurt	Interviewee inherited	Old	—	—	Yes	o	o	o
43	1935	Yurt	Youngest brother inherited	New	After democratization	?	Yes	o	o	o
44	1942	Yurt	—	Old	—	—	Yes	o	o	o
45	1951	Yurt	?	New	After democratization	?	No	x	o	o
46	1951	Yurt	Did not have any	New	1979	?	Yes	o	o	o
47	1952	House	?	New	After democratization	?	Yes	?	?	?
48	1952	Yurt	Disposed in about 1976	New	After democratization	?	No	o	o	o
49	1954	Yurt	?	None	—	—	?	?	?	?
50	1962	Yurt	Did not have any	None	—	—	No	x	x	x
51	1965	Yurt	Did not have any	None	—	—	Yes	o	o	o
52	1974	Yurt	?	None	—	—	Yes	o	x	o
53	1974	Yurt	?	None	—	—	No	o	?	?
54	1974	Yurt	Still at parents' house	None	—	—	Yes	o	o	o

Notes: 1. 'Old' means that the interviewee has Buddha statues inherited from their parents; 'new' means interviewee has statues they acquired themselves.

2. Interviewees 7, 12, 20, 25, 27, 39 are Christians.

3. All information is as of the survey time, conducted from January to March 2004.

Many ritual tools and charms were kept in the yurts. Members would place charms such as weasel's fur at the entrance to protect them from evil and sacred cloth called *hadag* (хадаг) over the skylight, known as *tono* (тооно). The hearth at the center of the yurt was worshiped as the symbol of the yurt itself. The inheritance of a yurt was described as the 'inheritance of the hearth (or fire)'. When the children were ready to become independent and build their own yurt, a ritual to 'share the hearth (or fire)' (таслах) was conducted. The innermost place looking from the entrance of the yurt was called *hoimor* (хоймор: seat of honor) and was considered the most sacred place in the dwelling. This was the location where statues and pictures of the Buddha (hereinafter 'Buddha images') and various ritual tools such as the Scripture, Mani wheel, incense burner, auspicious pouch (даллагын уут) and offering plate were placed. The guardian Buddha, determined according to the birth year of the head of the family, was the main object of worship for the family and was to be placed in the *hoimor*. The youngest son of the family usually inherited this Buddha. In nomadic society, the sons would set up for themselves once they reached adulthood and would leave the parents' yurt with some of the family's livestock. The last son was thus left to inherit the parents' yurt (inheritance of the hearth). The inheritance of the Buddha basically also followed suit.

The purge that began in 1937 brought drastic changes to people's religious environments. As far as household rituals were concerned, people could no longer openly place their Buddha statues or religious tools in the *hoimor*, so they either disposed of them or hid them in the wardrobe box. In the survey, there were some who spoke of how they had disposed of their Buddha statues during the years of purge (Inrweviewees 2, 16), but not many. In fact, according to a social survey conducted at the end of the 1970s, 17.9% of the households actually owned Buddha statues (Vandangombo 1985: 4). Considering the majority of the households secretly possessed Buddha statues and that the nation's population had more than doubled from 1940 to 1980 (730,000 to 1,640,000), the survey result suggests that a high proportion of the Buddha statues that were worshiped in the yurts prior to the purge were actually maintained during the time leading to democratization.[20] Conversely, there were also cases even after the purge where Buddha images had to be abandoned for various reasons. We now examine a few of such cases.

The father of Interviewee 13 was a lama, but returned to secular life during the purge of 1937 and lived as a nomad since that time. The yurt had many Buddha images and scriptures but he secretly kept them all in the wardrobe box. The father continued to offer tea to the god of fire, the heavens and the Buddha every day and secretly read scriptures at people's houses when asked. However, when the father passed away in 1977, the interviewee entrusted all the Buddha images, scriptures and ritual tools to the Gandan Temple because he was not able to worship the Buddha in the proper way. Many other interviewees also cited the notion that 'one should not have a Buddha image if one cannot worship properly'. One of the interviewees mentioned this as a reason for not having a Buddha image in the house at this time (Interviewee 54). This notion was often accompanied by the concept of 'curse'. The father of Interviewee 8, who used to be a lama, also secretly possessed many Buddha images and ritual tools. However, when the father passed away in 1969, the older brother who inherited the Buddha statue fell ill and a lama with whom they consulted told them that the 'Buddha is angry because there is no one to worship'. So, the brother took the Buddha to this lama and had it burnt. Interviewee 44's uncle was a *khubilgan* (хувилган: reincarnation of a high priest), and his older brother inherited the Buddha images on his passing. However, the brother's child passed away in a traffic accident in 2003. The brother thought that 'the Buddha was angry as he was not in the hands of the person who was supposed to be worshiping', and so the Buddha statue was passed on to the interviewee. As we can see from here, people's deaths were often associated with the concept of 'curse' and became the trigger for the loss of statues.

Another factor that contributed to the disappearance of Buddha images from homes was children's independence from their parents' household. During the socialist era, there were occasions when Buddha images vanished but hardly any opportunities for the introduction of new ones.[21] Therefore, an increase in the number of children going independent signified a rise in the number of households without any Buddha images. This was also evident in the survey as households headed by generations born in the 1960s and after rarely owned Buddha images.

The survey also found that many households who did not own Buddha images still offered sacred light and tea at a special place in the house, such as the *hoimor*. Portraits of the deceased were often cited as the target of such rituals. Displaying portraits of the deceased was a custom introduced after photos became available in Mongolia, which would have been in the 1930s at the earliest and had become quite common by the 1940s and 50s. In some cases, pictures of the deceased were displayed instead of photos, but these pictures were drawn from the photos so they would have also been introduced at about the same time. It was obvious that these photos acted as substitutes for the Buddha images in an era where it was forbidden to keep such images in the *hoimor*. We already mentioned that people's deaths often prompted the loss of Buddha images from homes, but at the same time they also induced the reproduction of household rituals using photos of the deceased.

There were also some households that conducted rituals in front of empty *hoimor* (Interviewees 1, 6, 19, 36, 38, 40, 53). While Interviewee 34 said that they did not offer the sacred light because they did not have a Buddha image, Interviewee 39 said that they offered the sacred fire to the *hoimor* for his deceased father even though they did not have Buddha images or photos of the deceased because the head of the household was Christian. As such, the *hoimor* played a role in terms of offering the space for household rituals, and this contributed to the survival of rituals and the reproduction of their sacredness.

When you visit yurts in Mongolia, you will notice that household items are arranged in a very similar way.[22] Even modern household items such as washbowls, refrigerators and televisions are almost always placed in the same locations in all yurts (refer to Figure 7.1). In the pre-socialist era, the space in the yurt was categorized into territories that related to male, female, age and religious values. These regions were divided radially with the hearth at the center. The diameter connecting the entrance and *hoimor* formed an axis and looking from the hearth, the entrance side was called 'front' (өмнө), the *hoimor* side of the hearth was 'rear' (хойно), the left side of the axis looking from the entrance was 'right' (баруун) and the

Figure 7.1 Spatial configuration in a yurt

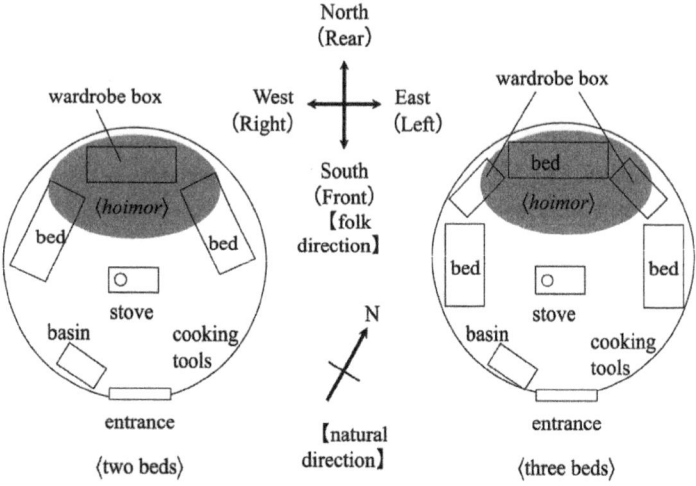

right side was 'left' (зүүн). The 'right' was regarded as men's territory and 'left' as women's territory but in a yurt, the master's position would be in the 'left rear', the wife's in the 'left front', the guests in the 'right' and the guest of honor in the 'rear' (= *hoimor*). The placement of yurt members also defined the way household items were located. The 'left front', the women's space, was where the cooking tools, plates and utensils were stored. The 'left rear', the men's space, was where hunting tools and horse gear used to be stored.[23]

As we have seen, the direction from the hearth determines the spatial division in the yurt. In the old days, the wall of the yurt was divided into twelve sections according to the twelve horary signs, and people could tell the time from where the sunlight from the skylight hit the wall (Hasumi 1993: 11). The direction in the yurt was extended to the recognition of direction in the outside world as well. In other words, the four directions were recognized based on the direction the entrance was facing. In the Mongolian language, 'front' and 'south', 'rear' and 'north', 'right' and 'west', 'left' and 'east' were represented by the same words. In some regions, the entrance of the yurt faced the southeast. However, the description that 'yurts are generally built facing south or southeast' (Hasumi 1993: 11) would not be accurate. To be precise, the entrance of the yurt faced 'south' in terms of the folk direction, and this 'south' sometimes leaned towards the southeast in the natural direction (refer to Figure 7.1).[24] There were many rituals based on the sense of direction centering on the yurt. According to the survey, offering tea outside was the most universal ritual of all and this tea was to be offered to all four directions. Another ritual was called 'leave the trace (мөр гархах)' and was conducted in the Lunar New Year, where one would walk towards the auspicious direction and then return home.

Everyday life in the yurt had always been practiced based on this sense of direction, so new household items were naturally arranged in the same manner. For example, the hearth in the yurt used to use the trivet, but when wood-burning stoves with chimneys were introduced by the Soviets in the 1940s, they were placed in a way so that the fire hole faced the left (east) because the territory of the women who used fire for cooking etc., was on the left. However, during the survey, yurts with their fire holes facing the right (west) side were noted (Interviewee 4, 30). These yurts switched the direction of the fire hole of the stove from left to right, as advised by the lama, when they had concerns about the slow growth of their babies. Considering the period the stoves became popular, it was obvious that these meanings were given during the socialist era.

The order and meanings of matters in the yurts were constantly reproduced in everyday lives and were extended to the world outside the yurts. The orders of the yurts were transferrable and remained unchanged even through migration and settlement. Indeed, it was this structure of the yurt that formed the axis for the maintenance and transformation of household rituals. The structure also affected how changes in the post-democratization religious environment were accepted. For example, while many households placed the Buddha statues back in the *hoimor*, the Bahaists placed the photo of the founder Baha'u'llah and the Christians placed the Bible (Interviewee 12) or the cross (Interviewee 25) in the *hoimor*. Interviewee 27 converted to Christianity a couple of years prior to the survey and while her husband was still a Buddhist, she entrusted the many Buddha statues and ritual tools inherited from the husband's parents to Gandan Temple. Instead, they now have a photo of their deceased child in the *hoimor* and offer cups of tea to it. Interviewee 20 is also a Christian. They do not offer tea or sacred light to the *hoimor* but offer tea outside to the heavens. In the Mongolian language, there are two variations for the translation of 'God'; 'the master of the world' (Ертөнцийн Эзэн) and 'Buddha' (Бурхан) (Nagayama 2001: 138). While there are discussions as to which is more appropriate, the Interviewee 20 interpreted that it should be 'the master of the world' and explains that because the God is not 'Buddha', they would offer the tea to the God of heaven and not to the *hoimor*. These examples show that the spatial order in the yurt was still acting as the axis for the reproduction of household rituals and religious interpretation in the post-democratization era.

What influences did the residential switch from yurts to individual houses and apartments have on household rituals? We have not seen typical spatial order, similar to that found in yurts, in any other housing styles. In addition, individual houses and apartments tend to have different household structures. As there are a number of rooms and it is possible for each room to house a separate household, individual houses and apartments are often occupied by extended or multiple families.[25] As such, households living in yurts and other styles of housing are different in many ways, but we have not been able to identify any major differences in how they conduct household rituals in the survey. The impact on household rituals of the changes to housing styles and the settled lifestyle will be a subject for future investigation. However, what we can say at this stage is that the shift from yurts to individual houses and apartments in the Mongolian society is neither conclusive nor irreversible. There are many examples where people left individual houses or apartments and moved into yurts, such as when people moved from a regional area to the capital city or became independent from their parents' household (Interviewees 25, 30).

Conclusion

The religious situation in today's Mongolia is extremely diversified and individualized. However, to attribute this solely to the liberalization of religions achieved through democratization would be to disregard so many other social and historical factors. In order to overcome this issue, we had to find a paradigm in which we could assess the socialist era and the following period continuously. In this paper, we have focused on 'household rituals' from this perspective and discussed their dynamics.

Household rituals were not just reminiscence of customs from the pre-socialist era. While religions were excluded from the public arena due to the purge and socialistic systematization, 'home' became an important place for the expression of religion and it had managed to reproduce the household rituals while responding flexibly to the changes in the social environments brought about by settlement and modernization. Here, the symbolic order of the 'yurt' acted as the axis for such reproduction. We also suggest that the nomadic social relationship, as seen in *hashaa*, has prevented the symbolic order that was represented in the yurt to be completely incorporated into the socialistic systematization. In comparison to the 'visible' administrative regions with the non-religious principle, the non-territorial 'invisible' network played an important role in various aspects of social life. It was indeed a network that directly connected families to other families, transcending the public space in between. Lamas, who played active roles in occasions of death and sickness, even during the socialist era, were also part of this network. As a matter of fact, religious practices were always performed and reproduced within people's homes. It is true that household rituals were lost in many households during the socialist era. However, even this may be regarded as one of the diversified developments because the unit of maintenance, transformation and loss of household rituals was the individual household.

When the virtual rule of the Soviet system was lifted through democratization, the principle of non-religiosity vanished instantly. Buddhism was established as a semi-state religion and policies to actively protect religions were introduced by the Mongolian People's Revolutionary Party, the very party that led the anti-religious policy for nearly seventy years. Religion spatially expanded rapidly from people's homes to the whole world, with the inflow of foreign religions.[26] As a result, the religious scene in Mongolia is now seeing extremely diversified developments. However, the process involved a unique factor that no capitalist countries have experienced. We have to realize that Mongolia had, as a starting point, the individuality and diversity of the household rituals that have been nurtured for some fifty years.

Acknowledgements

I wish to acknowledge and express my deepest gratitude to the informants who provided vast amounts of valuable information on the reality and history of household rituals and Mr. Batbayar, who provided great support in various forms as a guide and a driver during my fieldwork in Mongolia. This paper was produced as a part of the research achieved through the Ministry of Education, Culture, Sports, Science and Technology's FY2003/2004 Grants-in-Aid for Scientific Research (Grant-in-Aid for JSPS Fellows).

Notes

Chapter 1

1. First published in Japanese as 'Shakai no Tagenka to Tasōka' (Increase in diversification and stratification of Taiwan society) in Numazaki Ichiro and Satō Yukihito (eds.) *Kosaku suru Taiwan shakai* (Complexities in Taiwan society), Tokyo: Ajia Keizai Kenkyusho, 37–68.
2. Throughout this chapter, I use the word 'Taiwan' as a politically and ethnically neutral adjective, as in 'Taiwan society' or 'Taiwan families', and do not use 'Taiwanese' which is often loaded with politically pro-Taiwan independence as well as ethnically Hoklo-centric sentiments.
3. All Chinese words and names hereafter in this chapter and the list of references will be transliterated using the *pinyin* system of Romanization. However, conventional spellings are used to transliterate the names of politicians.
4. Political and social conflicts between 'Waishengren' who migrated to Taiwan with the Kuomintang (Chinese Nationalist Party) government after the Second World War and 'Benshengren' who had been living in Taiwan since before Japanese colonial rule. Since children retain the provincial origins of their fathers, descendents of the two groups also belong to either Waishengren or Benshengren even though they are born and raised on the island of Taiwan. Waishengren and Benshengren have been conventionally translated as 'Mainlanders' and 'Taiwanese' in much of the English literature but I shall not use these translations in this chapter and just use the transliterations, Waishengren and Benshengren, for either Mainlander or Taiwanese is increasingly a misnomer as will be discussed in more detail below.
5. Violent clashes over land and water between groups of different origins or lineages, such as Hoklo and Hakka, or peoples of Changzhou and Chuanzhou backgrounds within the Hoklo population.
6. It is said that the terms 'Waishengren' and 'Benshengren' came into common use after November 1945. According to Tzeng (2009: 136–138), these terms were first used in a newspaper called *Min Bao*.

7 The term 'zuqun' was originally a Chinese translation of the social scientific term 'ethnic group'. It came to be used not only by scholars but also by politicians and social activists, disseminated throughout Taiwan society via the media, and became part of the common vocabulary from the 1990s. Although it is an 'imagined classification system', as stated by Wang Fuchang (2003), it has come to possess political and social realities in Taiwan today.
8 See Tanoue (2012) and Wu Tiantai (ed.) (2008) for 'cultural pluralism' in Taiwan.
9 The official designation in law is currently 'Yuanzhuminzu' (Aboriginal peoples). However, 'Yuanzhumin' (Aborigines) is used in the present chapter as the ethnic group name according to the commonly accepted designation.
10 Official English translation from the Office of the President, ROC (Taiwan) http://english.president.gov.tw/Default.aspx?tabid=1037#10.
11 Among collected papers on new immigrants, Xia Xiaojuan (ed.) (2009) is a comprehensive collection. For foreign workers in general, see Xia Xiaojuan et al. (eds.) (2008). Detailed monographs about the state of foreign domestic workers include Wu Feinu (2006) and Lan Pei-Chia (2006) and Lan Peijia (2008). See Xia Xiaojuan (2002), Xia Xiaojuan (ed.) (2005) and Yan Guoxuan (2006) for foreign brides. Zhang Hanbi (2007) presents a monograph on the subject of marriage between Hakka men and Southeast Asian women in particular.
12 For more detailed analysis of *laoban*, see Numazaki (1997).

Chapter 2

1 We can glean some information about the existence of considerable numbers of *hain* (people of subordinate status) in local communities at the beginning of the twentieth century from diaries left by Yu Jeyang and his grandchild Yu Yŏngŏp, who belonged to the main household of a gentry lineage in Gurye County, Jolla Province (*Gurye Yu-ssi-ga ŭi saenghwal ilgi* (Diaries of the Yu family in Gurye)). Further, in the rural part of Sŏngju County where I conducted a survey in the early 1980s, the framework of village organization was premised on the existence of the *hain* population until after the end of the colonial period (Shima 1983).
2 I was informed by Yoshida Mitsuo, specialist on Chosŏn period history, that these government posts were often purchased with rice.
3 According to the genealogy of the U clan, Na Jip, the head of the household into which Hansari transferred, was an in-law of Sŏkjang's sister.

4 There was a male slave named Myŏnggŭm (age sixty-four) in the household of U Sŏkjun (Sangin-ri, household no. 1-2), a nephew of Yŏjun, of the Danyang U lineage but there is no record of his marital relations. It is impossible to rule out the possibility that this man and Juyang's husband Myŏnggŭm were the same person. If this is the case, the record has an entry about this male slave Myŏnggŭm that states, 'father Minnae, slave of the same owner, mother, Hŏnmae, slave of the same owner', and therefore confirms that Myŏnggŭm's parents were both slaves belonging to the U lineage (probably in the household of Baesŏn, later succeeded by Dalhae). In that case, it is surmised that Juyang and her husband were both slaves of the U lineage since Baesŏn's times who married one another. However, there is a possibility that this man was a different person with the same name, because the recorded status of Myŏnggŭm as the father of Juyang's children was not a slave of the same owner. Further analysis is required as to the possibility of male and female slaves belonging to the same owner marrying one another in the case of a lineage owning a large number of slaves, as did the U lineage.

Chapter 3

1 Taira (ed.) (1972–1982) and *Shizankō jike kiroku* (Documents of Date Yoshimura) in the possession of Sendai City Museum were used.
2 Documents contained in Tokyo Teikoku Daigaku Bunka Daigaku Shiryō Hensan Gakari (1908–1911) were used.
3 A comprehensive collection of records on Date Masamune, authored by Date Shigezane. The version revised and annotated by Kobayashi (1967) was used.
4 In his final years Date Masamune told various stories to his page, who recorded them. Koikawa (ed.) (1997) was used.
5 A compilation of accurate historical records that were considered useful for Date Masamune's biography, chronologically arranged and gathered based on the same topics. Zaidan Hōjin Hanso Date Masamune Kō Kenshōkai (ed.) (1938) was used.
6 See Matsuzaki (2004a, 2004b) for details of the analysis. Matsuzaki (2011) examines the roles of women and gender order in early modern and modern Japan, based on the examples of the Shimazu family of the Satsuma domain and the commoner families.
7 In Japan, people maintain the custom of cleaning house at the end of each year. Especially at castles and temples, this it is called *susuharai*. This tradition originates from a religious custom in which people

cleaned their home altar and rooms to welcome the god of the New Year.

Chapter 4

1 There have been many studies on the subject of feuds (Niida 1948; Kitamura 1950; Nakamura 1981; Maeda 1984; Lamley 1990; Segawa 1991, 1993, 2005; He 2003).
2 A lineage in China, especially in the southeastern region, is a patrilineal descent group with marked collectivity.
3 See Kawaguchi (2008) for the detailed process of lineage formation in the Pearl River Delta.
4 Anthropological studies of boat dwellers were actively conducted from the 1960s to the 1970s. Because mainland China was closed to researchers in those days, Hong Kong was the main field for anthropological research. Major studies include Ward (1965), Kani (1970) and Anderson (1972).
5 Other than members of the funeral party, no one approaches or watches a funeral procession unless they are anthropologists. For example, once I was walking with one of my informants in D village and we came across a funeral procession in front of us. He said, 'It's inauspicious (*m hou yiteo*) Let's wait here for a while', and we stood there for ten minutes or so waiting for the funeral procession to pass. See Watson (1988) about the abhorrence of death among the Cantonese and Kawaguchi (2004) for details of contemporary funeral rites in this region.

Chapter 5

1 This is reported collaterally, particularly in studies related to the 'revival' of the patrilineal group known as *zongzu* (宗族). For example, in recent studies, Fan (2002) reported how large sums of donations from powerful overseas immigrants and local magnates have been used to rebuild the shrine as the symbol of the *zongzu* and how they are contributing to the integration of the *zongzu*. Similar cases have been confirmed at the author's survey site.
2 The term 'elders' in Village X refers to those aged above sixty. Most are unemployed.
3 Waidiren began to move into the area in the 1980s. They rent houses in Village X and work at nearby factories. Today, they form the major workforce when conducting festivals and ceremonies in the village.
4 Fuzhou region includes all districts (区), county-level cities or *xiànjí* shì (県級市) such as Changle City (長楽市) and Fuqing City (福清

市), and counties or *xiàn* (県) such as Minhou County (閩候県) under the jurisdiction of Fuzhou City. The language spoken in these regions is Fuzhou language. From hereafter the term 'Fuzhou region' is used in this context.
5 The farmers referred to here indicate those who are registered in the farming village.
6 According to 'The Statistical Yearbook of Chinese Farming Villages' (中国農村統計年鑑) 2009, one yuan is equivalent to fifteen yen.
7 'Baomu' are usually women in their fifties and above and are from the surrounding farming villages. Some commute on a regular basis and some live with their clients. The average monthly wage for the former is around 1,000 yuan and the latter is around 1,500 to 2,000 yuan.
8 On the other hand, when a wife passes away, her husband participates in the funeral and acts as host.
9 The remains are placed in a coffin with refrigeration features (冰棺) at home. This type of coffin has been used since the 1990s in Village X. When I asked why such a coffin is used, they answered that 'it is used to wait for the return of the children'.
10 Funerals in Village X are on an invitation basis. Only those who received the notice of death from the mourning family can attend the funeral, and people are expected to attend the funeral procession if not anything else. The notice of death comes with a ticket to attend the feast and only those with tickets are allowed to eat and drink at the banquet hall.

Chapter 6

1 The capital of North Tapanuli Regency, the city of Taratung, is a typical Toba Batak residential area. The headquarters of the Protestant Batak Christian Church (HKBP) are also located here.
2 HKBP church home page (http://www.hkbpchurch.org/organization.html).
3 2,083,156 people, according to 2007 statistics.
4 According to 1930 population statistics, Toba Batak numbered 820 out of Medan's population of 76,584, accounting for a mere 1.07 percent of the total (Purba 1998).
5 I have previously taken up the narrative of a young person who prayed for a child at his lover's house, dumbfounding his father (Kimura 2005: 6).
6 STM is an acronym for the Indonesian phrase '*serikat tolong menolong*', meaning 'mutual aid society' in Indonesian. *Tapian Nauli* is an ornate expression for one's homeland, meaning 'beautiful spring (of water)' in Toba language.

7 There are several versions of Toba Batak lineage, and differing versions also give different numbers of generations of Batubara. In this paper, I have used the lineage handed down in the Batubara Clan. Otherwise, Gultom places Balasahuma and Datutala Dibabana between Borbor and Datudalu, and views Batubara as the ninth generation (Gultom 1992: 145f). On the other hand, Hutagalung adds the renowned Tarombo to the above two, placing Datu Ponpangbalasaribu between them, and shifting Batubara down one further generation (Hutagalung 1991: 127f).

8 Other *marga*, descendents of Borbor three generations previously, namely Harahap, Parapat, Matondang, Sipahutar, Tarihoran, Rambe, Saruksuk, Lubis and Pasaribu, are considered to form one group, and there is consciousness of these *marga* as constituting the boundaries of a taboo against intermarriage.

Chapter 7

1 According to the questionnaire survey conducted by the Science Academy of Mongolia in 1994, 71.1% of the respondents believed in some form of religion. Among the respondents, 59.7% answered they were Buddhists, 2.8% were Christians and 8.7% were Muslims (Tsedendamba 2003: 154).

2 Suganuma (1996, 2001, 2002a, 2002b, 2002c), Nakamura (1998), and Mani (2001) have documented the developments of post-democratization Mongolian Buddhism at the religious group level, as has Jambal (1998) on Islam, Umezawa (2002) on Christianity and Tsedendamba (1998, 2003) on the holistic situation.

3 Please refer to Kanaoka (2000:230) and Tanaka (1992:263) for the number of purge victims.

4 For reference, the decrease in the number of Russian Orthodox Churches during this period was from 39,000 (1928) to 4,200 (1941) (Powell 1975: 41).

5 'The percentage of atheists among Russians has dropped from 25% during the socialist era to 5%' (Froese 2004: 48). In the case of Mongolia, 'according to a survey in 1994, 71.1% of the participants disclosed that they believed in religion to some extent. However, according to a survey conducted in the mid-1980s, 80.4% answered they had nothing to do with or did not believe in religion (Tsedendamba 2003).

6 In the case of Kazakhstan, the First Five-Year plan aimed for the swift introduction of collectivization, targeting the settlement of 544,000 out of the total of 566,000 households of nomadic and semi-nomadic

people around at the time, but only succeeded in settling 50,699 households during the period from 1929 to 1930. This indicated the difficulty of settling nomads as well as the influence of the tribal leaders who had maintained their social power (Kimura 1999: 175).

7 For example, 'the basic unit of social organization in the nomadic society of Kazakhstan is a patriarchal blood (rod) relationship' and 'the basic structure of this social organization survived the farming collectivization process by the Soviet Union in 1920–1930 and was integrated into the *kolkhoz* without being dismantled' (Kimura 1999: 163).

8 Refer to Цэрэнханд (1987: 120). Onuki classified the *hot ails* into three main types according to the interrelationships of the constituents, i.e., the families; namely, 1) a union of independent families running their business based on small scale production; 2) a relationship based mainly on blood connections; and 3) a combination of affluent families with livestock and wealth and underprivileged families (Onuki 1993: 261–262). In any case, *hot ails* had the aspect of 'internal exploitation within the community based on inequality in private possessions or financial status, but the community also played a major role in maintaining its democratic nature as a community and protecting the constituents from attack from the feudal lords' (Onuki 1993: 264–265).

9 For example, wealthy households with large numbers of livestock could not form a *hot ail* together.

10 In the pre-socialist era, there were lineages and clans that were basically paternal with multi-layered structures depending on the depth of the generation. However, the use of the lineage name was abolished in 1926 and only the father's surname was to be used (in other words, surnames would only date back one generation). Furthermore, clans were reorganized into the seventeen 'tribes' (ястан) formerly recognized by the government, and many people no longer recognized the other clans.

11 Agricultural and stock farm cooperatives, equivalent to *kolkhoz* of Russia.

12 Private ownership of livestock was permitted, but the number was limited.

13 'The rapid population increase, which more than doubled in thirty years, and the change in the industrial structure, where the pastoral people which only amounted to one third of the population had to support the other two thirds of the population, meant that each pastoral family had to look after a higher than ever number of livestock. By the end of the *negdel* system, *soris* that used to be formed by two or three

families were almost all made up of just one family, and families had to live in isolation in the vast grassland' (Onuki 1993: 272–3).
14 As previously stated, the regional organizations form the foundation. In some locations, the family's territory and the regional territory may coincide. In such cases, the family identity often takes precedence over the regional identity. However, today knowledge of the pre-socialistic social organization itself has often been lost.
15 Besides the ritual *oboos*, there are *oboos* with various functions such as those for signposts and indications of boundaries. They are all targets of respect, but the *oboos* used for rituals are distinguished from others.
16 Here it is called *buleg* (бүлэг) and has the proper name of Olziiochir (Өлзийочир).
17 Humphrey also reported a case study of a joint *oboo* ritual which was conducted by a regional organization continuously for a certain period of time but was ceased due to the death of the main organizer (1999: 124).
18 Here we are assuming the Mongolian term *ail* (айл) as the term equivalent to 'household'. *Ail* has the same origin with the Turkish word *aile* which means family. The range covered by the term *ail* subtly varies according to era or region, but here we have chosen the term *ail* as 'household' which includes both the residential space and the people who live in it.
19 The targets here were households who lived in *hashaa*. The pastoral people and residents of apartments were not included. The targets of the suvery conducted in Ulan Bator were mainly natives of the western regions. As there was bias in the target group, we cannot assess as to what extent the collected material reflected the average reality, but I believe we have achieved, to a certain extent, the purpose of grasping the big picture and clarifying the issues surrounding household rituals through these case studies.
20 In the case of the nomads, 'maintain' does not simply mean to keep them, but also to courteously carry them every time they migrate.
21 However, there were several cases in the 1980s where people placed Buddha statues upon marriage (Interviewee 23) or retirement (Interviewee 3) when signs of liberalization began to appear.
22 For example, Omoya produced and compared a number of layout plans of the yurts (1997: 87–89) and mentioned 'the way household items are arranged are very similar in all the yurts, to the extent that it made me wonder why they are all so uniform' (1997: 93).
23 For the 'traditional' arrangement and order in the yurt refer to Hasumi (1993:11), Maidar (1988[1981]: 105), Batnasan (1987: 137), Nansalmaa (1987: 280–281), Maidar (1972: 14–15) and Maidar and Darisuren (1976: 109–111).

24 There are examples of folk direction being determined based on the seasonal wind etc. in Japan (Suzuki 1978: 69; Oguchi 1983: 10), and the same goes for Mongolia where the winter seasonal wind has an effect on the folk direction.
25 That is why, according to the records of the National Statistics Office (NSO), who records the residence, including yurts, individual houses and apartments, as the household units, the percentage of households composed of extended and multiple families is higher in the city regions than in the rural regions (NSO 2001: 154).
26 For example, there is currently a church in Denver managed by Mongolian pastors for the Mongolian people.

Bibliography

Ahern, E.M. and H. Gates (eds.) (1981) *The Anthropology of Taiwanese Society*. Stanford: Stanford University Press.

Anderson, E.N. (1972) *Essays on South China's Boat People*. Taipei: Orient Cultural Service.

Ashiwa, Y. (2000) 'Chūgoku tōnan bu ni okeru bukkyō fukkō no dōtai – Kokka, shakai, toransunashonarizumu' (Dynamics of the Buddhist revival movement in South China: State, society, transnationalism). In M. Hishida (ed.) *Gendai Chūgoku no kōzō hendō 5 shakai – kokka tono kyōsei kankei* (Structural change in contemporary China 5 Society: Symbiotic relations with the state). Tokyo: Tokyo Daigaku Shuppankai, 239–274.

Batnasan (Батнасан), G. (1987) 'Орон Сууц ' (Residence). In Mongolian Academy of Science (ed.) *БНМАУ-ын Угсаатны Зүй* (Ethnography in the Mongolian People's Republic), vol.1. Ulaanbaatar: National Publishing Office, 129–146.

Bourdieu, P. (1979[1990]) *Disticntion I* (Disticntion I). Y. Ishii (trans.). Tokyo: Fujiwara Shoten.

Bourdieu, P. (1988[1980]) *Jissen kankaku I* (Sense of practice I). H. Imamura and T. Minatomichi (trans.). Tokyo: Misuzu Shobo.

Bovill, J.B. (1986) 'Toba Batak Marriage and Alliances'. PhD Thesis, Illinois University.

BPS SUMUT (2008) *Sumatera Utara dalam Angkah*. Medan: Badan Pusat Statistik Provinsi Sumatera Utara.

Bruner, E. (1961) 'Urbanisation and ethnic identity in North Sumatra'. *American Anthropologist*, 63(3): 508–521.

Bruner, E. (1972) 'Batak ethnic associations in three Indonesian cities'. *Southwestern Journal of Anthropology*, 28(3): 207–229.

Chan, S.C. (2005) 'Temple-building and heritage in China'. *Ethnology*, 44(1): 65–79.

Chen, T. (1939 [1939]) *Nanyō Kakyou to Kanton, Fukken shakai* (Southern Ocean societies and Guangdong and Fujian societies). Y. Sakai (trans.). Mantetsu Tōa Keizai Chōsakyoku (Mantetsu East Asiatic Economic Investigation Bureau, Tokyo).

Copper, J.F. (1996) *Taiwan: Nation-State or Province?* Second edition. Boulder: Westview Press.

Corcuff, S. (2008) *Gaishōjin no genzai – Henyō suru kokka to aidentitī* (Taiwan's Mainlanders: The changing state and identity). H. Kamizuru and K. Nishimura (trans.). Tokyo: Fūkyōsha.

Ebrey, P. and J.L. Watson (eds.) (1986) *Kinship Organization in Late Imperial China: 1000–1940*. Berkeley: University of California Press.

Editorial Committee of Zhen Journal of Village X (2010) *Journal of Village X*. Fujian: Fujian People's Publishing House.

Endō, Y. (2003) 'Sengoku ki Ōu ni okeru Hoshunin no hataraki – Sengoku jidai no heiwa iji to josei' (Hoshunin's activities in Ōu during the Warring States period: Preservation of peace and women in the Warring States period). *Nihon shi kenkyū* (The journal of Japanese historical studies), 486: 26–55.

Freedman, M. (1980[1958]) *Lineage Organization in Southeastern China*. New York: The Athlone Press.

Froese, P. (2004) 'Forced secularization in Soviet Russia: Why an atheistic monopoly failed.' *Journal for the Scientific Study of Religion*, 43(1): 35–50.

Fukuda, C. (2005) 'Kinsei chūki ni okeru Hikone Ii ke no okumuki' (Oku of the Ii family in the Hikone domain in the middle of the Edo period). Hikone Han Shiryō Chōsa Kenkyū Iinkai, *Hikonejō hakubutsukan sōsho 6: Buke no seikatsu to kyōyō* (Library of Hikone Castle Bibliography Museum 6: Life and culture of the samurai family). Hikone: Hikone Castle Museum, 90–111.

Fukuda, S. (1998) 'Shakaishugi kyōiku ron 5 – Sobieto, Roshia ni mirareru kokka to shūkyō to seishin no kyōiku' (A study of socialist education 5: Relations between the state and religion, moral education in the USSR and Russia). *Tsuru Bunka Daigaku Kenkyū Kiyō* (The Tsuru University review), 49: 47–68.

Gultom, D.J. (1992) *Dalihan Na Tolu: Nilai Budaya Suku Batak*. Medan: Armanda.

Han, M. (2001) *Social Change and Continuity in a Village in Northern Anhui, China: A Response to Revolution and Reform*. Osaka: National Museum of Ethnology.

Hasselgren, J. (2000) *Rural Batak, Kings in Medan: The Development of Toba Batak Ethno-religious Identity in Medan Indonesia 1912–1965*. Uppsala: Swedish Institute of Missionary Research.

Hasumi, H. (1993) 'Geru no kosumorojī' (The cosmology of the yurt). In *Yūbokumin no kenchikujutsu – Geru no kosumorojī* (Architecture of the nomadic people: The cosmology of the yurt). Tokyo: INAX Corporation.

He, G.-Q. (2003) 'Zongzu lishi yu zuqun hudong- yi Fengshun xian Tangnan zhen Luoshi zongzu wei li' (History of clans and interaction among clans: Taking the Luo clan of Tangnan town in Fengshun county as an example). In D. Zhou et al. *Dangdai Huanan de zongzu yu shehui* (Contemporary clans and society in south China). Haerbin: Heilongjiang Renming Chubanshe, 65–105.

Hiraki, M. (1971) 'Jūshichi hachi seiki ni okeru nuryōsai shosei no kizoku ni tsuite' (On the affiliation of children born to male slaves by their commoner wives during the 17th and 18th centuries). *Chōsen Gakuhō* (Journal of the academic association of Koreanology in Japan), 61: 45–75.

HKBP. (1998) *Almanak HKBP*. Pematang Siantar: Percetakan HKBP.

Hobsbawm, E. and T. Ranger (eds.) (1983) *The Invention of Tradition*. Cambridge: Cambridge University Press.

Hu, T. (1989) 'Ethnic identity and social condition of veteran-Mainlanders in Taiwan'. *Revue Europeenne des Sociences Sociales*, 27(84): 253–266.

Hu, T. (1993) 'Yuzi yu fanshu—Taiwan rongmin de zuqun guanxi yu renting' (Taro and yam: Ethnic relations and identity of Taiwan's *rongmin* population). In M. Zhang et al. *Zuqun guanxi yu guojia renting* (Ethnic relations and state identity). Taipei: Yejiang chubanshe, 279–325.

Huang, S. (2010) 'Quanqiuhua yu Taiwan yuanzhumin jiben zhengce zhi yanbian yu xianzhuang' (Globalization and the changes and current conditions of basic policies toward Taiwan's indigenous peoples). In S. Huang and Y. Zhang (eds.) *Taiwan Yuanzhumin zhengce yanbian yu shehui fazhan* (Changes in Taiwan's policies toward indigenous peoples and social development). Taipei: Institute of Ethnology, Academia Sinica, 15–50.

Humphrey, C. (1999) 'Rural institutions'. In C. Humphrey and D. Sneath, *The End of Nomadism?: Society, State and the Environment in Inner Asia*. Durham: Duke University Press, 68–135.

Hutagalung, W.M. (1991) *Pustaha Batak: Tarombo dohot Turiturian ni Bangso Batak*. Medan: Tulus Jaya.

Ishida, H. (1996) *Chūgoku dōzoku sonraku no shakai keizai kōzō – Fukken dentō nōson to dōzoku nettowāku* (Socio-economic structure of lineage villages in China: Kinship in rural China). Osaka: Kansai Daigaku Shuppanbu.

Ishigaki, N. (2012) 'Gendai Taiwan shakai wo meguru "kyushinryoku·enshinryoku" to genjumin—Bunun no jirei wo chusin toshita shohoteki kentō' (The 'centripetal/centrifugal forces' in contemporary Taiwan and the indigenous peoples: An exploratory case study of the Bunun). In I. Numazaki and Y. Satō (eds.) *Kosaku suru Taiwan shakai* (Complexities in Taiwan society). Tokyo: Ajia Keizai Kenkyusho, 101–137.

Jambal (Жамбал), A. (1998) 'Монгол дахь Ислам Шашны Уламжлал, Өнөөгийн Байдал' (The recent situation of Islamic tradition in Mongolia). In Mongolian Academy of Science, Institute of Philosophy, Sociology and Law (ed.) *Төр, Сүм Хийдийн Харилцаа: Орчин Үе* (The relationship between the state and the temple: Recent times). Ulaanbaatar: Bambi-san, 53–73.

Ka, G. (He Yilin) (2003) *2.28 jiken – 'Taiwan jin' keisei no esunoporitikusu* (The February 28 incident: The formation of 'Taiwanese' ethnopolitics). Tokyo: Tokyo Daigaku Shuppankai.

Kamata, T. and T. Yoneyama (1994) *Shinban Kangorin* (Character dictionary, new edition). Tokyo: Taishūkan Shoten.

Kamizuru, H. (2012) 'Taiwan no hondoka go ni mieru gaishōjin ishiki' (Identities of Waishengren after Taiwanization). In I. Numazaki and Y. Satō (eds.) *Kosaku suru Taiwan shakai* (Complexities in Taiwan society). Tokyo: Ajia Keizai Kenkyusho, 139–173.

Kanaoka, H. (2000) *Mongoru wo shiru tame no 60 shō* (Sixty chapters to get to know Mongolia). Tokyo: Akashi Shoten.

Kani, H. (1970) *Honkon no suijō kyomin – Chūgoku shakai shi no danmen* (Boat people of Hong Kong: A cross section of Chinese social history). Tokyo: Iwanami Shoten.

Kawaguchi, Y. (2004) 'Kyōsan tō no seisaku ka ni okeru sōsō girei no henyō to jizoku – Kanton shō Shukō Deruta no jirei kara' (Changes and continuities in funeral rituals under communist rule: A case from a village in the Pearl River Delta). *Bunka Jinruigaku* (Japanese journal of cultural anthropology), 69(2): 193–210.

Kawaguchi, Y. (2008) 'Kinship organizations and social stratification in late imperial China: A study based on lineage in the Pearl River Delta'. In M. Shima (ed.) *Status and Stratification: Cultural Forms in East and Southeast Asia*. Melbourne: Trans Pacific Press, 63–94.

Kazato, M. (1999) 'Yūbokumin to shizen to kachiku – Yūdō to kachiku kanri' (Nomadic people, nature and livestock: Nomadism and livestock management). In M. Shimazaki and T. Nagasawa (eds.) *Mongoru no kazoku to komyunitī kaihatsu* (The family and community development in Mongolia). Tokyo: Nihon Keizai Hyouronsha, 21–50.

Kim, Y. (1997) *Chosŏn-sidae sanobi yŏngu* (A study on slaves owned by individuals during the Chosŏn dynasty period). Seoul: Jipmundang.

Kimura, T. (2005) '"Bunmyakuka sareta kyōkai" kara "ethnic church" e: Tōnan Ajia toshi shakai ni okeru Kirisuto kyōkai no dōkō ni kansuru ichikōsatsu' (From a 'contextualised church' to an 'ethnic church': A study on trends in Christian churches in South-East Asian urban society). *Tōhoku daigaku bungaku kenkyūka kenkyū nenpō*, 54: 80–64.

Kimura, Y. (1999) 'Chūō ajia no shakai kōsei ni tsuite no ichi shiron – 20 seiki zenhan ni okeru shakai shoshūdan no kōsei to tokuchō' (An essay on the social constitution of Central Asia: The constitution and characteristics of social groups in the first half of the 20th Century). In Y. Kimura (ed.) *Gendai chūō ajia no shakai henyō* (Social transformation in modern Central Asia). Sendai: Centre for Interdisciplinary Research, Tohoku University, 145–197.

Kitamura, H. (1950) 'Shindai kaitō no ichi kōsatsu' (The conflict among the clannish groups in the Ching dynasty)'. *Shirin* (Journal of history), 33(1): 64–77.

Kobayashi, S. (ed.) (1967) *Date shiryō shū (jō)* (Collected historical records of the Date family, vol. 1). Tokyo: Jinbutsu Ōraisha.

Koikawa, Y. (ed.) (1997) *Date Masamune genkō roku – Kimura Uemon oboegaki* (The words and actions of Date Masamune: Kimura Uemon memoranda). Tokyo: Shin Jinbutsu Ōraisha.

Kolarz, W. (1961) *Religion in the Soviet Union*. London: Macmillan.

Kuper, A. (1988) *The Invention of Primitive Society: Transformation of an Illusion*. London: Routledge.

Lai, T., R.H. Myers and W. Wei (1991) *A Tragic Beginning: The Taiwan Uprising of February 28, 1947*. Stanford: Stanford University Press.

Lan, P. (2005) 'Jiecenghua de tazhi—Jiawu yigong de zhaomu, xunlian yu zhongzuhua' (Stratified others: Recruitment, training and racialization of migrant house maids). *Taiwan shehuixue kan*, 34: 1–57.

Lan, P. (2008) *Kuaguo huiguniang* (Transnational Cinderella). Taipei: Xingren chubanshe.

Lan, P.-C. (2006) *Global Cinderellas: Migrant Domestics and Newly Rich Employers in Taiwan*. Durham: Duke University Press.

Lamley, H.J. (1990) 'Lineage and surname feuds in southern Fukien and eastern Kwangtung under the Ch'ing'. In K.-C Liu. (ed.) *Orthodoxy in Late Imperial China*. Berkeley: University of California Press, 255–278.

Lewis, D.C. (2000) *After Atheism: Religion and Ethnicity in Russia and Central Asia*. Richmond: Curzon.

Li, G. (2008) 'Jiguan, sida zuqun yu duoyuan wenhua—guojia renting zhi xia de renlei fenlei' (Origin, four major ethnic groups and multiculturalism: Classification of human beings under state identity). In H. Wang, G. Li and X. Gong (eds.) *Kuajie—Liudong yu Jianchi de Taiwan shehui* (Steps in forbidden zones: Changes and continuities of Taiwan society). Taipei: Junxue chuban, 93–110.

Li, M. (2003) 'Lixiang, kuahai, yuanjia, zuo"ta"fu—You Yuenan xingbie wenhua kan "Yuenan xinniang"' (Leaving home, crossing the ocean, becoming the wife of 'the other': Looking at 'Vietnamese brides' from the perspective of gender culture). In X. Xiao (ed.) *Taiwan yu dongnanya—Nanxiang zhengce yu Yuenan xinniang* (Taiwan and Southeast Asia: South-oriented policies and Vietnamese brides). Taipei: Center for Asia-pacific Area Studies, Academia Sinica, 215–247.

Lin, K. (2006) 'Kuajie Yuenan nüxing zuqun bianjie de weichi—shiwu juese de tanjiu' (Transnational Vietnamese women's maintenance of ethnic borders: Exploration of the role of food) *Taiwan Dongnanyaxue kan*, 3(1): 63–82.

Lin, Zhongzheng (Lin Heling) (1993) 'Taiwan diqu gequn de jingji chayi' (Economic disparities between ethnic groups in Taiwan). In M. Zhang et al. *Zuqun guanxi yu guojia renting* (Ethnic relations and state identity). Taipei: Yejiang chubanshe, 101–160.

Lin, Zonghong (2009) 'Taiwan de hougongyehua—jieji jiegou de zhuanxing yu shehui bupingdeng, 1992–2007' (Taiwan's postindustrialization: Transformation of class structure and social inequality, 1992–2007). *Taiwan Shehuixue kan*, 43: 93–158.

Maeda, K. (1984) 'Shindai no Kanton ni okeru dokyaku taikō ni tsuite' (A consideration on the problem of the opposite relation between the native community and the company community at Kuang Tung in the Ch'ing era). *Kokushikan daigaku bungaku-bu jimbun gakkai* (Transactions of the academic society of the humanities), 16: 69–80.

Maidar (Майдар), D. (1972) *Монголын Архитектур ба Хот Байгуулалт* (Mongolian architecture and urban construction). Ulaanbaatar: National Publishing Office.

Maidar, D. (1988 [1981]) *Sōgen no kuni Mongoru* (Mongolia, the country of grassland). K. Kato (trans.). Tokyo: Shinchosha.

Maidar (Майдар), D. and L. Darisuren (Дарьсүрэн) (1976) *Гэр: Орон Сууцны Түүхэн Тойм* (Yurt: The brief history of Mongolian residence). Ulaanbaatar: National Publishing Office.

Mani, K. (2001) '*Yomigaetta bukkyō* – Mongoru to Roshia no kako to genjō' (The revival of Buddhism: The relations of the Mongol-Russia of today and yesterday). *Nihon Bukkyō Kyoikugaku Kenkyū* (Journal of the Nippon Buddhist Education Research Association), 9: 149–161.

Matsuo, M. (2008) 'Shōgunke okumuki no keizai – goyō toritsugi minarai no kiroku kara' (The economy of Okumuki of the shogun family: Based on the record by an apprentice to goyo toritsugi). *Tokyo to Edo Tokyo hakubutsukan kenkyū hōkoku* (Research report of the Edo-Tokyo Museum), 14: 47–61.

Matsuzaki, R. (2004a) 'Kinsei buke shakai no jendā shisutemu to josei no yakuwari – Kinsei chūki no Sendai han Date ke wo jirei to shite' (The gender system of the Buke society in the Edo period and the role of women: The case of the Date family in the Sendai han in the middle period of the Edo period). *Rekishi* (Tohoku historical journal), 103: 101–126.

Matsuzaki, R. (2004b) 'Tenka tōitsu bakuhan sei kakuritsu ki ni okeru buke josei no yakuwari – Sendai han Date ke wo jirei to shite' (The roles of the samurai-class women in the unification period and the shogunate-domain system establishment period: The case of the Date family in the Sendai domain). *Kokushi danwa kai zasshi* (Journal of the society of the department of Japanese history at Tohoku University), 45: 1–19.

Matsuzaki, R. (2011) 'Women's roles and gender order in early modern and modern Japan'. In K. Kimura (ed.) *Minorities and Diversity.* Melbourne: Trans Pacific Press, 31–50.

Nagano, H. (1990) 'Bakuhansei kokka no seiji kōzō to josei – Seiritsu ki wo chūshin ni' (Women and the political structure of Japan under the shogunate and domain system: The establishment phase). Republished in H. Nagano (2003) *Nihon kinsei jendā ron – 'Ie' keieitai, mibun, kokka* (Gender theory in early modern Japan: 'Ie' management entity, status and state). Tokyo: Yoshikana kōbunkan, 197–235.

Naganuma, S. (2010) *Kanton no suijō kyomin – Shukō deruta kan zoku no esunishitī to sono henyō* (Water dwelling people of Guangdong: Ethnicity of the Han in the Pearl River Delta and its transformation). Tokyo: Fūkyōsha.

Nagayama, H. (2001) 'Gendai Mongorugo seisho no keikiteki shinka nitsuite' (Regarding successive evolution in the modern Mongolian bible). *Nihon Mongoru Gakkai Kiyō* (Bulletin of the Japan Association for Mongolian Studies), 31: 129–150.

Nakamura, J. (1981) 'Minkoku shonen Kanton shō no sonraku no kaitō ni tsuite – Hakura ken shūsai hōkokusho ni yoru' (Village's struggles (Hsieh-tou) in the Kwangtung province between 1916–1917). In Ichiko Kyōju Taikan Kinen Ronsō Henshu Iinkai (ed.) *Ronshū kindai Chūgoku kenkyū* (Studies in modern China). Tokyo: Yamakawa Shoten, 233–252.

Nakamura, R. (1998) 'Mongoru bukkyō no genjō' (The current status of Mongolian Buddhism). *Shūchiin Daigaku Mikkyō Shiryō Kenkyūjo Kiyō* (Bulletin of the Research Institute for the Materials of Esoteric Buddhism, Shuchiin College), 1: 61–69.

Nansalmaa (Нансалмаа), D. (1987) 'Ардын нэв заншил, зан үйл' (People's customs and rites). In Mongolian Academy of Science (ed.) БНМАУ-ын Угсаатны Зуй (Ethnography in the Mongolian People's Republic), vol.1. Ulaanbaatar: National Publishing Office, 270–340.

National Statistical Office of Mongolia (NSO) (2001) *2000 Population and Housing Census of Mongolia: The Main Results.* Ulaanbaatar: NSO.

Nie, L. (1992) *Ryūho – Chūgoku tōhoku chihō no sōzoku to sono henyō* (Liu Village: Lineages and change in northeastern China). Tokyo: Tokyo Daigaku Shuppankai.

Niida, N. (1948) 'Shina kinsei dōzoku buraku no kaitō' (Lineage village feuds in early modern China). In Ono Takeo Hakushi Kanreki Kinen Ronbunshū Kankōkai (ed.) *Tōyō nōgyō keizai shi kenkyū* (The study of East Asian agrarian economic history). Tokyo: Nihon Hyōronsha, 65–100.

Numazaki, I. (1989) 'Gendai Taiwan ni okeru minkan daikigyō no shoyū to keiei – Jōjō kigyō no bunseki' (Ownership and management of large private corporations in contemporary Taiwan: An analysis of listed companies). *Ajia keizai* (Asian economies), 30(12): 79–102.

Numazaki, I. (1997) 'The Laoban-led development of business enterprises in Taiwan: An analysis of Chinese entrepreneurship'. *Developing Economies*, 35(4): 440–457.

Numazaki, I. (1998) 'Esunishitī to shakai kaisō' (Ethnicity and social stratification). In M. Wakabayashi (ed.) *Motto shiritai Taiwan dai 2 han* (Knowledge of Taiwan, second edition). Tokyo: Kōbundō, 46–68.

Numazaki, I. (1999) 'The real community under imagined states: The social-economic transformation and the rise of the new Taiwan consciousness in contemporary Taiwan'. In S. Huang and C. Hsu (eds.) *Imagining China: Regional Division and National Unity*. Taipei: Institute of Ethnology, Academia Sinica, 253–264.

Numazaki, I. (2002) 'Genjitsu no kyōdōtai, kakū no seitai – Taiwan shakai no henyō to "atarashii Taiwan ishiki" no shutsugen' (The real community under imagined states: The socio-economic transformation and the rise of the new Taiwan consciousness in contemporary Taiwan). *Tōhoku jinruigaku rondan* (Tohoku anthropological exchange), 1: 19–29.

Numazaki, I. (2004) 'Kōdo keizai seichō ki Taiwan ni okeru "rōban" teki kigyō nettowāku no seisei to tenkai – 1949 nen–1989 nen' (Birth and growth of the laoban-led business network in Taiwan during the rapid economic development period). *Tōhoku Daigaku bungaku kenkyū ka kenkyū nenpō* (The annual reports of the graduate school of arts and letters, Tohoku University), 53: 210–194.

Oguchi, C. (1983) 'Kasōkan ni miru kūkan hyōka no sōtaisei – Saitama ken ni okeru "Fuji muki" denshō to eki tono taihi kara' (Relativity in the evaluation of space in the house physiognomy view: The comparison of 'Fuji direction' folk tales and divination in Saitama Prefecture). *Rekishi Chirigaku* (Historical geography), 122: 1–14

Oka, H. (2002) 'Mongoru ni okeru chihō shakai no dentōteki kōsei tan-i Otog bag nitsuite – Mongoru koku, Hentii aimag Galshar sum chōsa hōkoku' (Regarding the traditional constituent unit, otog and bag, in

Mongolia's regional society: Report of the survey in Galshar district, Hentii province, Mongolia)'. In H. Oka (ed.) *Mongoru kenkyū ron shū* (Mongolia research paper collection). Sendai: Centre for Northeast Asian Studies, Tohoku University, 209–233.

Omoya, S. (1997) 'Gendai Mongoru ni okeru jūseikatsu to seikatsuzai – Sono kōgengaku teki cōhsa' (Goods and housing for people living in modern Mongolia). *Ningen Bunka: Shiga Kenritsu Daigaku Ningen Bunka Gakubu Kenkū Hōkoku* (Bulletin: School of Human Cultures, the University of Shiga Prefecture), 3: 84–98.

Onuki, M. (1993) *Sekai gendai shi 4: Mongoru gendai shi* (Contemporary history of the world 4: Contemporary history of Mongolia). Tokyo: Yamakawa Shuppansha.

Pan, H. (2002) *Gendai tōnan chūgoku no kanzoku shakai: Min Nan nōson no sōzoku soshiki to sono henyō* (Han society in contemporary South East China: Transformation of lineage organization in rural Minnan). Tokyo: Fukyosha.

Pederson, P.B. (1970) *Batak Blood and Protestant Soul: The Development of Nasional Batak Church in North Sumatra*. Michigan: William B. Eerdmans.

Pelly, U. (1998) *Urbanisasi dan Adaptasi*. Jakarta: LP3ES.

Potter, S.H. and J.M. Potter (1990) *China's Peasants: The Anthropology of Revolution*. New York: Cambridge University Press.

Powell, D.E. (1975) *Antireligious Propaganda in the Soviet Union: A study of Mass Persuasion*. Cambridge: MIT Press.

Purba, O.H.S. and E.F. Purba (1998) *Migran Batak Toba: Di Luar Tapanuli Utara*. Medan: Monora.

Ruan, Y. (2005) *Chūgoku no sōzoku to seiji bunka – Gendai 'gijo' kyōson no seiji jinruigaku teki kōsatsu* (Chinese lineage and political culture: A political-anthropology monograph of contemporary Yixu village in Eastern Fujian). Tokyo: Sōbunsha.

Saitō, E. (1995) 'Edo chūki bakuhan kan no girei ni tsuite – Date Munemura no kekkon' (Rituals performed between the shogunate and the domain in the middle of the Edo period: The marriage of Date Munemura). *Miyagi ken nōgyō tanki daigaku gakujutsu hōkoku* (Scientific reports of the Miyagi Agricultural College), 43: 1–10.

SCKDSL (1931) *Indisch Verslag*. Batavia: Landsdrukkerij.

Scott, J.C. (1976) *The Moral Economy of Peasants: Rebellion and Subsistence in Southeast Asia*. New Haven: Yale University Press.

Se, A., S. Chin (Chen Junliang), S. Kyo (Xu Shiping) and A. Katsurada (2007a) 'Chūgoku tairiku oyobi Tōnan Ajia no gaikokuseki haigūsha imin no haikei kara kōsatsu suru "shin Taiwan no ko" no kyōiku mondai to sono taisaku' (A study on Taiwan's educational problem and policy on 'new children of Taiwan' from the background on spouses immigrating from Mainland China and South-east Asia). *Fukuoka Daigaku kenkyū ronshū A* (Fukuoka University Review Series A), 6(6): 121–138.

Se, A., S. Chin (Chen Junliang), S. Kyo (Xu Shiping) and A. Katsurada (2007b) 'Taiwan ni okeru gaikoku seki oyobi Chūgoku tairiku seki haigūsha no genjō to tenbō' (Research on the present situation and future prospects of South-east Asian and Mainland Chinese spouses in Taiwan). *Fukuoka Daigaku kenkyū ronshū A* (Fukuoka University Review Series A), 6(6): 139–154.

Segawa, M. (1991) *Chūgokujin no sonraku to sōzoku – Honkon Shinkai sonraku no shakai jinruigaku teki kenkyū* (Chinese village and lineage: Social anthropological study of the New Territories of Hong Kong). Tokyo: Kōbundō.

Segawa, M. (1993) *Hakka – Kanan Kanzoku no esunishiti to sono kyōkai* (Hakka: Ethnicity and boundary of Han-Chinese in South China). Tokyo: Fūkyōsha.

Segawa, M. (2004) *Chūgoku shakai no jinruigaku – Shinzoku, kazoku kara no tenbō* (Anthropology of Chinese society: A view from kinship and family). Kyoto: Sekai Shisōsha.

Segawa, M. (2005) 'Shukō Deruta seibu chiiki ni okeru sōzoku, kaitō, kaigai ijū' (Lineage, feud and overseas immigration in the western Pearl River Delta region). In Y. Mio (ed.), *Minzoku bunka no saisei to sōzō – Higashi Ajia enkai chiiki no jinruigaku teki kenkyū* (Revival and creation of folk cultures: Anthropological study on East Asian coastal areas). Tokyo: Fūkyōsha, 183–212.

Shen, Y. (2004) 'Fujian new immigrants in the United States: A case study on illegal immigrants in Fuzhou district in the 1990s'. *World Ethno-National Studies*, The Institute of Ethnology and Anthropology, Chinese Academy of Social Sciences, Beijing, 1: 53–59.

Shima, M. (1983) 'Hanguk nongch'on ch'onrak kujo yŏngu nout' ŭ' (A note on the structure of a Korean village). *Hanguk Munhwa Inryuhak* (Korean cultural anthropology), 15: 177–191.

Shima, M. (1997) 'Zoku fu no konsutorakushon' (Construction of lineage genealogy). In A. Tamotsu et al. (eds.) *Iwanami kōza bunka jinruigaku dai 4-kan Ko kara suru shakai tenbō* (Iwanami seminar cultural anthropology, vol. 4: Society from an individual viewpoint). Tokyo: Iwanami Shoten, 97–127.

Shimamura, I. (2002) 'The roots-seeking movement among the Aga-Buryats: New lights on their Shamanism, history of suffering, and diaspora'. In Y. Konagaya (ed.) *Mongolian Cultural Studies IV: A People Divided: Buriyat Mongols in Russia, Mongolia and China*.

Cologne: International Society for the Study of the Culture and Economy of the Ordos Mongols, 88–110.
Siahaan, N. (1982) *Adat Dalihan na Tolu*. Jakarta: Grafina.
Siu, H.F. (1989) *Agent and Victims in South China: Accomplices in Rural Revolution*. London: Yale University Press.
Sneath, D. (1999) 'Kinship, network and residence'. In C. Humphrey and D. Sneath, *The End of Nomadism?: Society, State and the Environment in Inner Asia*. Durham: Duke University Press, 136–178.
Su, G. (2008) 'Taiwan de suode fenpei yu shehui liudong zhi changqi qushi' (Taiwan's income distribution and the long-term trend of social mobility). In H. Wang, G. Li and X. Gong (eds.) *Kuajie—Liudong yu jianchi de Taiwan shehui* (Steps in forbidden zones: Changes and continuities of Taiwan society). Taipei: Junxue chuban, 187–217
Su, G. (2009) 'Jieji yu jieceng' (Class and stratification). In Z. Wang and H. Ju (eds.) *Shehuixue yu Taiwan shehui, di III ban* (Sociology and Taiwan society, 3rd edition). Taipei: Juliu tushu gongsi, 103–128.
Su, G. and W. Yu (2007) 'Taiwan zuqun bupingdeng de zai yantao— jieshi bensheng/waisheng zuqun chayi suojian' (Reexamination of inequality between Taiwan's ethnic groups: Interpreting the reduction of disparities between bensheng and waisheng ethnic groups). *Taiwan Shehuixue kan*, 39: 1–63.
Sugano, N. (2008) 'Buke josei no shakai wo toraeru me – "Chiri zuka nikki" no kentō kara' (Perspective of a woman of the samurai family on society: Analysis of 'Chiri zuka Journal'). *Teikyō shigaku* (Teikyo journal of history), 23: 53–99.
Suganuma, A. (1996) ' 'Mongoru bukkyō no genjō – Dan-atsu kara fukkō e' (The current status of Mongolian Buddhism: From oppression to revival). *Chuo gakujutsu kenkyu jo kiyō* (Annual review of the Chūō Academic Research Institute), 25: 25–48.
Suganuma, A. (2001) '"Mongoru bukkyō" no miryoku' (The attraction of Mongolian Buddhism). *Shunjū* (Shunjū), 435: 12–15.
Suganuma, A. (2002a) 'Sora ni matta kyōten – Mongoru koku no bukkyō dan-atsu' (The scripture that flitted in the air: The oppression of Buddhism in Mongolia). *Shunjū* (Shunjū), 436: 19–22.
Suganuma, A. (2002b) 'Kokyō Karakorumu to shūhen no bukkyō jiin' (Their hometown of Kharakhorum and the surrounding Buddhist temples). *Shunjū* (Shunjū), 437: 12–15.
Suganuma, A. (2002c) 'Mongoru bukkyō no sōhonzan, Gandan Dera' (The head temple of Mongolian Buddhism, Gandan Temple). *Shunjū* (Shunjū), 438: 20–23.
Suzuki, M. (1978) 'Nansei shotō ni okeru hōi kan no kenkyū – Kūkan ninshiki no shiten kara' (The study of orientation in the south-west

(Ryukyu) islands: An approach to spatial perception). *Jinbun Chiri* (Human geography), 30(6): 61–74.

Taira, S. (ed.) (1972–1982) *Date jike kiroku* (Documents of the Date family). Sendai: Hōbundō.

Takizawa, K. (2002) 'Gendai Mongoru ni okeru Kirisuto-kyō no juyō wo megutte: Minshuka ikō no shūkyō saikaishaku no naka de' (The reception of Christianity in current Mongolia: The process of the reinterpretation of religions after the collapse of communism). *Indogaku Shūkyūgakkai Ron Shū* (Studies in Religions East and West), 29: 45–64.

Tanaka, K. (1992) *Mongoru: Minzoku to jiyū* (Mongolia: ethnicity and freedom). Tokyo: Iwanami Shoten.

Tanoue, T. (2012) 'Tabunkashugi gensetsu ni okeru shin imin mondai' (The problem of new immigrants in the discourse of multiculturalism). In I. Numazaki and Y. Satō (eds.) *Kosaku suru Taiwan shakai* (Complexities in Taiwan society). Tokyo: Ajia Keizai Kenkyusho, 175–207.

The National Bureau of Statistics of Rural Social and Economic Investigation Division (ed.) (2009) *China Rural Statistical Yearbook 2008*. Beijing: China Statistics Press.

Tian, J. and H. Wang (2006) 'Nanxing qipo yu "qu" de kuaguo hunyin—weihe Taiwan nanzi yao yu Yuenan nüzi jiehun?' (Manliness and 'wife-taking' in transnational marriage: Why Taiwan men wish to marry Vietnamese women?) *Taiwan Dongnanyaxue kan*, 38(1): 3–36.

Tokyo Teikoku Daigaku Bunka Daigaku Shiryō Hensan Gakari (1908–1911) *Dai Nihon komonjo ie wake dai 3 Date ke monjo no 1–7* (Historical documents of Japan by family: The Date family documents 1–7). Tokyo: Tokyo Teikoku Daigaku Bunka Daigaku Shiryō Hensan Gakari.

Tsedendamba (Цэдэндамба), S. (1998) 'Уламжлал ба Уламжлал бус Шашны Харилцааны Асуудал' (The problem of the relationship between traditional and non-traditional religion).' In Mongolian Academy of Science, Institute of Philosophy, Sociology and Law (ed.) *Төр, Сүм Хийдийн Харилцаа: Орчин Үе* (The relationship between the state and the temple: Recent times). Ulaanbaatar: Bambi-san, 44–52.

Tsedendamba (Цэдэндамба), S. (2003) *Монгол Улс дахь Шашины Нөхцөл Байдал: XX-XXI Зууны Заагт Үе* (Religious situation in Mongolia: At the turn of the 20th and 21st centuries). Ulanbaatar: National University of Mongolia, The Research Centre for Buddhist Culture; London: Tibet Foundation.

Tserenhand (Цэрэнханд), G. (1987) 'Хот Айл, Нутагшил' (Hot ail and settlement). In ШУА (ed.) *БНМАУ-ын Угсаатны Зүй* (Ethnography

in the Mongolian People's Republic), vol.1. Ulaanbaatar: National Publishing Office, 119–125.
Tzeng, S. (2009) *From Honto Jin to Bensheng Ren: The Origin and Development of Taiwanese National Consciousness.* Lanham: University Press of America.
Vandangombo (Вандангомбо), R. (1985) 'Шашны Улдэгдлийн Илрэл, Оршин Буй Шалтгаан' (The expression of the remnants of religion, and the recent phase). In Mongolian Academy of Science, Institute of Philosophy, Sociology and Law (ed.) *Хөдөлмөрчдийн Шашингүй Хүмүүжлийн Өнөөгийн Асуудал* (The recent problem of atheistic education). Mongolian Academy of Science Publishing Factory, 47–78.
Vergouwen, J.C. (1964) *The Social Organisation and Customary Law of the Toba Batak.* The Hague: Nijhoff.
Wagner, E.W. (1974) 'Social stratification in seventeenth-century Korea: Some observations from a 1663 Seoul census register'. *Occasional paper on Korea*, 1: 36–54.
Walthall, A. (2001) 'Ōoku – Seiji to jendā no hikakushi teki kōsatsu' (A comparative-historical study on politics and gender in the Ōoku). In Y. Sakurai, N. Sugano and H. Nagano (eds.) *Jendā de yomitoku Edo jidai* (The Edo period explained in terms of gender). Tokyo: Sanseidō, 3–43.
Wang, F. (1993) 'Shengji ronghe de benzhi' (The essence of provincial amalgamation). In M. Zhang et al. *Zuqun guanxi yu guojia renting* (Ethnic relations and state identity). Taipei: Yejiang chubanshe, 53–100.
Wang, F. (2003) *Dangdai Taiwan de zuqun xiangxiang* (Ethnic imagination in contemporary Taiwan). Taipei: Qunxue chuban youxian gongsi.
Wang, H. (2008) 'Taiwan de yimin jieshou zhengce yu guojia rentong' (Taiwan's immigration policy and state identity). In H. Wang, G. Li and X. Gong (eds.) *Kuajie—Liudong yu jianchi de Taiwan shehui* (Steps in forbidden zones: changes and continuities of Taiwan society). Taipei: Junxue chuban, 111–126.
Wang, H. and J. Tien (2009) 'Who marries Vietnamese brides? Masculinities and cross-border marriages'. In H.Z. Wang and H.H. Hsiao (eds.) *Cross-Border Marriages with Asian Characteristics.* Taipei: Center for Asia-Pacific Studies, Academia Sinica, 13–37.
Wank, D.L. (2000) 'Bukkyō fukkō no seijigaku – Kyōgōsuru kikō to seitōsei' (The politics of Buddhism revival: Competing organizations and legitimacy). In M. Hishida (ed.) *Gendai Chūgoku no kōzō hendō 5 Shakai – kokka tono kyōsei kankei* (Structural change in contemporary

China 5 Society: Symbiotic relations with the state). Tokyo: Tokyo Daigaku Shuppankai, 275–304.
Ward, B.E. (1965) 'Varieties of the conscious model of the fishermen of south China'. In M. Banton (ed.) *The Relevance of Models for Social Anthropology*. London: Tavistock Publications, 113–137.
Warneck, J. (1909) *Die Religion der Batak* (The religion of the Batak). Göttingen: Van den Hoeck & Ruprecht.
Watson, J.L. (1988) 'Funeral specialists in Cantonese society: Pollution, performance, and social hierarchy'. In J.L. Watson and E.S. Rawski (eds.) *Death Ritual in Late Imperial and Modern China*. Berkeley: University of California Press, 109–134.
Watson, J.L. (1995[1975]) *Imin to soūzoku: Honkon to London no Man shi ichizoku* (Emigration and the Chinese lineage: The Man family in Hong Kong and London). M. Segawa (trans.). Kyoto: Aunsha.
Watson, J.L. and E.S. Rawski (eds.) (1994[1988]) *Chūgoku no shi no girei* (Death rituals in China). Tokyo: Heibonsha.
Wu, F. (2006) *Wojia de wailao* (Foreign worker in my home). Sanchong: Xinlu chubanshe.
Wu, N. (1997) 'Binglang yu tuoxie—Taiwan jieji liudong de zuqun chayi ji yuanyin' (Betel nuts and sandals: Ethnic difference in Taiwan's class mobility and its causes). *Taiwan shehuixue kan*, 1: 137–167.
Wu, T. (ed.) (2008) *Duoyuan wenhua* (Multiculturalism). Taipei: Eryu wenhua shiye.
Xia, X. (2002) *Liuli Xunan—zibenguojihua xia de 'waiji xinniang' xianxiang* (Drifting away and searching a shore: The phenomenon of 'foreign brides' under the globalization of capital). Taipei: Taiwan shehui yanjiu zazhishe.
Xia, X. (ed.) (2005) *Buyao jia wo waiji xinninang* (Do not call me a foreign bride). Xindian: Zuoan wenhua chuban.
Xia, X. (ed.) (2009) *Saodong liuyi* (Migration trouble). Taipei: Taiwan shehui yanjiu zazhishe.
Xie, C. (1987) *Rentong de wuming—Taiwan yuanzhumin de zuqun bieqjian* (Stigma of identity: Ethnicity of Taiwan's indigenous peoples and its transformation). Taipei: Zili wanbaoshe.
Xingzhengyuan Zhijichu (2010) *Jiushibanian jiating shouzhi diaocha baogao* (2009 household income survey report). Taipei: Xingzhengyuan Zhijichu.
Xue, C. (2004) 'Taiwan diqu pingqiong nüxinghua jianshao zhi tantao—yi 1990 nian wei li' (Exploration into the decrease of feminization of poverty in Taiwan: A case from 1990). *Renkouxue kan*, 29: 95–121.
Xue, C. (2008) 'Taiwan diqu ershao pingqiong—1991–2005 nian de qushi yanjiu' (Poverty among children and the youth in Taiwan: A study of trends from 1991 to 2005). *Taiwan shuhuixue kan*, 40: 89–130.

Yamakawa, K. (1983) *Buke no josei* (Women of the samurai family). Tokyo: Iwanami Shoten, 22–23.

Yan, G. (2006) *Jialai Taiwan—xinxing yimin de hunyin gushi* (Marrying into Taiwan: Stories of marriage among new immigrants). Xizhi: Xinxinwen wenhua shiye.

Yanagiya, K. (2001a) 'Josei ni yoru buke no sōzoku – Morioka han Sendai han no jirei kara' (Succession of the samurai-class family estate by women: The cases of the Morioka domain and the Sendai domain). Republished in K. Yanagiya (2007) *Kinsei no josei sōzoku to kaigo* (Female succession and nursing care in early modern times). Tokyo: Yoshikawa Kōbunkan, 61–85.

Yanagiya, K. (2001b) 'Sendai han Date ke no "okugata" – Nanadai Shigemura no jidai wo chūshin ni' (The 'oku' of the Date family in the Sendai domain: Centering on the seventh feudal lord Shigemura's times). Republished in K. Yanagiya (2007) *Kinsei no josei sōzoku to kaigo* (Female succession and nursing care in early modern times). Tokyo: Yoshikawa Kōbunkan, 132–157.

Yanagiya, K. (2003a) 'Jōka no kazoku to josei' (Family and women in a castle town). *Sendai shi shi tsūshi hen 4 Kinsei 2* (A history of Sendai City 4: Early modern 2). Sendai: Sendai Shi, 365–386.

Yanagiya, K. (2003b) 'Buke shakai to josei' (Samurai society and women). In M. Ōishi (ed.) *Nihon no jidai shi 16 Kyōhō no kaikaku to shakai henyō* (Japanese history by periods 16: The Kyōhō reforms and social transformation). Tokyo: Yoshikawa Kōbunkan, 243–277.

Yi, Y. (2001) 'Sippal/sipku-segi Daejŏri ŭi sinbun kusŏng gwa jachi jilsŏ' (Status composition and the order of self-government in Daejŏri village during the 18th and 19th centuries). In B. An and Y. Yŏnghun (eds.) *Matchil ŭi nongmindŭl- Hanguk gŭnse ch'onrak saenghwalsa* (Peasants in the village of Matchil: Rural social life conditions during early-modern Korea). Seoul: Ilcho-gak, 245–299.

Yoshida, S. (1999) 'Keizai ikōki no shinzoku nettowāku bunseki: Kita Kurugusutan, Sofuhōzu no kaisan katei kara' (An analysis of kin networks in the period of economic transition: From the process of the dissolution of a sovkhoz in northern Kyrgyzstan). *Minzokugaku Kenkyū* (The Japanese journal of ethnology), 64(2): 149–172.

Yu, J. and Y. Yu (1990) *Gurye Yu-ssi-ga ŭi saenghwal ilgi* (Diaries of the Yu family in Kuye). S. Kim (ed.). Seoul: Hanguk Nongchon Gyŏngje Yŏngguwŏn.

Zaidan Hōjin Hanso Date Masamune Kō Kenshōkai (ed.) (1938) *Date Masamune kyō denki shiryō* (Resources for the biography of Lord Date Masamune). Sendai: Zaidan Hōjin Hanso Date Masamune Kō Kenshōkai.

Zhuang G. (2006) 'Nearly 30 years of Chinese immigrants: A case study on immigrant from Fuzhou'. *World Ethno-National Studies*, The Institute of Ethnology and Anthropology, Chinese Academy of Social Sciences, Beijing, China, 3: 38–46.

Zhang, H. (2007) *Dongnanya nüxing yimin yu Taiwan kejia shehui* (Female immigrants from Southeast Asia and Taiwan's Hakka society). Taipei: Center for Asia Pacific Area Studies, Institute of Humanities and Social Sciences, Academia Sinica.

Zhang Y., J. Lin and Q. Liu (2010) 'Taiwan yuanzhumin de jianyi ji shehui jingji diwei zhi bianjian yu xiankuang' (Movements of indigenous peoples and the changes and current situation of their social and economic status in Taiwan). In S. Huang and Y. Zhang (eds.) *Taiwan Yuanzhumin zhengce yanbian yu shehui fazhan* (Changes in Taiwan's policies toward indigenous peoples and social development). Taipei: Institute of Ethnology, Academia Sinica, 51–120.

Index

ancestral hall 3, 78, 80–3, 85–9, 93

Benshengren 8, 11–16, 23, 27, 30, 144
boat dweller 3, 75–80, 84, 147
Bruner, E. 1, 113, 115, 117–20, 126
Buddha 135–9, 141–51
Buddhism 127, 129, 143, 149

ceremonial cloth 122–3, 125
channel 72–3
Christian 115–16, 136, 139, 141, 148
Christianity 5, 115, 127–8, 141, 149¬
clan 67, 69, 113–15, 117, 119–21, 123–6, 132, 145, 149–50
collectivization 76, 80, 128, 130–34, 149–50
Communist Party 78, 80, 83, 92, 100
compensatory function 125
concubine 39, 63–5

Danjia 79–80
death pollution 89
debt 102, 109–10
democratization 4, 7, 12, 128, 133, 136–8, 141–3, 149
domestic roles 61, 63, 65, 69
donation 4, 106–9, 111, 147

economic role 3, 66, 73

emigrant community
  see qiaoxiang
ethnic association 1, 4, 113, 114–15, 117–21, 123–6
ethnicity 1, 7–8, 13–18, 23–4, 28–30, 75
external roles 61, 63, 65–6, 70–1, 73

feud 3, 75–6, 83, 92
female messenger 66, 70, 71–2
foreign brides 18, 22, 24, 28, 145
foreign workers 16, 18, 19, 21–2, 24, 28, 145
Freedman, M. 79, 93
funeral 4, 65, 70, 89–91, 99–100, 103, 108–9, 111, 115, 119–20, 122–5, 147–8
Fuzhou 95, 97–101, 147–8

gender system 2, 55–7, 63, 72–3
genealogy 3, 35, 37, 39, 41, 45–51, 81–2, 92–3, 124, 145
Green Card 3, 103–3, 110

Hakka 10, 13, 15–16, 18, 23, 30, 144–5
Hasselgren, J. 116, 118–19
Hoklo 10, 13–6, 18, 30, 144
home renovation 104–5, 111
homecoming 4, 102–4, 111
household ritual 127–8, 130, 135–9, 141–3, 151

ie 55, 73–4

individualization 2, 7, 24, 28, 30, 127
intermarriage 2, 8–9, 13, 23, 30, 32–3, 38–40, 43, 45, 52, 149
internationalization 2, 7, 24, 28, 30

lineage 2, 3, 31, 35, 37, 40–5, 47–8, 50–2, 66, 75–6, 78–86, 88–93, 113, 132, 144–7, 149–50

Mongolia/Mongolian 4–5, 127, 128, 129, 130, 131, 134, 139–40, 142–3, 149, 151–2
multitiering 1, 7–8, 16, 18, 24, 28–30

new disparities 24, 26
new immigrants 11, 16, 18, 24, 28, 30, 145
nobi-jongmoje 2, 31–2, 43, 52
nomadic society 130–2, 137, 150

oegŏ nobi 32, 42, 158
oku 2, 56–7, 60–8, 70–3, 146
omote 2, 30, 56, 60–3, 65–6, 68, 72–4

Pearl River delta 75–6, 78–80, 147
pluralization 1, 7– 8, 16, 18, 23–4, 28–30
purge 4, 127–9, 132 3, 138, 142, 149

qiaoxiang 95–6, 99–101

remittance 98, 102, 109
revolving loan 1, 4, 120, 126

settlement 77, 114–15, 127–8, 130–2, 134–5, 141–2, 149
socialism/socialist 4–5, 100, 112, 127–35, 139, 141–2, 149–51
solgŏ nobi 41–2
Soviet 128–31, 141, 143, 150
Suharto regime 4, 113, 118
'New Order' 118
symbolic capital 3, 95, 97, 111

Taiwan 1–2, 7–28, 30, 97, 144–5

unsuccessful immigrants 95, 102, 110–11

Waishengren 7, 11–18, 27, 30, 144

Yuanzhumin 14, 16–18, 30, 145
yurt 131, 134–42, 151–2